PRENTICE-HALL

HISTORY OF MUSIC SERIES

H. WILEY HITCHCOCK, editor

second edition
BAROQUE MUSIC

second edition

# BAROQUE MUSIC

CLAUDE V. PALISCA
*Yale University*

PRENTICE-HALL, INC., ENGLEWOOD CLIFFS, NEW JERSEY 07632

*Library of Congress Cataloging in Publication Data*

PALISCA, CLAUDE V
  Baroque music.

  (Prentice-Hall history of music series)
  Bibliography:  p.
  Includes index.
  1. Music—History and criticism—17th century.
  2. Music—History and criticism—18th century.
  I. Title.
ML193.P34–1979     780'.903'2     79-22140
ISBN  0-13-055954-7
ISBM  0-13-055947-4 pbk.

Editorial/production by
  Penny Linskey and Frank Hubert
Page layout by Ana Hernandez
Manufacturing buyer: Harry P. Baisley
Cover photograph: Bernardo Buontalenti's design for
Jacopo Peri as Arion in the Fifth Intermedio of 1589.
Florence, Biblioteca Nazionale Centrale. In the background,
Peri's *Euridice*, Florence, 1601.

Printed in the United States of America

10  9  8  7  6

PRENTICE-HALL INTERNATIONAL, INC., *London*
PRENTICE-HALL OF AUSTRALIA PTY. LIMITED, *Sydney*
PRENTICE-HALL OF CANADA, LTD., *Toronto*
PRENTICE-HALL OF INDIA PRIVATE LIMITED, *New Delhi*
PRENTICE-HALL OF JAPAN, INC., *Tokyo*
PRENTICE-HALL OF SOUTHEAST ASIA PTE. LTD., *Singapore*
WHITEHALL BOOKS LIMITED, *Wellington, New Zealand*

TO JANE

# CONTENTS

# FOREWORD

Students and informed amateurs of the history of music have long needed a series of books that are comprehensive, authoritative, and engagingly written. They have needed books written by specialists—but specialists interested in communicating vividly. The Prentice-Hall History of Music Series aims at filling these needs.

Six books in the series present a panoramic view of the history of Western music, divided among the major historical periods—Medieval, Renaissance, Baroque, Classic, Romantic, and Contemporary. The musical culture of the United States is viewed historically as an independent development within the larger Western tradition, and a similar approach is accorded to the music of Latin America. A book devoted to the traditional music of India draws comparisons with Western music. In another pair of books, the rich yet neglected folk and traditional music of both hemispheres is treated. Taken together, the eleven volumes of the series will be a distinctive and, we hope, distinguished contribution to the history of the music of the world's peoples. Each volume, moreover, may be read singly as a substantial account of the music of its period or area.

The authors of the series are scholars of national and international repute—musicologists, critics, and teachers of acknowledged stature in their respective fields of specialization. In their contributions to the Prentice-Hall History of Music Series their goal has been to present works of solid scholarship that are eminently readable, with significant insights into music as a part of the general intellectual and cultural life of man.

H. WILEY HITCHCOCK, *Editor*

# PREFACE

This book invites the reader to study with ear and eye some typical examples of baroque music. It is not a comprehensive survey of this period or a gallery of the most famous composers. Certain important figures are hardly named, while others lesser known are treated at length, and this goes also for the various categories of composition. The emphasis is upon giving the reader an entry into the most significant manners of composition through concrete examples. My hope is that the reader will gain a method of approaching the principal styles of baroque music, a key as it were to intimate understanding and further exploration. The approach to analysis is based as much as possible on criteria and terminology common in the period under study even if at times this conflicts with accepted modern standards and usage.

In preparing this second edition I have profited from the criticisms and suggestions of numerous reviewers and from the kind advice of teachers who used the book. I wish to thank especially William S. Newman, who volunteered a friendly detailed list. I have added two new chapters, "Lute and Harpsichord Music in France" and "Organ and Clavier Music in Germany"; and I expanded the chapters "The Rise of the Sacred Concerto" and "Sonata, Concerto, and Sinfonia." I am indebted to Kerala Snyder for reading the chapter on German keyboard music and offering expert counsel. To my wife, Jane, I owe the thoughtfully devised index. Despite these additions and many smaller changes, I recognize that there are still obvious gaps that even a third edition will not bridge. But I hope to have come nearer to the goal of introducing the reader to a wealth of approaches to musical composition in this lively and fondly relived period of this art's history.

CLAUDE V. PALISCA

second edition
# BAROQUE MUSIC

# ONE

# THE BAROQUE IDEAL

Many terms now used to designate historical periods in music were first applied by art historians and subsequently adopted by music historians. Among these are *gothic, romanesque, renaissance, rococo,* and *impressionist. Baroque,* however, is not one of these. It was applied to music as early as to any of the other arts. At first it had a restrictive and derogatory connotation. But in the literature on music since the late nineteenth century it has denoted comprehensively the music of the period from approximately 1580 to 1750.

Baroque music as conceived today comprises such diverse manifestations as the madrigals of Gesualdo, the early musical pastorals of Peri and Monteverdi, the tragicomedies of Scarlatti, and the *tragédies lyriques* of Rameau. In instrumental music it includes such categories as the toccatas of Merulo, the trio sonatas of Corelli, and the concertos of Vivaldi. In baroque church music are embraced styles as opposed as the passions of Schütz and the cantatas of Bach.

1

Is it justifiable to lump together into one stylistic period and under one label such diverse modes of musical expression? Many have asked this question as the music of this period has become better known, particularly since Manfred Bukofzer's pioneering study, *Music in the Baroque Era* (1947). The appropriateness of the term *baroque* itself has been questioned. Because these doubts have been raised, we must examine at the outset of this book whether a unifying concept exists in the period we call baroque and, indeed, whether the term is a fitting one.

The French philosopher Noel-Antoine Pluche used the word *baroque* in 1746 to characterize the style of playing of Jean Pierre Guignon as opposed to Jean Baptiste Anet, then the most celebrated violinists in Paris. Guignon, he says, aims to show off his great agility, to amuse and surprise. Baptiste, on the other hand, prefers a sustained expressive style that aspires to the lyricism of the human voice. He disdains pure display, which "for him is to wrest laboriously from the bottom of the sea some baroque pearls, when diamonds can be found on the surface of the earth."[1] This comparison leads Pluche to distinguish two kinds of music common to both France and Italy. There is the *musique chantante*, rich in melodies that are natural to the voice, effortless, artless, and without grimace. The other kind of music seeks to amaze by the boldness of its sounds and turns, and to surpass the native capacities of the singer with its rapidity and noise. This is what he calls a *musique baroque*.

The term continued to be in vogue when in 1768 Jean-Jacques Rousseau gave this entry in his music dictionary:

> A *baroque* music is that in which the harmony is confused, charged with modulations and dissonances, the melody is harsh and little natural, the intonation difficult, and the movement constrained. It seems that this term comes from *baroco* of the logicians.[2]

Etymologists still disagree on whether *baroque* comes from the Italian *baroco*, an adjective applied to a far-fetched mode of argumentation by syllogism, as Rousseau believed, or from the Portuguese *barroco*, used to describe an oddly shaped pearl, as Pluche believed.

Odd pearl or strained syllogism, baroque music was to both Pluche and Rousseau bizarre, extravagant, and unnatural. To be sure, both were bent on disparaging the style, living as they did in a time that rejected the baroque. But the deprecating tone aside, were Pluche and Rousseau not speaking of the same music that today we call baroque? Might not the

---

[1]Noel-Antoine Pluche, *Spectacle de la nature*, Vol. VII (nouvelle éd.; Paris: Frères Estienne, 1770), p. 129.

[2]Jean-Jacques Rousseau, *Dictionnaire de musique* (Paris: la Veuve Duchesne, 1768), "Baroque," p. 41.

**EXAMPLE 1-1**   J. S. Bach, *BWV 21, Ich hatte viel Bekümmernis*, No. 3, Aria

passage from an aria of J. S. Bach which we give as Example 1-1 be described as confused in its harmony, charged with dissonance and modulation, unnatural in its melody, which is difficult to intone, and constricted in its rhythm by the persistent repetition of a formula? It is possible to admit this without judging the aria faulty, because we recognize that the unusual means here are justified by the text, which the composer sought to express forcefully. But a Frenchman of the mid-eighteenth century had little sympathy for Bach's attitude toward expression, and all he could hear was the bizarre quality. Similarly, the violin concertos of Vivaldi and Albinoni which Guignon played at the *Concerts spirituels* in Paris abound in passages of extravagant virtuosity, difficult leaps, and surprising configurations; outbursts of fire and fury alternating with moments of intense lyricism. Pluche and his contemporaries were not against virtuosity so much as the passion, impetuosity, and enthusiasm that were behind *baroque* virtuosity. Mondonville, Pluche's favorite song composer, wrote music that required agility, but it tended toward the playful, elegant, and static arabesques of the preclassic period.

Behind the traits that mark music as baroque, then, are their reason for being: the passions, or as they were more often called then, the affections. Affections are not the same as emotions. A sixteenth-century poetic critic, Lorenzo Giacomini, defined an affection as "a spiritual movement or operation of the mind in which it is attracted or repelled by an object it has come to know."[3] He described it as a result of an imbalance in the animal spirits and vapors that flow continually throughout the body. An abundance of thin and agile spirits disposes a person to joyous affections, while torpid and impure vapors prepare the way for sorrow and fear. External and internal sensations stimulate the bodily mechanism to alter the state of the spirits. This activity is felt as a "movement of the affections," and the resulting state of imbalance is the affection. Once this state is reached, the body and mind tend to remain in the same affection until some new stimulus produces an alteration of the combination of vapors.

*Affection* and *passion* are two terms for the same process, the former describing it from the point of view of the body, the latter from the standpoint of the mind. The alteration of the blood and spirits *affects* the body, while the mind *passively* suffers the disturbance.

This view of the mechanics of the affections perpetuated the belief, propounded earlier by Aristotle in his *Rhetoric*, that there exist discrete states known as fear, love, hate, anger, joy–to cite a few of those most common. From the last decades of the sixteenth century the arousal of the affections was considered the principal objective of poetry and music. There was much theorizing about the passions beginning about this time and continuing throughout the seventeenth and eighteenth centuries. One of the masques of the carnival of 1574 in Florence was even called "The Affections."

The most comprehensive study of the affections up to its time was the treatise of René Descartes, *The Passions of the Soul* (1649), in which this pioneer of rationalism elaborated, rather fancifully at times, upon the theory as it had been passed down to him. Johann Mattheson at the end of our period in his *Der vollkommene Capellmeister* (The Perfect Musical Director, 1739) still theorized at length about the affections and their representation in music. But by now psychology was turning away from this naive concept of emotional life toward theories of association of ideas and nerve activity. Daniel Webb, for example, saw the feeling of pleasure "not, as some have imagined, the result of any fixed or permanent condition of the nerves and spirits, but [as springing] from a succession of impressions, and [being] greatly augmented by sudden or gradual transitions from one kind or strain of vibrations to another."[4] Similarly, composers of the mid-eighteenth century found the affections too static, intellectual, and lifeless; they were enticed by the possibility of continuous dynamic flux and transition of sentiment.

If, then, there is any common thread that unites the great variety of music that we call baroque, it is an underlying faith in music's power, indeed

---

[3]Lorenzo Giacomini, "De la purgatione de la tragedia," in *Orationi e discorsi* (Florence: ne le case de Samartelli, 1597), p. 38.

[4]Daniel Webb, *Observations on the Correspondence between Poetry and Music* (London: J. Dodsley, 1769), p. 47.

its obligation, to move the affections. Whether it is a madrigal of Marenzio in the late sixteenth century or an aria of Bach or Handel in the 1730s, this belief strongly determines the musical style. If we want to ascertain whether we have crossed the boundary into the baroque or out of it, there is no better test than to ask whether the expression of the affections is the dominant goal in fashioning a piece of music. At one end of the chronological spectrum there is the art of such a composer as Adrian Willaert, who almost never sacrificed beauty of form, perfection of technique, and a prevailing harmoniousness for affective expression, though he always lavished great care on the enunciation and depiction of the text. But once across into the next generation, that of his pupil and countryman Cipriano de Rore, we have entered the beginnings of the baroque, because he was often more concerned with affection than form. Similarly, when we find Pergolesi, a contemporary of J. S. Bach, more intent upon balancing phrases, overwhelming the listener with spirited inventions, and weaving a spell of beautiful melody than upon turning out a steady stream of stereotyped affections, we recognize that we have crossed over into the esthetics of the early classic period.

Not all music can be subjected to this simple test. Certain categories of dance, instrumental, and church music are not so easily classified. Here we must apply rather arbitrarily the chronological lines drawn for music more easily characterized. Nor did the passage from one style to another at either boundary of the period arrive at the same moment in all countries. The baroque style was not evident in Germany until around 1610 and did not become the reigning style until decades later. Though its vogue declined in Italy in the 1720s, it suddenly flowered in France for a brief while. Even within a single country there were pockets in which the baroque persisted or was resisted: while Hasse's preclassical operas triumphed in Dresden in the 1730s, J. S. Bach's high baroque cantatas continued to inspire Leipzig worshipers and university audiences. Within a single composer's output or even within a single work, baroque and counter-baroque techniques existed side by side, as in the later operas of Alessandro Scarlatti and Handel.

Aside from the ideal of affective expression, there are external characteristics that run through much baroque music. The desire at the end of the sixteenth century to make the solo voice the principal bearer of the text and message of a musical setting led to the reduction of the instrumental accompaniment to a half-improvised chordal support that was outlined in a shorthand score. The ensuing thorough-bass manner of notation pervaded almost all vocal music and music for more than one instrument from shortly after 1600 to around 1770. In the last forty or fifty years of this period, however, much of the music written with thorough bass belongs to a tendency that is essentially counter-baroque. The *stile concertato*, which exploited contrasts and combinations of various instrumental timbres and groupings, originated in the Renaissance and gathered momentum during the seventeenth century to reach its greatest flowering around 1720 in the works of Vivaldi. Certain manners of *concertato* writing were almost exclusively a property of the seventeenth century, while others have subsisted until today. The thorough bass and the *concertato* style, then, were deeply ingrained in baroque music; but they were not exclusive to it.

Our period is thus unified and delimited more by an expressive ideal than by a consistent body of musical techniques. Nevertheless, several phases of baroque style can be recognized through changes in performance practices and compositional procedures. The first phase was one of preparation. This began as early as 1550 and gained an irreversible momentum by 1580. The desire to find new means for expressing extreme and conflicting affections that were earlier suppressed or moderated led to stylistic expediency and mannerism. At first composers were able to draw out their ideas and affections only for short spans until there evolved such means for expansion as the *ritornello, basso ostinato*, and strophic variation, and until they developed a surer sense of tonal relations.

By 1640 in Italy an accumulation of many techniques used in common marks the end of the individualistic experimental phase. Between approximately 1640 and 1690 a style that had been spontaneous and pragmatic became more and more regulated by rules and standards. The treatment of dissonance became uniform. Chords rather than freely counterposed melodic lines determined harmonic motion. Rhythm was subjected to rigid metrical control. Expressive devices, formal schemes, and compositional categories became stereotyped. The baroque style during this period spread throughout Europe.

In the last phase, 1690 to 1740, which we shall call the "high" baroque, the rules and standards evolved during the previous phase were accepted as fixed. Genres and forms were expanded and embellished but maintained their essential character. Expressive devices acquired symbolic value and were used out of context. The rendering of the affections tended to be intellectual and calculated. Reason often replaced inspiration.

Meanwhile, several counter-movements began. In the comic opera a new lightness, directness, and melodiousness was cultivated. In France popular elements blended with courtly elegance to produce the rococo style. The rationalistic approach of the affections-dominated esthetic provoked reaction from composers who wanted to express a more dynamic and unstable emotionalism. The outcome was the style of sentimentality, or *Empfindsamkeit*. These counter-baroque tendencies arose amid continuing but increasingly sporadic manifestations of the high baroque. By 1720 the baroque ideal was declining and by 1740 a new ideal swept through most of Europe.

# BIBLIOGRAPHICAL NOTES

A thoughtful survey of the uses of the term *baroque* is to be found in René Wellek, *Concepts of Criticism* (New Haven: Yale University Press, 1963), pp. 69–127.

For students who wish to pursue more deeply or multilaterally topics presented in this book, the constant companion should be Manfred F. Bukofzer, *Music in the Baroque Era* (New York: W. W. Norton & Co., Inc. 1947). A more complete short survey of the period than is attempted here may be found in Donald J. Grout, *A History of Western Music*, 3rd ed. (New York: W. W. Norton & Co., Inc., 1980), and the relevant bibliographies at the end of that volume are recommended. A broad view of music in the culture, esthetic outlook, and society of the period is offered in Friedrich Blume, *Renaissance and Baroque Music, a Comprehensive Survey*, trans. M. D. Herter Norton (New York: W. W. Norton & Co., Inc., 1967). Scholarly, though not always up-to-date, surveys of particular topics will be found in Anthony Lewis and Nigel Fortune, eds., *The New Oxford History of Music, Volume V: Opera and Church Music 1630–1750*, (London: Oxford University Press, 1974). The student should consult the many extended articles in *The New Grove Dictionary of Music and Musicians*, ed. Stanley Sadie (London: Macmillan, 1979) under "Baroque," names of composers, instruments, and genres of composition.

In Grout's *A Short History of Opera*, 2nd ed. (New York: Columbia University Press, 1965), the first fourteen chapters and the exhaustive bibliography in the back should be the first resource in any investigation in its area. The sections devoted to the baroque period in Oliver Strunk's *Source Readings in Music History* (New York: W. W. Norton & Co., Inc., 1950) should be read concurrently with the present text. The section on baroque music has been reprinted separately as a paperback.

Since some of the instruments mentioned in this book are not in common usage, the student should provide himself with a guide such as Anthony Baines, ed., *Musical Instruments Through the Ages* (Baltimore: Penguin Books, 1961).

# TWO

# THE BEGINNINGS
# OF THE BAROQUE STYLE

## THE "SECOND PRACTICE"

The years around 1600 were a time of wholesale experimentation in every aspect of composition. Not only did they see the emergence of the monodic style and the *basso continuo*, but there was a deeper and more general upheaval that these innovations should not be allowed to obscure. There is no better testimony to this than the polemics of those who were alarmed by the abandonment of past standards. The composer and theorist Giovanni Maria Artusi (1540–1613), a canon of the church of San Salvatore of Bologna, was the most outspoken critic of the new tendencies in his dialogue, *L'Artusi, overo Delle imperfettioni della moderna musica (The Artusi, or the Imperfections of Modern Music,* 1600). It is significant that the music attacked there is not monodic but polyphonic. One of the interlocutors, Luca, who usually took the conservative point of view, gave his reactions to some madrigals written by an unnamed composer which he had heard the previous day at a private salon. Actually they were by Claudio Monteverdi (1567–1643).

> The texture was not unpleasing. But, as Your Lordship will see, insofar as it introduced new rules, new modes, and new turns of phrase, these were harsh and little pleasing to the ear, nor could they be otherwise; for so long as they violate the good rules—in part founded upon experience, the mother of all things, in part observed in nature, and in part proved by demonstration—we must believe them deformations of the nature and propriety of true harmony far removed from the object of music, which, as Your Lordship said yesterday, is delectation.[1]

Sixteenth-century practice, as exemplified in such composers as Adrian Willaert (c. 1490–1562) and Palestrina (c. 1525–1594), recognized only certain applications of dissonances. The admission of seconds and sevenths and their compounds was severely limited, while augmented fourths, diminished fifths, and perfect fourths were treated somewhat more freely. The accepted ways of introducing dissonances are illustrated in Example 2-1 from a motet by Willaert: on strong beats through the prepared suspension (marked S); on

**EXAMPLE 2-1**   Adrian Willaert, *O magnum mysterium*

[1]Oliver Strunk, *Source Readings in Music History* (New York: W. W. Norton & Co., Inc., 1950), p. 396.

weak beats, and occasionally on strong beats, as passing notes (P); as modified passing notes called *cambiate* (C); or as certain other forms of auxiliary notes (A). The first and third beats in common time and the first, third, and fifth beats in six normally received consonances.

The nature of Monteverdi's departures from the established practice is evident in the madrigal *Ohimè, se tanto amate* (*HAM* II, 188)[2] from the same book of madrigals as one of those Luca heard, that is, the composer's fourth book, published in 1603 but mainly written before 1600.

The licenses Monteverdi took affect mainly the weak beats. The device he most exploited in this madrigal was a common vocal ornament, or *accento*, now known as *échappé*. It occurs in the clearest context in measures 27–28 of Example 2-2. The E and G in measure 27 "escape" from the d minor harmony[3] of the second part of this measure, and return to consonance by both dropping a third. The same technique, but veiled, produces the striking effect of measures 2 and 4. Here, if the harmony in the alto and tenor were assumed to continue over the barline and the canto and quinto were transposed down an octave, the same figure would result as in measure 28. But

**EXAMPLE 2-2**   C. Monteverdi, *Ohimè, se tanto amate*

**EXAMPLE 2-3**   C. Monteverdi, *Ohimè, se tanto amate*

[2]See *Abbreviations*, p. 290, of this book.
[3]Throughout this book capital letters will stand for major triads or keys, lower case letters for minor.

how much stranger and like a forbidden pleasure is Monteverdi's actual opening! (See Example 2-3.) Another daring use of this figure occurs in measure 17, in which the "escaped" notes B–D resolve by skipping down a fifth. As the bass is held, they meet it in a seventh chord. The sustained bass note under changing chords is one of Monteverdi's chief means of making the harmony strained yet smoothly cohesive. There are several other examples of this technique in measure 54 and between 62 and 64.

Aside from the use of dissonance, Artusi would have been shocked also at the numerous cross relations resulting from juxtaposing unrelated chords, such as A major and F major in measure 16 (Example 2-4); the same two chords in measure 26 (Example 2-2); or D major and B♭ major in measure 56. Usually the chords sought for this harsh effect are major triads whose roots are a major or minor third apart.

**EXAMPLE 2-4**   C. Monteverdi, *Ohimè, se tanto amate*

If smoothness of harmony and richness of consonance produce delectation, as Artusi rightly believed, what did Monteverdi gain by doing violence to them? This he explained in a too brief defense prefacing his fifth book of madrigals in 1605. He said that his method constituted a "second practice," superseding the "first practice" for which Gioseffo Zarlino (1517–1590) had given the rules of consonance and dissonance in *Le istitutioni harmoniche* (Harmonic Institutions, 1558). Claudio Monteverdi's brother Giulio Cesare, also a musician, fortunately amplified these cryptic remarks in the next book of madrigals in 1607. Claudio, he explained, aimed to make the text the mistress of the harmony rather than the reverse, as was true in much earlier music. The unorthodox procedures found in *Ohimè* and its companion works could therefore be justified, because the rules of counterpoint often had to be set aside.

The text always had a decisive influence on the composition of a piece of vocal music, but earlier it was the form of the text rather than its meaning that concerned the composer. A poem's structure in terms of the number of its stanzas, lines per stanza, syllables per line, refrains, metrical pattern: these determined the structure of a musical setting. This external correspondence was not what Monteverdi cared about; he wanted a deeper correspondence of meaning and feeling. The form of the poem *Ohimè* is of nine lines in which all but the second and fifth have seven syllables. This structure is almost completely disguised in the musical setting. The rhyme at the end of the third and fifth lines, *morire* with *sentire*, is respected by having both close through a full cadence followed by a rest. Otherwise, the line endings are elided, because the thought is not broken. Although symmetry is lost, continuity and sense are won. On the other hand, individual words or groups of words are singled out for special treatment. For example, "ohimè" is represented by a sighing, drooping figure, and "mill'e mille dolc'ohimè" is graphically rendered by sequential motion upon the original "ohimè" escape figure.

The changes of texture, rhythm, and style leave a disjointed impression. The composer sacrificed musical consistency to mirror the poet's every image. Only the carefully calculated tonal design—notice particularly the frequent return to the dominant and tonic harmonies—and the subtle insistence upon the opening figure save the work from disintegration; nevertheless, the madrigal remains manneristic and experimental. Monteverdi and his contemporaries soon realized that free poetizing in music was not coming to terms with the problems of musical composition.

Claudio Monteverdi's brilliant output spanned the formative period of baroque music. More a culminator than a creator of a new style, he rightly looked upon himself as one of a long line of innovators reaching back to Cipriano de Rore (1516–1565). Giulio Cesare Monteverdi four times referred to de Rore as having set precedents for the liberties his brother took, calling de Rore "the first renovator of the second practice," for this pioneer had made contrapuntal technique "a faithful servant of the text, without which these compositions would remain bodies without souls." He cited the madrigals *Dalle belle contrade* (*HAM* I, 131) and *Crudele acerba inesorabil morte* (Einstein, *The Italian Madrigal*, III, 114). Although de Rore, like Zarlino, had learned his rules from Willaert, he put ahead of them, according to Giulio Cesare, a principle set down by Plato. This required that the melody and rhythm follow the text and not the opposite.[4] Giovanni de' Bardi and Vincenzo Galilei in their writings around 1580 had professed similar beliefs, and they too hailed de Rore as their prophet.

---

[4]Plato, *Republic* 398D.

# DE RORE, PIONEER OF THE SECOND PRACTICE

Of the madrigalists, de Rore remains one of the most unjustly neglected in spite of the high rank assigned him by Alfred Einstein in *The Italian
Madrigal*. An analysis of one of de Rore's works will show how much secular
musical composition was becoming subject to the imagery and emotions of
poetic texts. It must be emphasized that at mid-century this was true only of
secular music; some decades later the tendency spread to sacred motets and
similar categories, though rarely to the mass. Thus de Rore was musically a
split personality. In his church music he continued to write in the traditional
way, but in his madrigals, particularly in those he composed in his last years,
he was indeed the prophet that the next generation revered. Here music
rivaled poetry in arousing the affections, as the musician matched the poet's
verbal images with clever and evocative sound pictures. Music became a
language in which every technical device of composition, both new and old,
was enlisted to communicate feelings and ideas.

*O Sonno*, from the *Second Book of Madrigals in Four Parts*, 1557, one
of the compositions singled out for praise by Giovanni de' Bardi[5] (1534–
1612), will serve as an example. The poem is an apostrophe to sleep by
Giovanni della Casa (1502–1556) in the form of a sonnet. Its lofty language,
elaborate imagery, and tone of despair are typical of the poetic tendency that
paralleled the early baroque in music. Sleep is likened in turn to a child of
darkness, to a large bird that spreads its wings protectively over the sleeper,
to a refuge from daylight, and finally to a prickly bed of painful memories.
As each image called forth from the composer a carefully chosen technique,
the music shifts from one manner of writing to another. The freedom with
which della Casa treated poetic form is equaled by de Rore's disregard for the
line as a unit of thought. A short phrase, even a word, may be isolated from
its context by a distinct musical thought and texture.

The two opening words, for example, stand by themselves, as the two
top voices address sleep in a plaintive descent (Example 2-5). Then the
"placid son" of night is characterized in a succession of smooth major triads
in root position, but the harmony is darkly colored by the shifts first down
the cycle of fifths from E to d, then up from B♭ to G. The syncopation in the
second measure abets the undercurrent of uneasiness. After a momentary
stirring of optimism (measures 6 and 7), de Rore blends the sweetness of
sleep and the bitterness of the evils it dispels in a gentle chromaticism. The
words "hard and tedious" are underlined by a reversion to *fauxbourdon*, the
fifteenth-century technique of parallel sixth chords, closing in on an open
fifth and octave, a piquant progression among the prevailing full root chords.

---

[5] *Discorso mandato a Giulio Caccini*, trans. in Strunk, p. 295.

EXAMPLE 2-5  C. de Rore, *O Sonno*

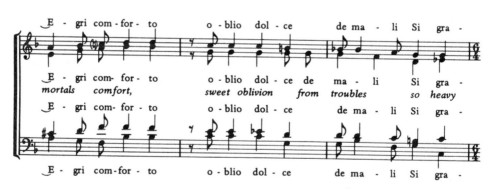

EXAMPLE 2-5 (Cont.)

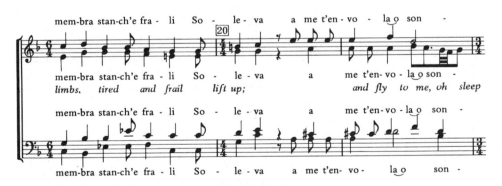

15

EXAMPLE 2-5 (Cont.)

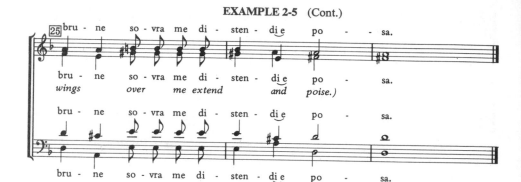

Suddenly de Rore turns to a popular-style tune in $\frac{6}{8}$ plus $\frac{2}{4}$ meter for the words "come to the aid of a heart." But the thought "languishes, and rests not" breaks the bright mood with its cross relations. The climax of the first part is reached in the appeal "fly to me, o sleep," repeated with an air of urgency begotten by the contracted measure 22.

It pays to dwell on this masterpiece, for it epitomizes the esthetic goals and musical apparatus of the emergent baroque style. The composer lost no opportunity to make his representation of the text vivid and moving. Sacrificing the homogeneity of style admired by the Renaissance, he created a melange that has been fittingly called *mannerism*. With breathless abandon he went from one rhythmic scheme to another, from diatonicism to chromaticism, from root chords to sixth chords, from sharp keys to flat keys. Still there is coherence, because de Rore was careful to return to the principal degrees of the tonality at frequent cadence points and to relate the end to the beginning. Monteverdi may well have learned these techniques from him.

The preference for chordal declamatory style concentrates the melodic interest in the top voice, and the lowest part becomes a supporting bass. These features make this madrigal very apt for solo performance by a soprano voice, the other parts being taken by accompanying instruments. Such arrangements were often practiced, and as often as not the top line was embellished. An embellishment of *O Sonno* was published by Girolamo dalla

EXAMPLE 2-6  G. dalla Casa, *Il vero modo di diminuir*

Casa in 1584 in his treatise *Il vero modo di diminuir* (The True Method of Making Divisions). Measures 13 to 18 are rendered there as shown in Example 2-6.

## THE RISE OF THE SOLO SINGER

The solo professional singer began to emerge as an important figure in musical life around 1570, according to a contemporary witness, Vincenzo Giustiniani. This is not to say that accompanied solo singing was truly an innovation. The poet-lutanist-singer was a familiar entertainer at courts throughout the Renaissance, but he was not primarily a musician who had trained himself as a vocal virtuoso, as were those who became famous in the last quarter of the sixteenth century: Giulio Cesare Brancaccio, Alessandro Merlo Romano, Giovanni Luca Conforto, Vittoria Archilei, Giulio Caccini, and others. Giustiniani described the technique of three famous women singers, Tarquinia Molza, Lucrezia Bendidio, and Laura Peperara at the court of Ferrara this way:

> ... they moderated or increased their voices, loud or soft, heavy or light, according to the demands of the piece they were singing; now slow, breaking off with sometimes a gentle sigh, now singing long passages legato or detached, now groups, now leaps, now with long trills, now with short, and again with sweet running passages sung softly, to which sometimes one heard an echo answer unexpectedly. They accompanied the music and the sentiment with appropriate facial expressions, glances and gestures, with no awkward movements of the mouth or hands or body which might not express the feeling of the song. They made the words clear in such a way that one could hear even the last syllables of every word, which was never interrupted or suppressed by passages and other embellishments.[6]

The principal composer for the three ladies was Luzzasco Luzzaschi (1545–1607), a pupil of de Rore. A notable part of the repertory he wrote for them was published in Rome in 1601 in *Madrigali . . . per cantare, et sonare a 1, 2, e 3 soprani*, all ostensibly composed before the death of their patron, Duke Alfonso II, in 1597. The madrigal for three soprani, *O dolcezze amarissime d'amore*, may be seen in Einstein's *The Italian Madrigal*, III, 310. An example of one of the solo pieces is *O primavera* on a text from the tragicomic pastorale by Guarini, *Il Pastor fido* (*GMB* 166). The keyboard part contains all the parts of what is essentially a four-part madrigal. Of these the soprano sings the top part, accompanying almost every harmonic close with brilliant cadenzas.

[6] *Discorso sopra la musica*, trans. Carol MacClintock, *Musica disciplina* XV (1961), p. 213.

A similar piece, one that can be precisely dated, is *Godi, turba mortal* by Emilio de' Cavalieri (d. 1602). It was written for the last of the six inter- mezzi staged at the marriage of Duke Ferdinand I of Tuscany in 1589. These intermezzi, performed between the acts of a comedy, were allegorical stage extravaganzas that united singing, dancing, and instrumental music with elaborate cloud and other stage machinery and rich costuming. The soloist, Onofrio Gualfreducci, sang to the accompaniment of a *chitarrone*—a large lute with extra bass strings—which played the four parts of this madrigal. As in Luzzaschi's madrigal, the soloist doubles the top part, but the ornaments are not limited to cadences (Example 2-7). It is instructive to compare the top instrumental part and the voice line, for this reveals the process by which the top line of a polyphonic texture was embellished. The sixteenth-note run usually begins on the note it replaces, but sometimes the diminution takes the place of several notes of the simple version. On the word "felice," for example, it departs from the first note of the original and joins this again only on the fourth note. This process takes on the character of a variation upon a melody. This, it will be seen, was one of the principal techniques of solo music in the seventeenth century.

EXAMPLE 2-7   E. de'Cavalieri, *Godi, turba mortal*, from *Intermedio VI* (1589)

That these florid examples should have originated in response to the demands of virtuoso singers is significant. Composers are not alone in creating new styles. Much of what is novel at the beginning of the seventeenth century was the result of a gradual transformation of performance practice as it adapted to the tastes of public and patrons. The singer, being in direct contact with audiences, was sensitive to their eagerness to be moved by music they could understand and their admiration for brilliant technique and soaring, smooth vocality. Dalla Casa and de' Cavalieri were singing masters, and Giulio Caccini (d. 1618), Francesco Rasi, and Jacopo Peri (1561–1633) were very successful singers who turned to composition in order to create for themselves a repertory for the changing times, since the professional composers had defaulted. Only after the new style became popular did men who were primarily composers, such as Sigismondo d'India and Monteverdi, begin to imitate and refine it.

## THE BASSO CONTINUO

A similar development is observable in instrumental practice. Within a few months between October 1600 and February 1601, musical scores by three of these singers and singing masters were published containing a new shorthand method of notating instrumental harmony. These were Cavalieri's *Rappresentatione di Anima et di Corpo*, Caccini's *Euridice*, and Peri's *Euridice*. The first of these to be issued was Cavalieri's. Formerly, whatever instrumental parts were printed appeared in partbooks, tablatures, or scores. A glance at the accompaniment of Cavalieri's *Godi turba mortal* (Example 2-7) shows why the new method was needed. The four-part accompaniment shown there represents the published viol parts. We know that in the 1589 performance the accompaniment was played by a chitarrone, for which such a score is cumbersome, if not superfluous. With only the treble and bass before him, a player of a keyboard instrument, harp, or lute could improvise an accompaniment that better suited his instrument and his hands. The necessary treble-bass sketches must have existed years before they began to appear in print in 1600. Viadana claimed to have used them as early as 1594, and unembellished versions of some of Caccini's songs of *Le nuove musiche* written in this way survive in an English manuscript whose sources probably go back to an even earlier date.[7]

The following page, reproduced from Cavalieri's score of 1600, shows the method used by him, and Peri and Caccini as well. The only instrumental part given under the voice is a bass line. Over the notes of the bass appear

[7]See Nancy Maze, "Tenbury Ms. 1018: A Key to Caccini's Art of Embellishment," *JAMS*, IX (1956), pp. 61-63.

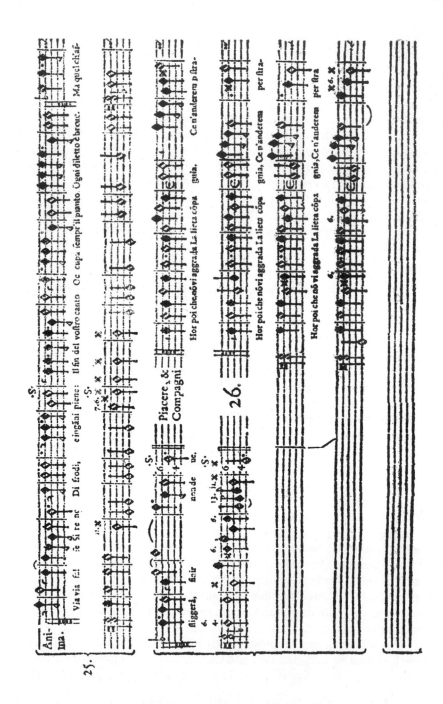

20

numbers and signs such as 11, 7, and $\frac{6}{4}$. The numbers instruct the player of a keyboard or lutelike instrument to include in the chord over the bass the eleventh, seventh, or sixth and fourth notes, counting the bass note as 1. For example, 11 over the D calls for the G an octave-plus-fourth above. When no number occurs over a bass note, the player builds a chord with the third or tenth above the bass, major or minor, whichever belongs to the key. If the composer wished a major third or tenth when the key contained a minor one, he placed a ♯ over the bass note, or if the reverse was true he marked a ♭ above the bass. Normally a fifth or twelfth above the bass is also played, but when the number 6 is present, the sixth or one of its compounds replaces the fifth as a component of the chord. A ♯ before a 6 means that the sixth is raised a semitone from that found in the key. A sharp after 11, 4, or 7 means that immediately after the note designated by the number should follow the major tenth, third, or sixth above the same bass note. This usually occurs in connection with a suspension. A solution—or "realization" as it is usually called—of Cavalieri's bass may be seen in *TEM* 37.

This practice of "figuring" basses continued throughout the baroque period and beyond, but after the first years of the seventeenth century composers stopped specifying the octave in which they wanted the dissonances, writing a 4 instead of an 11, for example. Not all later composers took the pains to figure their basses; some assumed that the player would judge which chord was necessary by reading the upper part or parts. Italian opera composers tended to be lax in this, although Corelli and Bach, for example, figured their basses punctiliously.

Whether figured or not, a bass that was meant to serve as the foundation for an improvised accompaniment was called a *basso continuo* or thorough bass. It was called this because it was continuously present, even when there were rests in the bass voices or instruments. In this it differed from the earlier *basso seguente*, which duplicated in a part for a keyboard instrument the lowest voice of a polyphonic texture. Normally one or more bass instruments played the bass line, while a keyboard instrument or one belonging to the lute or harp class, or a combination of several of these, played the chords implied by the bass and its figures.

It is obvious that the *basso continuo* was a handy device for the accompanist, who was thereby spared the onus of reading a score containing numerous parts written usually in several different clefs. This alone would not have made it almost universal within a few decades into the seventeenth century had it not also served the purposes of composers. Its adoption by them is the surest sign that they were losing interest in the thick texture of equal parts moving in more or less independent lines throughout the musical fabric. More appealing now was the texture of one or two solo parts, very often in the treble range, highlighted against a bass. At first this bass was a static one, little more than the foundation for a series of chords, but soon it acquired rhythmic momentum and melodic interest which restored some balance between it and the upper parts. Composers became quite indifferent to the specific details of the chordal filling that closed the gap between these outer parts. The duty of completing the composition fell to the performers.

## THE MONODIC AIR AND MADRIGAL

The new secular solo songs, or monodies, as they are often called, were mainly of two kinds: strophic and through-composed. Strophic songs took over the technique of the Renaissance air and were usually called *arie*. Through-composed songs followed the procedures of the madrigal. They were often indeed designated as madrigals, and the texts were of the same sort that had served the earlier polyphonic madrigal composers. Both madrigals and airs were eventually infused with the style of the recitative.

The history of the air in the sixteenth century is mainly an unwritten one. Court poet-singers who improvised upon standard or original tunes rarely recorded their settings. The airs sung in sacred or secular plays are almost all lost. A few tunes survive in instrumental variations and dances and in published or manuscript compilations. Some are designated with terms such as *aria di terza rima, aria di sonnetti, aria di capitoli*, or *aria di ottava rima*. These labels mean that the tune is suitable for singing any poem that follows a certain form, such as *terza rima* (three lines of eleven syllables each, rhyming ABA—the stanza form of Dante's *Divine Comedy*) or the sonnet (fourteen lines usually of eleven syllables, composed of two quatrains followed by two tercets). That this singing tradition was still very much alive in the seventeenth century is shown by the fact that several of the monodists published airs for singing poetry, among them Sigismondo d'India in 1609, Pietro Benedetti in 1613, and Biagio Marini in 1635. Vincenzo Galilei jotted down a scheme for singing sonnets in the back of a copy of *Fronimo*, his treatise on arranging vocal compositions for the lute, published in 1568. To show how the formula works, a Petrarchan sonnet, chosen at random, is here set over the tune (Example 2-8). The lutanist would sing the top line and play the lower three parts or all the parts as accompaniment. The many repeated notes and the cadence notes at the end of each line are characteristic of the air for singing poetry.

Both the opera and chamber air of the early seventeenth century are descendants of this improvised singing of poetry. The espousal of the air by the composers at the turn of the century may seem to run contrary to the new esthetic ideals, because when the same music must serve different strophes or even different poems, it cannot serve them all equally well. But there is another aspect of the new ideals that needs emphasis: the desire to return to the cultivation of melody. This was a reaffirmation of an Italian tradition represented at the beginning of the sixteenth century by the *frottola*, essentially a solo song with lute accompaniment. During the Italians' brief

**EXAMPLE 2-8**  V. Galilei, *Aria de sonetti*

1. Il  can-tar no - vo e'l  pian - ger de li au - gel - li
5. Quel - la c'ha ne - ve il vol - to, o - ro i  ca - pel - li
9. Co - si mi sve - glio a  sa - lu - tar  l'au - ro - ra
12. I' gli ho ve - du - ti al - cun gior - no am - be - du - i

Voice
and
Lute

2. In  su'l dì fan - no  re - ten - tir le  val - li,
6. Nel cui a-mor non  fur mai in - gan - ni ne  fal - li,
10. E'l  sol ch'è se - co, e più  l'al - tra on - d'io  fu - i
13. Le - var-si in se - me, e 'n un  pun - to e 'n un' or - a

3. E'l  mor-mo - rar  de' li - qui - di cris - tal - li,
7. Des - ta-mi al suon  de li a - mo - ro - si  bal - li,

4. Giù  per lu - ci - di  fre - schi ri - vi e snel - li.
8. Pet - ti - nan - do al suo vec - chio j bian - chi vel - li.
11. Ne' pri-mi an - ni a  ba - glia - to e son  an - co - ra.
14. Quel far le stel - le e que - sto spa - rir lu - i.

flirtation with the contrapuntal style brought in from the north, the lyric tendencies were submerged and somewhat vilified in the *villanelle, canzonette,* and *balletti,* in which trivial verse and often dialectal doggerel were melodiously and dancingly set. Galilei, spokesman for the new music, urged composers to imitate the simple tunes and means of the *frottole* and airs and to seek "beauty of air." By this he meant not only tunefulness but also clarity of harmonic movement, simplicity of texture, and rhythmic vitality. The aim was to ennoble the air style by bestowing it upon worthier poetry. For this purpose Giulio Caccini requested the noted poet Gabriello Chiabrera to provide him with fresh canzonet texts, some of which he set to music among the airs of *Le nuove musiche*.

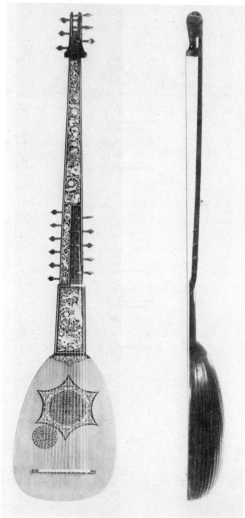

The chitarrone was the preferred instrument for realizing the thorough-bass accompaniment to a recitative or aria in the early seventeenth century. This instrument, built in Venice, had besides the normal complement of strings a set of bass strings for the continuo line. (Cliché Publimages. Musée Instrumental du Conservatoire de Paris.)

This collection, published in Florence in 1602,[8] contains some of the earliest composed examples of the new air as well as solo madrigals. It was not, however, the first such collection printed, having been preceded by about two months by that of Domenico Melli. But if we may believe Caccini, he had written some of his airs as early as 1585. All ten of the compositions designated *aria* by Caccini are set to poems which consist of several stanzas following a uniform scheme. The musical form is not always simply strophic, that is, repeating the same music for each stanza, as in *Udite, udite amanti*. Just as the improvising poets must have added certain nuances and ornaments to suit each stanza of a *terza* or *ottava rima*, so Caccini varied a single musical skeleton in the several stanzas of three of the airs. This procedure, one of the most important means of musical expansion in the baroque period, is illustrated in Example 2-9. Writing anew the music for the fifth stanza upon the skeleton of the first permitted Caccini to declaim the text more naturally and precisely and to underline the words *scorgono* and *piovono* with descriptive runs. The long passage on *piovono* (rain) required an expansion of the time value of the measure by a half. This process of varying the details of a melody while keeping its scheme and harmonic accompaniment is called strophic variation and will be met again and again in the baroque period.

Although in setting an air strophically the composer tried to capture the mood of the poem as a whole, the music usually remained the mistress and not the text. The solo madrigal, on the other hand, like its polyphonic counterpart, was the medium of choice for intense expression, because every significant portion of the text received due attention. Single words or short phrases could be repeated and used to build to a climax through sequences, as the thrice-repeated "Amarilli" in Caccini's *Amarilli mia bella* (*GMB* 173, measures 20–26, 36–45). Entire sections could also receive repetition, whether for formal reasons or emphasis, but never was the music separated from the words that engendered it. The burden of expression was, of course, on the single melodic line and its purely chordal accompaniment. Harmonic and melodic dissonances, chromaticism, changes of meter and rhythm were, as in the polyphonic madrigals, the principal resources. But well-placed ornaments, such as trills, shakes, and runs, accompanied by crescendos and diminuendos, contributed much to convey feeling incisively when performed by a skillful singer.

It is not to be wondered that such madrigals as *Perfidissimo volto* (*NAWM* 63), *Vedrò il mio sol*, and *Dovrò dunque morire* (*MM* 30) were greeted "with affectionate applause" in Florence among Bardi's circle of noblemen,

---

[8]The Florentine calendar, which began the year on the Feast of the Annunciation, March 25, has led to some confusion about certain dates in Florentine music history. The first performance of *Dafne* took place in 1597 Florentine style but 1598 our style; *Le nuove musiche* has 1601 on the title page but was not published until 1602 of our calendar, similarly Peri's *Euridice*, which was issued in February 1600, Florentine style, belongs in 1601.

**EXAMPLE 2-9**  G. Caccini, *Le nuove musiche,* aria ultima

First verse:
1. Chi mi con-fort' ahi - me, chi più con -
*(Who comforts me, alas? Who still con -*

Fifth (last) verse:
5. Deh se tue bel-le ci - glia ho - ra mi scor - - -
*O, if your beautiful eyes now pick me out,*

1. so - la-mi? Hor che'l mio sol che si bei
*soles me? Now that my sun, whom such*

5. go - no, Mi - ra che gl'oc-chi mie-i la - cri - me
*Look this way, for my eyes tears*

1. rag - gi a - dor - na - no....
*beautiful rays adorn.)*

5. pio vo - no.
*rain.)*

some of whom remembered it as Bardi's *Camerata*. We can also believe Caccini when he says that he was told later in Rome that

> they had never heard a melody of a single voice with a simple string instrument that had such power to move the affections of the soul as these madrigals. This was both because of their new style, and because when in those times madrigals printed for several voices were sung by a single one, it seemed to them that the artifice necessary to coordinate the parts prevented the soprano by itself from having any affection.[9]

This statement indicates that Caccini scored his first successes with the monodic style around 1590, since Bardi moved from Florence to Rome in 1592, and his *Camerata* (see Chapter 3) did not survive that date. Comparison of the other songs with those he named shows that Caccini's conception of the monodic style failed to develop beyond that point. For 1602, they are strangely conservative and untouched by the most important discovery of the age: the recitative style.

## BIBLIOGRAPHICAL NOTES

Alfred Einstein, *The Italian Madrigal* (Princeton, N. J.: Princeton University Press, 1949), Vol. II, gives a detailed and comprehensive picture of developments in the sixteenth-century madrigal that led to the second practice. A good brief survey that includes England and other northern countries is Jerome Roche, *The Madrigal* (London: Hutchinson University Library, 1972).

Einstein's Vol. III contains works by the main exponents of the new trends: de Rore, Wert, Marenzio, Luzzaschi, Galilei, and da Gagliano. Other examples are in *HAM* I, 131, 146, 155; *MM* 27; and *GMB* 165, 166. The madrigals of de Rore are edited by Bernhard Meier in the *Opera omnia* (American Institute of Musicology, 1959–1977), Vols. II-V. Two collected editions of the works of Marenzio are in progress, one by Les Editions Renaissantes, New York, of which the first volume, edited by Franklin B. Zimmerman and Hannah Rose, was issued in 1974; the other by Broude Brothers, New York, edited by Steven Ledbetter and Patricia Myers. Both are planned to contain the secular works in twenty volumes or more. The complete madrigals of Wert have been issued in his *Collected Works*, ed. Carol MacClintock, with the collaboration for the sacred music of Melvin Bernstein (American Institute of Musicology, 1961–1977), Vols. 1–12, 14–15. Selections of late madrigals are also edited in *CW* 80, 105, 109, 115, and 125.

The most authoritative statement of the standards of composition that Monteverdi called the first practice is Gioseffo Zarlino, *The Art of Counterpoint*, Part III of *Le Istituzioni harmoniche*, 1558, translated by Guy A. Marco and

---

[9]Foreword to *Le nuove musiche*, 1602. Translations in this book are by the author unless otherwise indicated.

Claude V. Palisca (New Haven: Yale University Press, 1968; New York: W. W. Norton & Co., Inc., 1976 [paperback]).

Monteverdi's madrigals illustrating the second practice are in G. F. Malipiero's edition of Monteverdi, *Tutte le opere* (16 vols., 1926–1942), Vols. 1–5. A reprint of this series, slightly corrected, is published by Universal Edition, Vienna, and distributed by Theodore Presser Co. of Bryn Mawr, Pennsylvania. A new critical edition, conforming to modern scholarly standards, has begun to appear under the editorship of Raffaello Monterosso (Cremona: Athenaeum cremonense, 1970–   ). Another critical edition, aimed particularly at assisting the realization of authentic performances, is that of Bernard Bailly de Surcy, issued by Editions Renaissantes, Paris and New York, 1972–   .

The most readable introduction to the music of Monteverdi and the one that best sets him in the context of contemporary styles is Denis Arnold, *Monteverdi* (London: Dent; New York: Farrar, Straus, & Giroux, 1963; rev. ed. 1975). Another authoritative, more leisurely study is that by Leo Schrade (New York: W. W. Norton & Co., Inc., 1950). Some detailed studies of Monteverdi's music and his thought, as well as translations of his most important letters and other writings, are in Denis Arnold and Nigel Fortune, eds., *The Monteverdi Companion* (London: Faber and Faber; New York: W. W. Norton & Co., Inc., 1968).

The basic source book on the *basso continuo* is Frank Arnold, *The Art of Accompaniment from a Thorough-Bass* (London: Oxford, 1931), which contains many translations from the manuals on accompaniment. Agazzari's instructions are in Strunk, *SR* 55. More oriented toward performance but still authoritative is Peter Williams, *Figured Bass Accompaniment*, 2 vols. (Edinburgh University Press, 1970).

Caccini's *Le nuove musiche* is available in several facsimile editions and in an excellent modern edition with English translations of the preface and texts by H. Wiley Hitchcock (Madison, Wis.: A-R Editions, 1970). See also the examples in *HAM* II, 184, *MM* 30, *GMB* 172, 173, Many monodies by Caccini and his contemporaries are in the excellent anthology by Knud Jeppesen, *La Flora* (3 vols.; Copenhagen: Hansen, 1949). Another large selection of solo songs is *The Solo Song, 1580–1730* (New York: W. W. Norton & Co., Inc., 1973), edited with English translations of texts by Carol MacClintock; it includes English, French, and German as well as Italian songs.

The music of the Florentine intermezzi of 1589 is printed in D. P. Walker, ed., *Les fêtes du mariage de Ferdinand de Médicis et de Christine de Lorraine, Florence 1589*, I: *Musique des intermèdes de "La Pellegina"* (Paris: Éditions du Centre national de la recherche scientifique, 1963).

A fine survey of the early solo song is Nigel Fortune, "Italian Secular Monody from 1600 to 1635." *MQ*, XXXIX (1953), 171–95. A good history of the art of making embellishments, and one that shows its key role in the baroque style, is Imogene Horsley, "The Diminutions in Composition and Theory of Composition," *Acta musicologica*, XXXV (1963), 124–53. Extensive examples are in *Die Improvisation*, ed. Ernest T. Ferand (Cologne: Arno Volk, 1956).

# THREE

# THE RECITATIVE STYLE

The recitative style has been compared at times to Greek music, to psalmodic chant, and to the singing of poetry to standard formulas. But it is like none of these. A true return to Greek practice would have been unpalatable to musicians of the early baroque, because it would have meant rejecting the Western tradition of regularly measured rhythm and the recently mastered triadic harmony. Greek music was purely monophonic, like psalmody. Neither the plainchant practice nor the manner of improvising on tunes to sing poetry was adequate to modern needs, because both were too insensitive to the meanings and feelings of the text. A new method was needed, and recitative was a truly progressive solution, because it built on the most recent advances in the use of triadic harmony and controlled dissonance. Like these other modes of singing, it depended on an interaction between speech inflection and melody, but its essential novelty was that it navigated the straits between speech rhythm and measured rhythm, and between free dissonance and triadic harmony. For, in recitative, melodic declamation was at once free from and controlled by harmony and measured rhythm.

If the recognition of the triad as a basic harmonic building block in the sixteenth century prepared the way for recitative, the immediate stimulus for its invention was external to purely musical development. It was the wish to imitate an ancient practice of singing. This was fed by a critical interpretation of the ancient sources by the erudite musical scholar Girolamo Mei (1519–1594), a product of the humanist movement. From reading every ancient piece of writing extant on music in the original Greek and, equipped with a key to their notation, studying a few surviving Greek hymns, Mei came to a number of important conclusions about the nature of ancient Greek music. It always consisted of a single melody even when many were singing and playing together. This permitted it to be a means for moving and moderating the passions, because it could imitate the rhythms and inflections of impassioned or ordinary speech and seek the regions of the voice used in various states of emotion. For this purpose the Greeks developed a system of keys through which they could raise or lower any melody to fit a particular region of the voice. Aside from instrumental music, which with or without dance could be imitative of actions, melody was a vehicle for the expression of the content of poetry. Considering the several genres of poetry that were used among the Greeks, Mei's interest was particularly drawn to the music of the tragedy because of his previous researches on the history of the Greek theater and his work in establishing the critical text of a number of tragedies of Euripides and Aeschylus. Mei decided, after much study, that the entire tragedies were sung and not, as some believed, only the lyric portions and choruses.

Although Mei lived and worked in Rome, he was a Florentine gentleman and kept up numerous contacts with his native city. He sent chapters of his Latin treatise, *De modis musicis antiquorum* (Concerning the Modes of the Ancients), as they were completed to his former teacher, the philosopher and classical scholar Piero Vettori, and several copies were made of this treatise for others. He also corresponded with the musical patron and amateur Giovanni Bardi and with Vincenzo Galilei (c. 1520–1591), both of whom used information and ideas they received from Mei in their writings. Galilei particularly urged a return to the ideals and procedures of ancient music, in his *Dialogo della musica antica, et della moderna* (Dialogue Concerning Ancient and Modern Music, 1581), in which he published several Greek hymns sent to him by Mei. He also experimented with a melodic style inspired by what he had learned of Greek music.

Through Bardi and Galilei, interest in these matters spread to others. Bardi was host at his home from at least 1573 to a circle of noblemen who gathered regularly as an informal academy to discuss literary and scientific matters and to make music and talk about it. The only musicians known to have attended these meetings are Caccini, Galilei, and the amateur Pietro Strozzi, but others must have been frequent visitors. Galilei wrote his *Dialogo* partly in response to the curiosity and eagerness for instruction of these gentlemen. This group, to which Caccini referred in 1600 as the *Camerata* of Bardi, probably broke up well before Bardi moved to Rome in 1592.

Galilei was also patronized by another wealthy nobleman, Jacopo Corsi (d. 1604), who perhaps more than Bardi was interested in the practical application of some of Galilei's theories. Corsi was host to a rival academy and also had the privilege of presenting occasional entertainments at the court of Ferdinand I of the Medici, Grand Duke of Tuscany. Together with the young poet Ottavio Rinuccini and the young singer Jacopo Peri, Corsi conceived of setting an entire dramatic pastoral, *Dafne*, to music in a *stile rappresentativo* inspired by the antique model. Although Peri later stated that they began work as early as 1594, the production was not shown until the carnival of 1598, when it was done both in Corsi's palace and at court. By this time two short pastorals had been similarly set to music by Emilio de' Cavalieri, whom the Duke had brought from Rome in 1587 as his superintendent of fine arts and entertainments. These were *Il Satiro* and *La Disperazione di Fileno*, performed at court in 1591. A few airs and one recitative section survive from *Dafne*, but nothing from Cavalieri's pastorals. We therefore have to accept Peri's acknowledgment that Cavalieri was the first to set an entire dramatic work to music, which Cavalieri himself boasted was the case. However, if we compare Cavalieri's music for his sacred *Rappresentatione di Anima et di Corpo* (Representation of the Body and the Soul), produced in Rome in February 1600, Peri's music for Rinuccini's *Euridice*, produced in Florence in October 1600, and Caccini's score for the same *Euridice*, it is clear that Peri's departs most radically from the solo music of the sixteenth century. Otherwise, all three works are similar in that they consist of airs, choruses, dances, and recitative sections.

It is obvious, then, that several composers competed to arrive at a satisfactory dramatic style. But Peri was the one who realized a solution that answered the needs of the stage and that was to become a model for others. His solution was to free the voice from the accompaniment both rhythmically and harmonically and yet derive musical coherence from its support. His own description is the best that has yet been written of his method. He begins by saying that he assumed the Greeks in their tragedies used a manner of singing that was intermediate between speech and melody. He therefore reasoned that he should find a middle course between the sustained, measured, and intervallic steps of singing and the fluent, hurried, continuous inflections of speech. He continues:

> I knew also that in our speech we intone certain syllables in such a way that a harmony can be built upon them, and in the course of speaking we pass through many that are not so intoned until we reach another that permits a movement to a new consonance. Keeping in mind those manners and accents that serve us in our grief and joy, and similar states, I made the bass move in

time with these, faster or slower according to the affections. I held it fixed through both dissonances and consonances, until the voice of the speaker, having run through various notes, arrived at a syllable that, being intoned in ordinary speech, opened the way to a new harmony.[1]

In this way he avoided repeating the notes of the bass, which would have grated against the dissonances; nor did the melody of the singer continually "dance to the movements of the bass," as in some earlier monodies.

## *PERI'S* EURIDICE

The lament in *Euridice* which Orpheus sings after hearing Daphne tell of Euridice's death from a snakebite (*NAWM* 68) exemplifies Peri's recitative technique. Certain syllables (italicized below) tend to be accented or prolonged in speaking, such as, in the first four lines: *pian-go*, *so-spi-ro*, Eu-ri-*di-ce*, *pos-so*, fe-*li-ce*. These receive the longer notes in the musical setting and meet the bass in consonances that form the nuclei of the chords of the accompaniment. The remaining syllables of these lines are pronounced hurriedly as in speaking. Often to give the illusion of the continuous or sliding pitch inflections of speech, these shorter syllables pass through dissonances, which occur mainly on secondary beats, but also, significantly, on primary beats. In Example 3-1 the dissonances are marked with asterisks.

The harmonic technique is indebted to the madrigalists but surpasses them in boldness of dissonance. Sudden shifts of harmony, as between E and g in measures 8 and 9, are familiar from the madrigal literature. Like the madrigalists too, Peri avoided cadences, preferring to divert the harmonic motion to unexpected regions. Unfortunately he tended to return too often to the same degrees, vacillating in this example between a and g. At other times the writing is distinctively monodic and shows Peri's sure instinct for the resources of the new genre. Nonchordal tones such as the B♭ of measure 4, the F♯ of measure 8, or the E against a D chord in measure 11, obviously anticipating the next harmony—these are difficult to classify even in present-day analytical terms, so special are they to the idiom Peri devised. These dissonances arise not only from an attempt to express the words but also from the manner of speaking them. As Marco Scacchi was to note in 1643, "in the compositions of the moderns one should consider not only the words of the songs but also, and first of all, the very manner of speaking, which changes according to the different affections of the soul."[2]

[1]Foreword, *L'Euridice*, reprinted in Angelo Solerti, *Le origini del melodramma* (Turin: Fratelli Bocca, 1903), p. 46.
[2]*Cribrum musicum* (Venice: A. Vincenti, 1643), p. 184.

**EXAMPLE 3-1** Peri, *Euridice*

Orfeo

Non pian-go e non so-spi-ro O mia ca - ra Eu-ri-di - ce,
*(I cry not and I sigh not o my dear Eurydice,*

Ché so-spi-rar, ché la-gri-mar non pos-so Ca-da - ve-ro in-fe-li - ce,
*For sigh and weep I cannot unhappy corpse.*

O mio co - re, o mia spe-me, o pa-ce, o vi-ta! Ohi - mè! chi
*O my heart, o my hope, o peace, o life! Alas, who*

mi t'ha tol - to, Chi mi t'ha tol - to ohi mè! do - ve se' gi - ta?
*from me has taken you, who from me has taken you, alas, where have you gone? )*

The recitation is mainly limited to a narrowly circumscribed range, perhaps following Galilei's counsel that modern singing should imitate the small range practiced by early Greek bards. For exclamations of despair, such as "O mio core" or "Dove se' gita," Peri reached for higher levels, while for thoughts of death, as at the end, he moved to a lower one. In this too he followed the theoreticians of the monodic movement. In some ways Peri's recitative has the earmarks of an ideology translated too literally into practice, and there are inevitably awkward moments. But there is an intensity, nobility, and realism that could not have failed to move its first auditors and that can still affect us today.

It would be a mistake, however, to assume that the entire pastoral contains nothing but this kind of intense declamation. Within the monodic passages alone several styles may be distinguished. Giovanni Battista Doni, writing in 1640,[3] recognized three types of dramatic monody: narrative, recitational, and expressive. The example discussed above he would undoubtedly have classed as expressive, though the illustration he gave is the lament of Arianna in Monteverdi's *Arianna* (*GMB* 177), which he described as "the most beautiful composition that has yet been seen in stage and theatrical music." A passage such as the messenger Dafne's account of the death of Euridice, which begins, "Per quel vago boschetto" he classified as narrative. This is characterized by many repeated notes, fast movement, and speechlike rhythm. The remaining style, which he called *speciale recitativo*, is not as pathetic as the expressive but more arioso than either the narrative or the expressive. It is the style used in the musical recitation of heroic and similar poems, and it contains many cadences marking the ends of line—too many for Doni's taste. Doni cited the prologue of *Euridice* as an example, noting that this was very similar to the way *ottave rime* were sung in Italy.

Besides the several levels of monody, Peri's pastoral was given variety by numerous choral canzonets or madrigals, powerful unison choruses, and tuneful solo airs. Some of this variety is exhibited by Example 3-2, from the same scene as the lament of Orpheus just discussed. After we hear Daphne, the Nymphs, and the shepherd Aminta voicing their sorrow, there is a break in the recitative style. The librettist Rinuccini may have given the composer the cue for the change. Normally he avoided closed or regular poetic forms, mixing seven- and eleven-syllable lines in irregular rhymes. Now he wrote a strophic poem of seven stanzas, each of four octosyllabic lines rhyming ABAB. The last two lines of the first stanza, "Sospirate aure celesti/Lagrimate, o selve, o campi," serve as a refrain after each subsequent stanza. Peri seized upon this as an opportunity for a grand refrain or *ritornello* form. (*Ritornello* literally means refrain, and it acquired a special meaning in the baroque, signifying the choral or instrumental tutti section that returns between diverse solo sections.)

The opening unison chorus was written in recitative style up to the middle of measure 5, when Peri turned to the air style for the two lines of refrain, and we hear monodically the music that is to be arranged for five voices in the choral *ritornello*. The air style is identifiable by the melody's "dancing to the movement of the bass," which Peri avoided in recitative. The two stanzas of the Nymph of the Chorus that follow are further clear examples of air style. The emphasis is on a regular, bouncing rhythm and

---

[3] *Annotazioni sopra il Compendio de' generi, e de' modi della musica* (Rome: Andrea Fei, 1640), pp. 60-62.

EXAMPLE 3-2　J. Peri, *Euridice*

EXAMPLE 3-2 (Cont.)

Peri's music for Orfeo's moving lament over the death of his bride, Euridice, in the original edition by Giorgio Marescotti, Florence, 1601.

a tuneful vocal part, with a certain neglect of textual interpretation. Peri avoided monotony by setting the stanza form not just once but in two alternating airs, and at the end, in a duet (omitted in the example).

Peri's *Euridice*, the first surviving dramatic work set entirely to music, received its premiere without fanfare in a small hall of the apartment of a nephew of the Grand Duke of Tuscany on October 6, 1600. The production, directed by Emilio de' Cavalieri, was Jacopo Corsi's offering to the festivities accompanying the wedding by proxy of Henry IV, King of France, to Maria de' Medici, niece of the Duke. *Euridice* was very much eclipsed by the spectacular production two days later of another pastoral, *Il Rapimento di Cefalo*, by Gabriello Chiabrera with music mainly by Giulio Caccini. Whereas *Euridice* was staged very simply and accompanied by a few instruments, among them a harpsichord, chitarrone, lira grande (a kind of bass viol), and a large lute, *Cefalo* featured about a hundred musicians and singers, elaborate and very expensive scenery and machinery—and this before an audience of 3,800. But *Cefalo*, except for the monodic airs of Caccini, was quite conventional, following in the tradition of the grand intermezzi of 1589. It was loudly praised but soon forgotten. *Euridice*, on the other hand, although it bored some of the princes and prelates, was performed again several times and undoubtedly persuaded many musicians of the promise of the new style.

Soon composers in Florence and other cities began to imitate Peri's manner. Two of them chose the same subject. One was Caccini, who had contributed a few choruses and airs to the 1600 performance and issued a setting of the libretto in January 1601, beating the publication of Peri's version by about a month; but Caccini's was not performed until December 5, 1602. The other was Monteverdi, who set in 1607 a new version of the tale of Orpheus and Eurydice by Alessandro Striggio, the chancellor of Monteverdi's employer, the Duke of Mantua. The following year Marco da Gagliano returned to the Rinuccini poem *Dafne*. The new recitative style also had wide repercussions in the field of the chamber monody and in church music.


## MONTEVERDI'S ORFEO


Striggio's *La favola d'Orfeo* is very similar in outline to Rinuccini's poem, though it tends more to emphasize the tragic elements of the story and preserves the ancient legend more faithfully. According to the myth, Orpheus goes to Hades to retrieve his dead bride from the powers of the underworld. So persuasive is his singing and pleading that she is returned to him on the condition that he not look back at her during the passage back from the realm of the dead. He does turn back and loses her again. He then conceives a hatred for womankind, and for this is vengefully torn in pieces by the Thracian maenads. Rinuccini had resolved the plot very simply. He set no condition for Eurydice's return, allowing Orpheus to bring her back triumphantly to their beloved Thracian fields for a scene of reunion and rejoicing. This suited the uncomplicated, sweet, idyllic nature of Rinuccini's poem, inspired more by the eclogue than by tragedy. Striggio preserved the legendary condition imposed upon Orpheus. Concerned for Eurydice's safety during their passage through Hades. Orpheus looks back and loses her once more. He forswears women, and an enraged group of Bacchantes threatens him, but he escapes. In Monteverdi's printed score the ending of the libretto is revised and Orpheus is rescued by Apollo, who takes him up in a cloud to gaze upon Eurydice among the stars. However, the endings of the libretto and score are not incompatible. A *moresca*, which in the theater is usually a battle dance, is the last item in the score. This may well have accompanied the hostile movements of the Bacchantes, from which Apollo provides Orpheus a convenient escape.

Neither Rinuccini's nor Striggio's libretto represents a return to Greek tragedy, nor was this their authors' aim. The sixteenth century had seen the staging of many translations and imitations of Greek and Roman tragedies in Italy, some with choral music. By the end of the century enthusiasm for this genre gave way to the vogue of the pastoral tragicomedy, spurred by the success of Tasso's *Aminta* (1581) and Guarini's *Pastor fido* (1590). Indeed, Cavalieri's *Giuoco della Cieca*, a musical pastoral produced in Florence in 1595, is derived from an episode of Guarini's play. Tasso and Guarini consciously imitated many devices used by Greek and Roman playwrights, whether tragic or comic, and defended their procedures by the precepts of Aristotle's *Poetics*. Similarly, Rinuccini and Striggio embodied many of these elements in their plays, which are essentially tragicomic pastorals in the fashion of the time. So, if neither *Euridice* nor *Orfeo* satisfies the criteria of tragedy, this must not be held against their authors.

Peri, Caccini, and Monteverdi knew they were not setting tragedies to music, but they did consciously aspire toward some of the manners, functions, and effects of ancient theatrical music. There are many parallels among their scores. There are also notable differences. Caccini's recitative, as compared with Peri's, is diluted and sweetened and is more frequently interrupted by strophic and other airs. Monteverdi was closer to the spirit of Peri in that he often eschewed vocality and suavity for speechlike realism and passion. But he too leaned toward the air and madrigal for a large proportion of the score. The more ambitious format permitted by the Mantuan carnival celebrations of 1607 also deeply affected the nature of Monteverdi's setting. It was decided to make a major show of *Orfeo*, incorporating the large forces and spectacular staging usually reserved in Florence for intermezzi, so an orchestra of about forty players, a chorus of singers and dancers, and smaller ensembles were given abundant roles.

Monteverdi's debt to Peri, as well as some of his distinctive qualities, is strikingly revealed by a comparison of the lament quoted in Example 3-1 with the parallel lament of *Orfeo*, which begins as shown in Example 3-3 (the entire lament is in *NAWM* 69c).

The essential ingredients of Monteverdi's recitative style were derived from Peri. The principal pauses occur, as in Peri, at irregular intervals of time, creating an illusion of speech rhythm. However, Monteverdi maintained a more continuous line and rhythm, partly because of the nature of the text. Except in formal songs and choruses, Striggio, like Rinuccini, used a free mixture of seven- and eleven-syllable lines, but Striggio's is mainly blank verse. So the line endings were easier for the composer to ignore, and he did so to good advantage.

The treatment of nonchordal tones follows Peri's very closely. For example, the F♯ in measure 2, the G♯ in measure 4, the F♯s in measure 8, or the Bs and D in measure 12 are dissonances that were not permitted by even the freest rules of counterpoint. They are accounted for by Peri's theory in that they fall on rapidly enunciated syllables on the way to others that are sustained in speech and that in music receive consonance. Monteverdi chose the dissonant tones more deliberately than Peri. Very often they are leading tones or tones anticipatory to the following consonant chords.

Monteverdi followed Peri's precedent in borrowing from the madrigal the technique of juxtaposing alien harmonies. By coincidence the same two chords Peri used in Example 3-1—E and g—are contrasted to dramatize the opposition between Orfeo's "life," who is dead, and his own miserable breathing existence (measures 5 and 6). In general, Monteverdi's harmony is less stagnant and aimless than Peri's, revealing the hand of an experienced and gifted composer. He aims for a tonal goal, such as the F in measure 19, and, this realized, he heads for a new one (see the continuation of this passage in *MM* 31 or in *NAWM* 69c). This is also true of the melodic line, which moves in sweeping arches, climbing toward an apex and then stepping down. There are three such climaxes in the monologue—at the words "rimango" (Example 3-3, measure 14), "stelle," (*MM* 31, measure 26), and on the last words (Example 3-4). This last climax is approached by a technique that can best be called *recitativo arioso*, a free airy style—a melodious recitative, as it were, that exploits rhythmic repetition and melodic sequence.

As in Peri's example, high pitch is associated with excitement and despair; low pitch, with depression and death. More than Peri, who may have avoided them because they were so violently attacked by Galilei in his *Dialogue*, Monteverdi resorted to the word pictures of the madrigalists. "Stars" in this monologue gets the highest note; "profound abysses," the lowest one, which it shares with "death."

Important as pure recitative was at this stage of dramatic music, in *Orfeo* it does not play a preponderant role. The proportion of recitative on

**EXAMPLE 3-3**  C. Monteverdi, *Orfeo*, Act II

EXAMPLE 3-4   C. Monteverdi, *Orfeo*, Act II

the one hand to air, madrigal, and orchestral music on the other is less than one to four in the first act; in the second and third acts, which are more dramatic, it increases to about one to three; and it approaches nearly equal proportion in the final two acts.

The airs present a rich variety of types. The composer adapted his style to the poetic forms offered by Striggio. The Prologue (*NAWM* 69a), consisting of stanzas of four hendecasyllabic (eleven-syllable) lines rhyming ABBA, is in the elevated genre of the *canzone*. The musical style is based on the primitive improvised air, but it is enriched by elements of the recitative style. The slightly varied strophes are separated by a recurrent *ritornello*.

The airs of the shepherds in Act II, "Mira ch'a se n'alletta" and "In questo prato adorno," follow a similar procedure, but the style, as befits the uniformly seven-syllable lines, is borrowed from the dance song. In the first of these airs Monteverdi produced an interesting cross-rhythm by defying the natural accents of the text (see in Example 3-5 the accents added to the text), allowing the music to be dominated by the square-cut sequences in the bass.

Orfeo's air "Vi ricorda, o boschi ombrosi" (Example 3-6a; *NAWM* 69b) may best be called a canzonet. Its lines are uniform not only in their eight syllables but also in having iambic meter. Monteverdi repeated the first line at the beginning to get a balanced phrase and twice more at the end of the stanza for an ABA form. The unvaried strophes are preceded and separated by a *ritornello*. Both ritornello and air follow a rhythmic scheme in which $\frac{3}{4}$ and $\frac{6}{8}$ measures are mixed. This effect is known as *hemiola* (Greek for

**EXAMPLE 3-5** C. Monteverdi, *Orfeo*, Act II

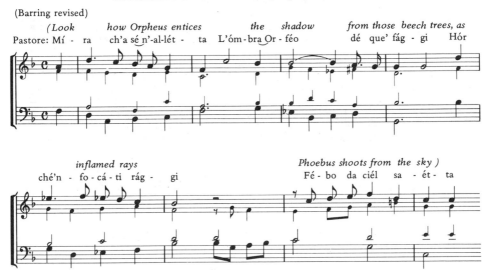

three against two) because simple triple meter alternates with compound duple. The particular rhythm of this song was taken by the monodists from the earlier *frottola* composers. Compare Monteverdi's melody (Example 3-6a) with that of Peri's chorus "Se de' boschi i verdi onori" (Example 3-6b) and with a *frottola* of approximately 1500, "Se de fede or vengo ameno" (Example 3-6c). Marco da Gagliano's chorus "Al mio dio" in *Dafne*, as well as numerous chamber monodies, also uses the same rhythm.

The most important of the strophic songs is Orfeo's appeal to Charon to ferry him across the river Styx after he has been led to its bank by Hope. "Leave every hope here, o you who enter," she puns, quoting the famous line of Dante's *Inferno*. Fittingly, Orpheus pleads with Charon in the form used in the *Divine Comedy*, the *terza rima*, or *capitolo*. This consists of interlocking stanzas of three hendecasyllabic lines rhymed ABA BCB CDC, etc., ending with an extra line that rhymes with the second of the final stanza, as, XYXY. The archaic manner of Striggio is matched by that of the composer, who took as his model the air for singing verses. Like Filippo de Laurana in his *Aer de capituli* of about 1500 (Example 3-7a). Monteverdi used a simple formula in which each line is set off by rests and ends with two even notes (Example 3-7b). To facilitate comparison, Striggio's first tercet and final line are here set to Filippo's tune.

Normally all the strophes were sung to the same three lines of music, with the extra phrase of music being applied to the final line. Monteverdi departed significantly from this conventional repetition. He made changes, as expected, in the rhythm and melody in various strophes, keeping the

**EXAMPLE 3-7a**   F. de Laurana, *Aer de capituli*

[Pos - sen - te   spir - to e   for - mi - da - bil
nu - me,   Sen - za   cui   far   pas -
sag - gio a l'al - tra   ri - va,   Al -
ma   da   cor - po   sciol - ta in
van   pre -   su -   me, . . . . . . . .

(Final line)
Con - tra   cui   ri -   gi - d'al -   ma
(Text from
Striggio, *Orfeo*)
in   van   s'im -   pe -   tra ]

**EXAMPLE 3-7b**   C. Monteverdi, *Orfeo* Act III

Pos - sen -   te   spir - to   e   for - mi - da -
[ *Mighty*   *spirit*   *and awesome*
- bil nu -   me,   Sen - za cui   far pas - sag - gio a l'al - tra
*god,*   *Without whom passage to the other*
ri - va   Al -   ma da cor - po sciol - ta in   van   pre - su -
*shore,*   *a*   *soul, from its body detached, in vain*
me, . . . . . . .   Con - tra cui   ri - gi - d'al - ma   in van
*attempts,*   *Against whom a stiff soul   in vain*
s'im - pe -   tra.
*batters.* ]

harmony and bass constant in the manner of the strophic variation, but there are also other important variants. Throughout the score Monteverdi exercised great restraint in writing embellishments of the sort singers were wont to add, intending undoubtedly to exhort them to equal moderation. But now he wanted Orpheus to weave a spell of coloratura around Charon. He indicated this by providing in the 1609 score a profusely ornamented alternate part for each of the first four strophes. For singers not agile enough to negotiate this or for those confident they could improvise effective "divisions" of their own, he gave the simple version too. Then in the fifth strophe he abandoned the formula altogether, as Orpheus, realizing he has failed to soften the callous boatman, resorts in desperation to a free madrigal style. In the sixth strophe Monteverdi wished the formula to return in its bare simplicity, since he gave no ornamented version.

As if to compensate further for his archaic procedure, Monteverdi provided a modern accompaniment exploiting the contrasting tone colors and sonority of the medium of voices with instruments. Different solo instruments play rapid figures in echo and in thirds during and between the strophes. In the first there are two violins; in the second, two cornetts—wood instruments with trumpetlike mouthpieces; in the third, a double harp; in the fourth, two violins and a bass lira. In the sixth, as Orfeo makes his final effort, the simple version of the tune is accompanied very softly by a quarter of viols playing sustained chords. During the entire song an organ with wooden pipes and a chitarrone play the chords and bass. Thus there are contrasted and merged two classes of instruments: a group of tutti or *ripieno* instruments, and a group of soloists. Bringing together in a harmony a variety of sounds and capabilities and at the same time contrasting them in this way is the essence of the new mixed vocal-instrumental style. By means of it Monteverdi built out of an archaic framework the most modern piece of the drama.

The most conservative music in *Orfeo* is that for the chorus, but it is not altogether so. The five-part "madrigals" follow the sixteenth-century practice, aside from the provision of a *basso seguente* and various ripieno instruments to double the voices. The madrigal style is used particularly when the chorus acts as a group of bystanders who reflect upon the action and point out a moral. "Nulla impresa," the chorus of infernal spirits for low voices in Act III, is the most ambitious of these compositions and the most decorative instrumentally, accompanied as it is by a regal (portable reed organ), a wood-pipe organ, five trombones, and three viols (two bass and one contrabass). "No undertaking of man is in vain," it instructs. The chorus of spirits for high voices in Act IV, "E la virtute un raggio," is also a moralizing one. Although Orfeo conquered Hell, it warns, he was conquered by his passion, and only he who masters himself will have eternal glory. These and other five-voice madrigals are set in a mixture of imitative and chordal style.

Each textual line or combination of them receives individual musical treatment in a rather formal exposition.

There are also two madrigals in modern style—for few voices with independent *basso continuo*. "Alcun non sia" in Act I, alternately for two and three voices, is a strophic variation in which the harmony and bass are the fixed elements. The same ritornello precedes and separates the strophes, which are purely musical units, since the text is formless blank verse. This chorus reflects upon Orfeo's happy springtime after a winter of adversity. A true strophic text is that of "Chi ne consola ahi lassi?" of Act II, but here Monteverdi did not pursue the variation form strictly. A novel feature is that each stanza is followed by the refrain chorus "Ahi caso acerbo," which was earlier heard as a choral response to Orfeo's lament. In this way this refrain helps knit together the latter part of Act II.

"Ahi caso acerbo" (*NAWM* 69c) is the most original of the choruses: it is in a polyphonic recitative style. The bass line is identical to the arresting speech sung by the Messenger earlier in the act when she interrupted the festivities with the news of Eurydice's death. Of the remaining choruses, "Lasciate i monti" is notable because it is a *balletto*, that is, a choral dance, and because here the chorus is an active participant.

This enumeration of the forms and styles contained in *Orfeo* and their sources shows that there existed no distinctive dramatic style at this time but only an aggregation of many current and older styles. The agglutinative process that is at the basis of the madrigal is applied on a broader time span. There results a collection of musical manners drawn from many sources. This reflects a similar tendency in the libretto. Despite the disintegrating forces of mannerism, Monteverdi achieved a certain unity within the several acts, thanks to judicious use of recurrent choruses, orchestral symphonies, and ritornels. That one feels an encompassing unity is also owing to the forceful personality that asserts itself throughout.

## THE LATER CONTINUO MADRIGAL

Caccini, we saw, showed hardly a trace of the recitative style in his airs and madrigals. Several of his younger contemporaries, though, embraced the new idiom with enthusiasm. Many of the madrigals of Sigismondo d'India (c. 1580–1629), for example, are virtual dramatic scenes in *stile recitativo*. In "Là tra le selve" (Example 3-8) d'India did not merely set words elegantly, agreeably, and expressively; he created a protagonist who projects a personal drama. This the polyphonic madrigal could not achieve, because it was too impersonal and undramatic a medium. The quilt of conceits, wordplay, and mannered devices of the polyphonic settings had succeeded in stimulating the intellect and imagination, to be sure, and occasionally also the emotions. They had done so by translating words into music, and this was both their strength and their limitation. Now, however, the music began where the word left off, reaching beyond it to bring the personage and situation behind the poem to life; for where the older solo airs and madrigals had been vehicles for the ideas and feelings of the poet, now the poet or his hero was virtually incarnated in the singer.

Some of d'India's madrigals are mixtures of the recitative style and the rhythmically more regular and melodically flowing arioso style. Still others derive their idiom mainly from the polyphonic madrigal. Example 3-8 departs from pure recitative only to underscore a few cadences with rapid divisions. The characteristic free use of dissonance and rhythm allies it with the recitative of Peri. But more like Monteverdi, d'India cultivated the long line and the calculated climax. The moving ascent starting in measure 4, followed by a melancholic descent of more than an octave, unites into one extended utterance three lines of text. Despite the dependence upon

EXAMPLE 3-8  S. d'India, *Là tra le selve*

the recitative, this madrigal is still indebted to the polyphonic madrigal, particularly in its chromaticism and the technique of evading cadences.

Chromaticism, whether in the sense of successive half-step motion or of deep modulatory forays, appealed only mildly to Peri, Caccini, and Monteverdi; yet this vein, like others mined by composers of the second practice, can also be traced to the circle around Cipriano de Rore. In addition to de Rore two others—his pupil Luzzaschi and his fellow student in Willaert's school, Nicola Vicentino (1511–1572)—were important early experimenters in chromaticism.

De Rore's most outré essay was the Latin ode *Calami sonum ferentes* (Example 3 9; see Burney, *History of Music*, Mercer ed., II, 256, for the entire piece). It was published along with a similar venture by Orlandus Lassus in 1555. Even at this early date de Rore showed a complete mastery of the chordal progressions demanded by the chromatic lines.

In the same year Vicentino proposed a revival of the chromatic and enharmonic genera of the Greeks in his treatise *L'antica musica ridotta alla*

**EXAMPLE 3-9**   C. de Rore, *Calami sonum ferentes*

*moderna prattica* (Ancient Music Adapted to the Modern Practice). The ancient chromatic genus proceeded in each descending tetrachord, or fourth, by a minor third and two semitones, while the enharmonic consisted of a major third followed by two microtones. Vicentino deliberately revised these scales, meant for monophonic music, to suit modern polyphonic music. In his chromatic and enharmonic scales the entire octave is divided into semitones and microtones, respectively. Vicentino published examples of both these modern genera and constructed an instrument capable of playing them. Although his enharmonic compositions were not found convincing, his sponsorship of chromatic writing and his own essays in this style had a lasting influence. His principle was that the expanded means should not be employed casually, but only in the service of expression. Indeed, Luzzaschi, who used to play one of Vicentino's instruments, drew powerful effects from chromatic progressions, both melodic and chordal, in his *Quivi sospiri* (1576).

The greatest master of the chromatic idiom after these pioneers was Gesualdo. The madrigal *Moro lasso al mio duolo* (1611; the entire composition in *TEM* 33) shows the extremities to which he was able to push chromatic motion and concomitant wandering modulations without losing either individuality of part movement or control of tonal direction. This example also illustrates a technique for evading a cadence that both Gesualdo and d'India favored. It consists of approaching the end of a passage with a 4–3 suspension over a bass note and then failing to have the bass proceed, as expected, a fourth up or a fifth down (see Example 3-10, measures 22 and 23, and Example 3-8, measures 2, 4, and 6). This method ties up a phrase neatly, if inconclusively, while absorbing none of the shock from a startling turn in the next phrase.

There were numerous other ways in which the solo madrigal depended upon its polyphonic counterpart. A few of these become evident if we compare the passage from Gesualdo with one from d'India's *O dolcezz' amarissime d'Amore* (1609; Example 3-11). The opening measured chromatic rise of the top voice, which owes nothing to recitative, is analogous to a similar descent in Gesualdo (Example 3-10, measures 23–26). When, three lines later, the poem turns to thoughts of happiness, the composer, as earlier madrigalists would have done, matched the poet's antithesis with a musical one (Example 3-12). A lilting diatonic melody, balancing two phrases, fits the new thought. This too has its parallel in Gesualdo: in measure 29, where life becomes the antithesis of death. The methods of the polyphonic madrigalist, therefore, continued to guide the composer. But now controlled a new cohesive structural support, the thorough-bass. Counteracting the scattering effect of the disparate styles, it knitted the separate periods into a tight whole.

It is evident that the composers of the monodic madrigal did not burn bridges from the sixteenth-century tradition. Although they courted the recitative and the air, they also preserved ties to the older forms. This eclec-

**EXAMPLE 3-10** C. Gesualdo, *Moro lasso al mio duolo*

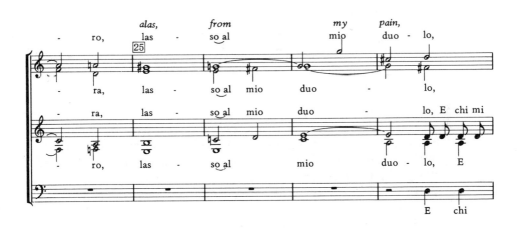

EXAMPLE 3-11  S. d'India, *O dolcezz'amarissime d'Amore*

EXAMPLE 3-12  S. d'India, *O dolcezz'amarissime d'Amore*

ticism was a transitional phenomenon. Eventually the taint of polyphony was washed away in the tide of the two reigning styles, the unmeasured recitative and the measured arioso or air. These styles may be found alternating in a single work, as in d'India's *Torna il sereno Zefiro* (1623; recorded in "Songs for Courtiers and Cavaliers"), or Monteverdi's *Et è pur dunque vero* (1632; *Five Songs*, p. 21). Also, the two styles may be separated, as in Monteverdi's air *Quel sguardo sdegnosetto* (1632; *Five Songs*, p. 2), which is a strophic variation, or in Se i languidi miei sguardi, a pure recitative that bears the subtitle "Love-letter for solo voice in *genere rappresentativo* to be sung without measure" (1619; *Five Songs*, p. 8).

The madrigal for two or more voices inclined naturally even more to vestiges of the polyphonic style, but here also eclecticism was the byword. Probably the most remarkable synthesis of the styles that combined to produce the continuo-madrigal is Monteverdi's duet *Ohimè dov'è il mio ben* (1619) on a poem by Bernardo Tasso (*NAWM* 65). Here a mixture of recitative, arioso, and polyphonic madrigal styles fills out a frame provided by the most famous of the airs for singing *ottave rime*, that known as the *Romanesca*. The *ottava rima*, consisting of eight hendecasyllabic lines rhyming ABABABCC, was the standard form for Italian sacred dramas in the fourteenth and fifteenth centuries and was adopted by Torquato Tasso for his *Gerusalemme liberata* (1575), an important source for musical texts. Each of the four couplets of an ottava rima would have been sung to the *Aria della*

*Romanesca* approximately the way the first couplet of *Ohimè dov'è il mio ben*
is hypothetically set in the upper staff of Example 3-13. It would have been
harmonized normally with chords in root position, whose bass notes are
shown in the lowest staff in each brace.

It is obvious that Monteverdi drew freely from this formula for his
melodic and harmonic material. He kept to the rhythmic scheme of the
original except for measures 4–5, 15–16, and 20–21, each of which com-
presses three beats into two. Monteverdi also repeated the second line
(omitted in Example 3-13). His three subsequent couplets, not shown in the
example, are variations on the first.

**EXAMPLE 3-13**   C. Monteverdi, *Ohimè dov'è il mio ben*

EXAMPLE 3-13  (Cont.)

co - re? Chi m'a
heart? Who conceals

co - re? Chi m'a - scon - de Chi m'a -

- re? Chi m'a - scon -

scon - de il mio ben e chi
my treasure and who

scon - de il mio ben e e chi me'l

- de il mio ben e e chi me'l to -

6

me'l to - glie? ]
takes it away? )

to - glie? Chi m'a - scon - de

- glie? Chi m'a - scon -

So completely did Monteverdi assimilate the various ingredients of style that one is conscious only of his forceful and personal interpretation of the text. The opening savors of the recitative style, but the acrid suspensions, the short imitative motives, and the evaded cadence (in measures 10–11) are pure madrigalisms. On the other hand, in the third couplet, the setting of "ambizios'e troppo lievi voglie" (ambitious and too trivial fancies), with its gay coloratura passage in dotted rhythms for "trivial," transmutes the graphic description of the madrigal into the new arioso. Each of the couplets abounds in fresh inventions inspired by the new texts. This composition achieves a brilliant reconciliation of the concrete expression of the through-composed madrigal and the concentration of material imposed by the strophic form. It is reinforced further by the strong, enduring spine of the *Romanesca* pattern.

## BIBLIOGRAPHICAL NOTES

An extensive commentary on the letters that sparked the monodic movement is in Palisca, *Girolamo Mei, Letters on Ancient and Modern Music to Vincenzo Galilei and Giovanni Bardi*, 2nd ed. (American Institute of Musicology, 1977), wherein the original documents are also published.

Peri's *Euridice* is available in several fascimile editions, among them those of Broude Brothers, New York, and Forni, Bologna, but in only a poorly edited modern edition in Torchi, *L'arte musicale in Italia*, VI. Caccini's version is also available in facsimile (Forni) and is partly edited in Eitner, *Publikationen*, X, which contains also some of da Gagliano's *Dafne*. Monteverdi's *Orfeo* is in his *Opere*, XI; some other acceptable editions are those of G. Benvenuti in *CMI*, IX (1942); A. Wenzinger (Kassel: Bärenreiter, 1955); Eitner, *Publikationen*, X; Malipiero (London: Chester, 1926); and Stevens (London: Novello, 1967).

Cavalieri's *Rappresentatione di anima et di corpo* is published in facsimile (Gregg Press, 1967), in a complete but revised edition by E. Gubitosi (Milan: Ricordi, 1956), and in an incomplete transciption in *CDMI*, X. Besides these more or less complete, more or less scholarly editions, there are several well-edited excerpts from the early music dramas in anthologies and histories: from Peri's *Euridice* in *HAM* II, 182, and *GMB* 171; from Gagliano's *Dafne* in *GMB* 176 and *MM* 31; from Peri's and Monteverdi's works in Elaine Brody, *Music in Opera: A Historical Anthology* (Englewood Cliffs, N.J.: Prentice-Hall, 1970), pp. 2–33.

Monteverdi, *Five Songs*, ed. George Hunter and C. Palisca (Bryn Mawr, Pa.: Theodore Presser, 1963), contains a representative selection of monodies. A large number of continuo-madrigals were published in Monteverdi's sixth, seventh, and eighth books of madrigals of 1614, 1619, and 1638, and in some other collections, all of which are transcribed in the Malipiero edition, vols. V, VI, VII, VIII, IX, and X.

For examples and discussion of the works of Sigismondo d'India see Nigel Fortune, "Sigismondo d'India, an Introduction to His Life and Works," *Proceedings of the Musical Association*, 81 (1954–55). 29–47; and Federico Mompellio, "Sigismondo d'India e il suo primo libro di musiche da cantar solo," in *Collectanea historiae musicae*, I (Florence: Olschki, 1953), 113–34. D'India's *Primo libro di musiche da cantar solo* is edited by Federico Mompellio in *Instituta et monumenta*, Ser. 1, Vol. 4 (Cremona: Athenaeum Cremonense, 1970).

The madrigals of Gesualdo are published in his *Werke*, vols. 1–6, ed. W. Weismann, (Hamburg: Ugrino). See also *HAM* I, 161; *TEM* 33; *GMB* 167; *NAWM* 55. Glenn Watkins's *Gesualdo, The Man and His Music* (Chapel Hill, N.C.: University of North Carolina Press, 1973) is a carefully documented portrait and sensitive commentary on the works.

# FOUR

# THE RISE OF THE SACRED CONCERTO

*FIRST AND SECOND PRACTICE IN THE CHURCH*

Three years after the staging of *Orfeo*, Monteverdi presented to Pope Paul V a large collection of sacred works that exhibits an even more bewildering profusion of stylistic directions than his pastoral. This was published in 1610 under the title *Mass to the Most Holy Virgin for Six Voices for Church Choirs, and Vespers for Many Voices, together with Some Sacred Harmonies Suitable for Chapels or Princes' Chambers.*[1] Several of the works do not fail to reflect the new tendencies in secular music, but the collection is generally conservative. This was probably in deference to the Pope, whose chapel was strongly bound by tradition. Nevertheless, the contents are indicative of a

[1] *Sanctissimae Virgini Missa senis vocibus ad ecclesiarum choros ac Vesperae pluribus decantandae cum nonnullis sacris concentibus ad sacella sive principium cubicula accommodata* (Venice: Ricciardo Amadino, 1610); in Malipiero edition, *Opere*, XIV.

57

ferment in religious music no less seething than that experienced by secular music.

The collection begins with a *Missa da cappella* for six voices written on subjects taken from a motet by the much earlier Flemish composer Nicolas Gombert. This, an exercise in mid-sixteenth-century style, cost Monteverdi much labor and study, since by now it was an academic idiom. Although he wrote other *a cappella* masses, none was so archaic, so unrelieved in its fugal texture, and so uncompromising as this tribute to the papal chapel. There follow music for a Vespers service, two settings of the Magnificat, and some assorted motets. The Vespers music is labeled *da concerto*, which here means simply that voices and instruments are combined in such a way that the instruments do not merely double the voices but sometimes have independent roles. There are sections in which a choir of instruments is pitted against a choir of voices (Domine ad adiuvandum), others in which the instruments play along with the voices and intersperse ritornelli (Dixit Dominus), others in which a single choir (Laetatus sum) or two choirs (Laudate pueri, Nisi Dominus, Lauda Jerusalem) sing with organ accompaniment. There is also a strophic variation on a harmonized plainchant hymn, Ave maris stella. Here the seven strophes are set variously for double choir, single choir, and solo voices, each except the last two followed by a ritornello. The two Magnificats add to this array various combinations of solo-voice groupings and instruments. Throughout the collection there is a parallel richness of compositional techniques: imitative polyphony, florid arioso, cantus firmus technique of a most original kind, homorhythmic choral chanting in triadic harmony known as *falsobordone*, and the homophony characteristic of double-chorus writing. The only works that show a clear link to secular monody are the devotional pieces probably intended for princely chambers: *Nigra sum*, *Pulchra es*, and Audi coelum. Here we find both the dramatic recitative and aria styles. Pulchra es is discussed in detail later in this chapter.

Thus the 1610 collection is a compendium of the sacred styles that coexisted during the earlier part of the baroque period. Such a plurality of idioms was not unusual in church music. Plainchant endured beside the newer organum in the twelfth century, not to mention later centuries. Leonin's organa, after he died, continued to be sung with *clausulae* composed by his successors. Fauxbourdon as a practice persisted long after it ceased to be fashionable as a technique for written compositions. So it is not surprising that in Monteverdi's collection some older styles should pass in review. Age and use do not make a style obsolete in the church as they do in secular entertainment; rather, they consecrate it.

In the early seventeenth century some composers wished to see a single polyphonic style, that of Palestrina, canonized as the only choral idiom acceptable in the church. This movement, emanating from Rome, failed. One of its most articulate opponents, Marco Scacchi, saw in the diversity of styles one of the great gains made by the music of his time.

Whereas the older music, he said in 1649, contained "only one practice and one style of using consonance and dissonance, the modern consists of two practices and three styles, that is, the styles for church, chamber, and theater." By "practices" he meant, of course, those defined by Monteverdi. The first, he said, took as its motto "Ut Harmonia sit Domina orationis"—"Let Harmony be the Mistress of the text"; the second: "Ut Oratio sit Domina harmoniae"—"Let the Text be the Mistress of the harmony."[2]

In a letter to a fellow composer, Cristoph Werner, of approximately 1648,[3] Scacchi presented a classification of the available styles that will help to organize our discussion. He divided church music into four types: 1) masses, motets, and similar compositions for four to eight voices without organ; 2) the same with organ, or for several choirs with organ; 3) similar compositions *in concerto*, that is, in which one or more choirs are mixed with instruments; 4) motets and concertos in modern style, or, in other words, in the second practice. That these types were valid as late as the eighteenth century is attested by Johann Joseph Fux (1660–1741), who adopted this classification with only slight modification in his *Gradus ad Parnassum* (1725).[4] Fux probably got it from Scacchi's pupil, the prolific writer Angelo Berardi (1635–c. 1700).

The strict style of writing for four to eight parts without obligatory instrumental accompaniment was known variously as *stile grave* (severe style), *stile da* or *a cappella* (choir style), *stile antico* (old style), and *stile osservato* or *legato* (strict or bound style). Each of these expressions refers to a different aspect of one and the same style. *Stile grave* denotes mainly the slowness of movement, as Pietro Ponzio showed in this definition in his *Ragionamento di musica:* "When one wishes to compose a motet, the manner or style is severe [*grave*] and quiet. The parts move with heaviness and particularly the bass part, and the composer must keep to this manner from the beginning to the end."[5] *A cappella* denotes the performance medium: the chapel choir, or *cappella*. *Stile osservato* and *legato* refer to the composer's obligation to observe a certain code of good counterpoint. All of these characteristics are implied in the retrospective term *stile antico*, used in the seventeenth century to distinguish the older style from the modern.

Scacchi cited the masses of Josquin, Lassus, and Palestrina among those considered models for the old style, but it was often referred to simply as "the style of Palestrina." How stereotyped and narrow was the seven-

---

[2]Marco Scacchi, *Breve discorso ~~sopra~~ la musica moderna* (Warsaw: Pietro Elert, 1649), trans. in Palisca, "Marco Scacchi's Defense of Modern Music (1649)," in *Words and Music: The Scholar's View*, ed. Laurence Berman (*Festschrift* for A. Tillman Merritt; Cambridge, Mass.: Department of Music, Harvard University, 1972), pp. 189–235.

[3]Printed in Erich Katz, *Die musikalischen Stilbegriffe des 17. Jahrhunderts* (Freiburg, 1926), pp. 83–89.

[4]*Gradus ad Parnassum, sive manuductio ad compositionem musicae regularem* (Vienna: Joannis Petrus Van Ghelen, 1725), Exercitium V, Lectio vii, De stylo ecclesiastico.

[5](Parma: E. Viotto, 1588), p. 154.

teenth-century conception of this style may be discerned from Scacchi's description of it, and from the examples discussed below.

Scacchi described the style for masses, motets, and similar compositions *da cappella* as follows:

> In this manner of composition, the norms for which are to be derived mainly from the composers cited, the following are principally to be observed. 1) The note values and measures should be ordered in binary time (which is commonly called *alla breve*). 2) No note shorter than a semiminim [quarter note] should receive a syllable. 3) No more than two *fusae* [eighth notes] should be placed in a row. . . . 4) The answer to a fugal statement should begin on a natural step [of the mode] and on a consonance. 5) The parts of the composition should proceed as much as possible by step. 6) The Alto should never go lower than the Bass, the Tenor only rarely. 7) The statement of a fugal subject should not exceed six or seven measures [or breves]. 8) The writing should be as full as possible, following the style of Palestrina and of other excellent authors.[6]

## MASSES IN STILE ANTICO

Monteverdi's mass on subjects taken from the motet *In illo tempore* of Gombert follows these norms to the letter. To be sure, a bass part is provided for organ. But it is merely a *basso seguente*—that is, it is not figured and it simply reproduces the lowest note of the texture at any moment, and therefore is expendable. On the other hand, the *Messa a 4 voci da cappella* by Monteverdi published posthumously in 1650 is in a style also based upon the norms of the a cappella idiom, but it is a baroque composer's parody of it rather than a slavish imitation. The continuo serves a real function, for the texture is not always full. The *alla breve* time is occasionally laid aside for textual expression, as in the "Et resurrexit" in fast triple time, and there is overall a sensitivity to the text not found in the abstract polyphony of the 1610 mass. Still it does not go beyond the limits of the *prima prattica*. The frequent occurrence of homophonic passages makes this mass truer to the sixteenth-century tradition than the 1610 mass, with its constant imitation, but the baroque composer is betrayed in the square-cut rhythms that swallow up the independent stresses of the voice lines in strong waves of metrical accent, and the counterpoint is conceived throughout in chordal terms. Nevertheless, the spirit, if not the letter, of Renaissance music resides here.

Intermediate in style between these two masses are the mass in four parts da cappella and a Magnificat for four voices *in genere da capella*, both

[6]Quoted in Katz, *Die musikalischen Stilbegriffe*, pp. 83–84.

in the collection *Selva morale e spirituale* (Moral and Spiritual Grove) of 1640 (Malipiero edition, Vol. XV). Here imitative texture pervades except for moments in triple time, but the contrapuntal means are much simpler. The verses of the Magnificat are unified by the use of the plainchant formula, which acts as a cantus firmus in the top voice or as a source for thematic building material.

These compositions of Monteverdi illustrate that what was preserved in the a cappella idiom of the seventeenth century was the shell rather than the core of Renaissance polyphony, the body without the soul. There was much more to be learned from sixteenth-century polyphony than this academic manner. The affective and imaginative word treatment of Andrea Gabrieli (c. 1520–1586), Giovanni Gabrieli (c. 1556–1612), Orlandus Lassus (1532–1594), Jaches Wert (1535–1596), and Filippo di Monte (1521–1603), to name only a few sixteenth-century polyphonists, made a deep impression on baroque music, although one would not suspect this from the a cappella masses. These composers forged a path for the second practice in the church, and their works bear witness to a continuity of expressive means that the ancient-modern antithesis obscures.

## POLYCHORAL STYLE

Scacchi's second category, compositions for several choirs with organ, follows the rules of the first practice but with more leeway. The greater the number of voices, he noted, the greater was the need for exceptions, and this was also true when voices were combined with instruments. Scacchi cited some special rules that governed this style. A chorus that has been silent should enter upon the closing chord of the active group, as in Example 4-1, from Giovanni Gabrieli's *Sacrae symphoniae*, Book I, 1597 (entire motet in *CW* 10). Where an appreciable pause intervenes, the entering chorus may attack on a new chord, as in Example 4-2 from Gabrieli's collection published posthumously in 1615 as *Sacrae symphoniae*, Book II (entire motet in *CW* 10 and *NAWM* 80).

Several other strictures enumerated by Scacchi are generally valid in this medium. The responses between the choirs should be related and proportionate to each other. The subject matter of the statements and responses should avoid complexity and too much speed of melodic motion, particularly when the choirs are placed in the church at a distance from one another. When instrumental forces are added, a balance between the instruments and the full choral sound should be sought.

Once again, Scacchi's conception of an older style is somewhat academic and based on classical models, in this instance the early works of

EXAMPLE 4-1   G. Gabrieli, *O Domine Jesu Christe*

Giovanni Gabrieli. By contrast, Gabrieli's late polychoral compositions are penetrated by many elements of the second practice. In Example 4-1, the words "ut vulnera" (that your wounds) are set in a fast dotted figure to bring out the implied violence, but this requires giving a syllable to a note shorter than a quarter, breaking a rule of the first practice. The "alleluia" section in Example 4-2 violates the rules in yet another way. Here the pretext is not so much text expression as a desire for a novel harmonic color. Gabrieli carried a G over from measure 16 into 17, where it is suspended against a diminished triad, producing the piquant sound of a minor triad with an added sixth. He then moved by way of resolution to a seventh chord. The same configuration is then repeated after a rest by the other choir, a fourth higher. Neither of these compositions, it must be added, is limited to the tones of any diatonic mode, as the severe style demands.

*Hodie completi sunt* contains several other features that reappear often in the motets for few solo voices and instruments in the seventeenth century. The "alleluia" section in triple time quoted above occurs twice, acting as a refrain to longer *alla breve* sections. Example 4-3, the latter part of the phrase "Hodie completi sunt dies pentecostes" (Today ended are the days of Pentecost), grows gradually to a full tutti, without losing the identity of the two choirs. The setting of the words "dies pentecostes" is madrigalistic in its rhythmic variety, with some syllables set to sixteenth notes, as is the cadential flourish—all departures from the severe style.

**EXAMPLE 4-2**  G. Gabrieli, *Hodie completi sunt*

**EXAMPLE 4-3**  G. Gabrieli, *Hodie completi sunt*

The remaining words of the motet are "Today the Holy Ghost appeared in splendor to the disciples and distributed the gifts of grace. He told them to preach and testify throughout the world. He who believed was both baptized and saved, alleluia." The words are grouped into small units not only to bestow upon each idea some appropriate musical conceit, but because short musical phrases tossed back and forth between the two choirs are the essence of this medium. The final "alleluia," which begins with a repetition of the passage in Example 4-2, is extended through a play with this word that will recall Monteverdi's similar treatment of "ohimè" in *Ohimè se tanto amate* (*HAM* II, 188). Here the distinction between the two choirs is obliterated as they merge to produce a stirring close.

Besides the organ, for which a continuo part is provided in the 1615 collection but not in that of 1597, other instruments are sometimes brought into play with the several choirs. In the *Concerti di Andrea, et di Giovanni Gabrieli, continenti musica di chiesa, madrigali, & altro, per voci & stromenti musicali: à 6, 7, 8, 10, 12, & 16* (1587), in which Giovanni published a large quantity of music by his uncle and a few pieces of his own, some of the works for many voices are described as "for singing and playing," but specific instruments are usually not indicated. In the *Symphoniae sacrae* of 1615, however, some of the motets call for particular instruments.

The deservedly famous *In ecclesiis benedicite Domino* is such a work. The parts here are very explicit. In addition to two choruses and organ there is an ensemble of instruments consisting of three cornetti, a tenor violin, and two trombones. This ensemble functions as a third choir, playing either as a group or not at all. (The complete score is in *HAM* I, 157.)[7] Gabrieli made magnificent use of the assembled resources. In some sections only one or two voice parts sing with organ or instruments. Other sections are for a single choir, for a single choir with a partial choir, or for two choirs and orchestra alternating and converging. There is also a *sinfonia* for the instrumental ensemble alone. More even than in the double-chorus works, no opportunity was missed to exploit the added dimension that comes from locating choirs in separate galleries and the delight in startling juxtapositions of different vocal and instrumental colors in the symmetry of statement and answer. As in *Hodie completi sunt*, an "alleluia" set in antiphonal style serves as a refrain at the end of each of the five lines of text. The verses are all in a lighter texture of one or two voices, with the exception of the final one, "Deus, adjutor noster in aeterno" (God, our helper in eternity), which is for full choir. The word "Deus" is four times set to a sequence of triads whose roots are a minor third apart, first F–D, followed immediately by G–E; then later B♭–G, followed by G–E. This and similar devices, employed by the madri-

---

[7]But there the basso continuo part is a reconstruction by the editor. Gabrieli's part is given in Frederic Hudson, "Giovanni Gabrieli's Motet *a 15* In ecclesiis," *Music Review,* XXIV (1963), 130–33.

galists only for words of pain, cruelty, and the like, appealed to Gabrieli for their sheer sound. The other verses tend to be broken into short segments, for which Gabrieli invented pregnant motives that are either imitated sequentially in the same voice or are passed from one voice to another. Bukofzer gave such ideas the fitting label "contrast motives." (*See* Example 4-4.)

**EXAMPLE 4-4** G. Gabrieli, *In ecclesiis* (Instrumental choir has been omitted.)

As often as not the musical gesture in this work seems to arise from a textual rhythm or a purely musical impulse rather than a verbal conceit. There is no trace of Florentine recitative in the music for one or two parts; rather, the style is that of reduced choral texture. Particularly in the duet quoted above, one has the impression that the top parts of two choirs have been skimmed off. Scacchi was quite right to think of this style as fundamentally a first-practice idiom. It remained so in Gabrieli, despite the infusion of some of the secular techniques of the second practice.

## THE MEANING OF CONCERTO

Compositions like *In ecclesiis* belong to Scacchi's third category—works for one or more choruses *in concerto*. The meaning in the early baroque of this noun *concerto* and the related parts of speech—the verb *concertare*, its present participle *concertante*, and its past participle *concertato*—need explanation, because they have been misused so often in modern writing.

The Italian noun *concerto* as used in the sixteenth century and most of the seventeenth refers to an ensemble of various instruments or voices or both, or a composition for such an ensemble. This is what the English then called a *consort*, a word which, however, appears to have a different root.

The Italian verb *concertare*, which may have been coined from the noun, means to coordinate or unite in a harmonious ensemble a heterogeneous group of players or singers, or both. It is equivalent to the English verb *concert*.

Many modern writers make much of the idea of opposition and contention in the *concerto*, invoking a bellicose image of instruments and voices attacking and counterattacking. It is doubtful that such an idea existed in the minds of seventeenth-century composers; rather, a great deal of evidence points to the contrary. The principal source for the idea of strife in the concerto is Michael Praetorius (1571–1621), whose etymologies for Italian terms in his *Syntagma musicum* (Musical Treatise, Part III, 1619) are notoriously fanciful. He derived the term from the Latin verb *concertare*, which means to contend or fight, but whose noun is *concertatio*. He was probably led off base by an innocent—if from the point of view of later history catastrophic and also prophetic—pun made by Ercole Bottrigari (1531–1612) in his dialogue *Il Desiderio* (1594).

The interlocutors of the dialogue, Gratioso Desiderio and Alemanno Benelli (anagram for Annibale Melone, a Bolognese music teacher and choirmaster and pupil of Bottrigari) have been speaking of the difficulty of uniting into a harmony (*concento*) instruments of different types—fretted and nonfretted string instruments, keyboard instruments, brass instruments with and without slides, woodwind instruments—each with its own system of tuning. Desiderio concludes that with the present confusion of tuning methods a *concerto* of such instruments is next to impossible to achieve. Alemanno then ventures into a play on words, a favorite sport at this time. "Rather," Alemanno replies, "by what we have said, we can, alas, make such *concerti*." After all, *concerto*, he explains, means contention and contrast, and he cites Cicero, Terence, and Pliny. The word *conserto*, he adds, is merely a Tuscan corruption of this. Desiderio upbraids his mentor for confusing the issue with his joke, and he asks again: Are *concerti* possible with so many different instruments? Alemanno replies:

> Both good and bad ones are to be heard. They should not be *concerti*, nor *conserti*, but *concenti* (harmonies). Such *concenti*, I believe, can be achieved, but with diligence. Otherwise the letter *n* will be changed to *r* or *s*, and instead of a *concento* we shall have a *concerto* or *conserto*. But in this discussion we shall use the terms *concento* and *concerto* interchangeably so as not to depart from common parlance.[8]

And so, Alemanno, admitting that his learned etymology is irrelevant, accepts the common usage of *concerto* as a harmonious aggregation of musical forces.

[8]Ercole Bottrigari, *Il Desiderio, overo De' concerti di varii strumenti musicali, dialogo, di Alemanno Benelli* (Venice: R. Amadino, 1594), pp. 8–10.

A group of concertizing singers and instrumentalists, each performing from a partbook one voice of a five-voice texture. Copper engraving by Abraham Bosse (1602–76). (Jules Ecorcheville, *Vingt Suites d'orchestre du xvii siecle français*, Berlin, 1906)

In a concerto, then, a harmonious cooperation is achieved among diverse musical performers. *To concert* is to secure this cooperation, and a *concerted* piece or style is one in which this union occurs. Since the term is used mainly when the means are diverse—and rarely when they are homogeneous, as in pure choral music—the desired agreement is always a triumph over some natural opposition. In the concerted madrigal, for example, there is such opposition between the singer or singers on the one hand and the instrumentalists playing the thorough bass and its filling on the other. But the composer, while respecting their separate roles, brings them into a coordinated scheme.

The term *concerto* does not imply the use of soloists, though it often occurs in connection with them. The ensemble of the three ladies of Ferrara was called a *concerto*. To take another example, the *concerti* of Adriano Banchieri (1568–1634) in his *Ecclesiastiche sinfonie* of 1607 are conceived for four soloistic parts, with frequent monodic or duet sections, all accompanied by a basso continuo, as opposed to the *sinfonie* in the same collection, which are choral motets in the old style accompanied by a *basso seguente*. On the other hand, in describing the ensembles of the Florentine intermezzi of 1589, the compiler of the music, Cristofano Malvezzi, used *concertato* and *concerto* for ensembles of voices and instruments in which the instruments, sometimes more than one to a part, double the voices of a chorus, as in the six-part madrigal *O qual risplende nube*: "The following madrigal was concerted [*concertato*] with four lutes, four viols, two basses [viols], four trombones, two cornetts, a cittern, a psaltery, a mandola, an arciviolata lira, violin, and 24 voices."[9]

Later in the century the term *concerto* and its derivatives truly acquired the ambiguity Bottrigari discovered. For example, Laurentius Erhard (1598–1669) in a Latin-German dictionary of musical terms[10] made the distinction between *concerto* used as a generic term, meaning motet or symphony, and used to designate a subspecies, as the equivalent of *concertatio*, "when the parts contend [*certiren*] with each other." Praetorius probably helped to bring about this cleavage, for he too recognized a general class called *concerto* and a species of music called *a concertando*. In any case this dual usage became pronounced in the middle of the century and continued throughout the later baroque.

## THE CONCERTO FOR A FEW VOICES

The first essays in the sacred medium of solo voices with basso continuo were based on polyphonic models. We saw that chamber singers extracted single voice parts from madrigals to contrive vehicles for themselves. Later they composed monodies based on these models. The same phenomenon is observable almost contemporaneously in sacred music, but the models were naturally motets and similar pieces. A product of this practice is the collection of motets for one and more voices with basso continuo published by Lodovico Grossi da Viadana (c. 1560–1627) in 1602 under the title *Cento concerti ecclesiastici* (One Hundred Church Concertos).

Viadana admitted in the preface that his principal aim was to relieve soloists of the necessity of reducing music written for many parts by singing one or more of the parts while the rest were played.[11] A disadvantage of this procedure was that when the part singled out waited its turn in a point of imitation, an awkward pause resulted in the singing. Moreover, the usual motet did not offer good opportunities for improvised florid passages, orna-

---

[9]D. P. Walker, ed., *Musique des Intermèdes de "La Pellegrina"* (Paris: Editions du Centre national de la recherche scientifique, 1963). p. LII.

[10]*Compendium musices* (Frankfurt a. M., 1660).

[11]This preface is translated in Strunk, *Source Readings*, pp. 419–23.

ments, and cadenzas. To replace the impromptu arrangements Viadana devised a pseudopolyphony in which one, two, or three voices were sufficient when complemented by a basso continuo. Often a voice imitated itself, or two voices kept up a round of interlocking imitations. Except for the runs, usually at cadences, Viadana's vocal style is that of part music. The bass for the organ moves like a vocal part. Although it is unfigured, the organist is expected to improvise a simple accompaniment upon it, adjusting this to the number and character of vocal parts.

This pseudo-polyphonic style is illustrated in Example 4-5, taken from Viadana's 1602 collection (entire piece in *HAM* II, 185). Each phrase of text is given separate musical sections marked off by cadences. Pseudo-imitation is seen at the words "a puero tuo." At "Quoniam tribulor" (measure 43) the organ bass announces the subject as if it were a vocal part. The run at "velociter" is both cadential and descriptive.

A setting of *Salve Regina* for soprano and tenor soloists (*GMB* 168) shows that Viadana was not unaware of the special opportunities and demands of the ensemble of few voices. The composer set only the odd-numbered verses and final verse of this antiphon to the Blessed Virgin Mary, the other verses being sung in plainchant according to the traditional alternating style. The relationship between the two voices is enlivened by imitation at a close interval of time. Occasionally the composer took advantage of the seductive qualities of the solo voice, as in the willowy undulations of the verse "O clemens, o pia." The bass for organ doubles the tenor part throughout most of the concerto.

Similar tendencies may be found in the sacred concertos of several of Viadana's contemporaries, such as Agostino Agazzari (1578–1640) in Rome, Adriano Banchieri in Bologna, and Giovanni Croce (c. 1560–1609) in Venice. More than Viadana, these men betray the influence of the polychoral style in their proclivity for breaking up vocal lines into short motives conferred upon bits of text. Although their compositions still fall into discrete sections framed by cadences, a section may contain a variety of heterogeneous material. The contrast motives of the polychoral idiom are often combined with an independent bass line to produce a style that is much more indigenous to the medium of solo voices and organ than the transparently hybrid efforts of Viadana.

These early sacred concertos belong to a category of writing that, like the airs of Caccini, is a compromise between an elegant style of vocal performance with chordal accompaniment then in vogue and the ideals of the first practice. A shift to a new kind of melody based on the ideals of the second practice is not conspicuous in sacred music until the second decade of the seventeenth century.

As in the secular field, it was Florence that pioneered the use of the monodic style in the church. Though none of Caccini's or Peri's works for

EXAMPLE 4-5   L. Grossi da Viadana, *Exaudi me, Domine*

the church are extant, two important cycles of compositions for Holy Week by Cavalieri are preserved. Vincenzo Galilei had set the Lamentations and Responses for Holy Week in a monodic style in 1582. These are lost, but they may have exerted some influence on Cavalieri. The latter's settings are for solo voices, ensembles of soloists, chorus, and basso continuo. They were probably first performed in Florence or Pisa in the last years of the sixteenth century, and there is evidence that Vittoria Archilei sang the solo soprano part. The vocal line, which lacks the independence from the bass of Peri's recitative, relies upon affective skips and chromaticism rather than on dissonance for its expression. Example 4-6, from the First Lesson of the First

**EXAMPLE 4-6** E. de' Cavalieri, *Lamentationes Hieremiae Prophetae*, Prima die, lectio prima

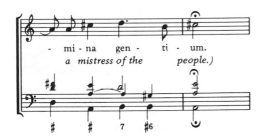

Day from the first cycle, is typical. The technique here is consistent with Galilei's instructions in his unpublished treatise on counterpoint of 1589–1591 as to how to express sorrowful affections by false melodic and chordal connections without using contrapuntal dissonances.[12] Cavalieri also experimented with enharmonic music in passages of the second set of Lamentations. For the performance of such music he had an organ built that accommodated the unusual tunings.

Although Cavalieri's music is highly original and prophetic, it is outside the main stream of development of the sacred concerto for few voices. This is best represented by Monteverdi and Alessandro Grandi (d. 1630). In their early creations in this medium they show a smooth transition from

[12]The illustration Galilei provided is printed in Fabio Fano, *La camerata fiorentina*, Istituzioni e monumenti de l'arte musicale italiana (Milan: Ricordi), IV (1934), pp. 277–78.

the pseudo-polyphonic style to the new sacred monody. The two styles are often juxtaposed within a single composition, as in Grandi's four-voice *Plorabo die ac nocte* (*CW* 40, pp. 8–12) of approximately 1615, in which tight fugues for two, three, and four voices alternate with passages of solo recitative. Another such composition is Monteverdi's *Pulchra es amica mea* from the 1610 collection. It is on a text paraphrased from the *Song of Songs*. The section in modern style in Example 4-7 stands in the midst of more conventional writing.

With a work such as this we come to Scacchi's fourth category: motets in the modern concerted style. Again he is our perceptive guide:

> We now come to the motets or concertos in the modern style that belongs to the second practice. . . . This type of composition must be so fashioned that it is distinct from the theatre and chamber styles and takes a middle course. This second practice requires that consonances and dissonances be disposed otherwise than in the previous practice. . . . It was invented by the Italians to compose works in their vernacular tongue for the highest advance of musical art, and also . . . for the music that is customarily made in oratories. Indeed, to put this into practice in composing vocal pieces in the secular idiom, it is advisable to take as examples Jacopo Peri, Luca Marenzio, Luzzasco Luzzaschi, and, among the first, Claudio Monteverdi, who brought this genre to the highest form of perfection.
>
> Further, this second practice requires a melody different from the old, and the natural expression of the words must be sought as much as possible.[13]

These remarks are from Scacchi's letter to Werner. In his printed essay, he elaborated on what he meant by the middle course:

> Two manners are distinguished in the recitative style. One is the simple representative style, which is that accompanied by gestures in the theatre. The other is called *imbastardito* [hybrid], that is, the mixed style, in which one goes along representing the text in the recitative style and then suddenly varies this with florid passages and other melodic movements.[14]

This mixed style, he said, was used in the church.

This description fits Monteverdi's approach perfectly. The passage in Example 4-7 begins in recitative style, with the characteristic drop of the sixth, but almost immediately the composer begins to repeat words, making sequences on "a me." Suddenly, to illustrate the words "me avolare," he breaks the free rhythm with a faster fluent triple-metered melody. This returns later as a refrain. The remainder of the example is truly in a mixed

---

[13]Quoted in Katz, *Die musikalischen Stilbegriffe*, pp. 85–86.
[14]Scacchi, *Discorso*, fol. 9v.

style, wavering between recitative with its free dissonance, as in measures 39–40, on the one hand, and coloratura and airlike passages on the other. The dry declamation of the stage is made liquid and the hard dissonances softened by the flow of sweet consonant vocality. Expressiveness is not lost withal; rather, it is enhanced.

Outstanding among the contemporaries of Monteverdi who were heading in the same direction is Alessandro Grandi. His *O quam tu pulchra es*

**EXAMPLE 4-7**   C. Monteverdi, *Pulchra es amica mea*

(published 1625; *NAWM* 82) on a somewhat different text from the *Song of Songs*, contains a similar mixture of recitative and flowing triple-time airlike passages (ed. Rudolf Ewerhart in *Drei Hoheliedmotetten*, "Cantio sacra" [Cologne: Verlag Edmund Bieler], Vol. 23).

It is of some significance that both the motets are based on the *Song of Songs*, whose sensual imagery and amorous theme naturally call for a secular treatment. Solomon's song elicited from both Monteverdi and Grandi early departures from the conventional religious music making, but by the 1620s settings of religious texts containing more purely devout feelings can hardly be distinguished in style from these. The collection of motets for one voice by Grandi published by Gardano of Venice in 1628, for example, contains both a *Tata pulchra es amica mea* and a *Quam pulchra es o Maria*, treated in a like manner and in a style hardly distinguishable from their neighbors, which are on a variety of sacred texts.

Monteverdi, throughout his career in Mantua and from 1613 as choirmaster at St. Mark's in Venice, continued to commit to the divine service the craft he acquired in writing madrigals, pastorals, and ballets for courtly entertainments. The resultant mixed genres are evident in two sacred miscellanies, the *Selva morale e spirituale* of 1640 and the posthumous collection, *Messa a quattro voci, et Salmi* (Mass for four voices and psalms, 1650), both containing works composed probably over a period of thirty years or more.

The strophic song with ritornelli for two violins and bass, familiar from *Orfeo* and developed particularly in the *Scherzi musicali* of 1607 (Malipiero edition, X), is the model for the hymn *Sanctorum meritis* (XV, 606). All stanzas of the hymn are sung by one voice to the same easily flowing triple-time melody, which, the composer noted, could serve also for singing other hymns of the same meter (iambic hexameter). By contrast, the hymn *Jubilet* (XV, 748), a through-composed dialogue for a single voice, alternates this song style with sections in recitative.

In a number of settings of the psalms for Vespers, Monteverdi adapted the mixed madrigal and recitative styles that he consolidated in the Seventh (1619) and Eighth (1638) books of madrigals. Psalm 126, *Nisi Dominus* (English no. 127; 1650; XVI, 299), mixes sections for one, two, or three solo voices and two violins over a quasi-ostinato bass, with sections for one or two voices in recitative (Example 4-8). The last verse begins in *falsobordone*, an idiom originating in the church, if assimilated by Monteverdi into the madrigal. The doxology brings back the music of the beginning, a framing device that Monteverdi favored in his late works. The free dissonance of the second practice, mentioned by Scacchi as a mark of the modern motet, is particularly effective in the passage of Example 4-9, which is repeated on several different tonal levels.

**EXAMPLE 4-8** C. Monteverdi, *Nisi Dominus*

Basso: va-num est, vo - bis an - te
*(vain it is for you before*

lu - cem sur - ge - re
*day break to get up)*

Tenore: sur - gi - te sur - gi - te sur - gi - te

Canto: sur-gi-te sur-gi-te sur -gi -te    sur-gi -te sur-gi-te sur -gi -te

Tenore: sur- gi-te sur-gi-te sur- gi -te

**EXAMPLE 4-9**  C. Monteverdi, *Nisi Dominus*

**EXAMPLE 4-10**  C. Monteverdi, *Laetatus sum*

EXAMPLE 4-10 (Cont.)

## THE GRAND CONCERTO

For the festive occasions that earlier called forth the polychoral *symphoniae sacrae* of Gabrieli, Monteverdi wrote concertos in both the first and second practices. Psalm 115/116, *Credidi*, for two choirs (*Selva morale*; XV, 544), is in *alla breve* severe style, with the psalm formula of the fourth tone cited intermittently in the soprano of the first choir. Psalm 121/122, *Laetatus sum* (1650; XVI, 231) for six voices and two violins, is entirely in a modern manner. Except for the beginning of the doxology, the entire psalm is sung over a one-measure ostinato that imposes a recurring progression—tonic-subdominant-dominant—on the vocal and instrumental parts. The violins and two voices exchange a running figure in the first verse (Example 4-10) that resembles the violin figuration in the madrigal *Chiome d'oro* of the Seventh Book. Although the music has the flavor of the *ciacona*, the ostinato does not conform to the *ciacona* bass of this period, which followed the harmonic succession I–V–vi–V or I–V–vi–iii–IV–V, the latter used in Monteverdi's famous *Zeffiro torna* (*Scherzi musicali*, 1632; IX, 9). In Psalm 116/117, *Laudate Dominum omnes gentes* (*Selva morale*; XV, 481), Monteverdi drew together the modern resources of the concerto for few voices with violins and that of the full choir doubled by either four *viole da braccio* or trombones. Voice pairs exchanging music with the violin duet over a quasi-ostinato bass alternate with homorhythmic tutti sections, written not in the old fashioned *falsobordone* but in choral recitative. A fugue on the text "misericordia," set to a chromatic subject—a rare occurrence in Monteverdi—involves at first only the tenor and violins, but, after a solo episode over the quasi-ostinato walking bass, it returns to be developed in ten vocal and instrumental parts (Example 4-11).

In these large-scale, probably late, works Monteverdi completed the transference of the new secular resources to key texts of the liturgy.

**EXAMPLE 4-11**    C. Monteverdi, *Laudate Dominum omnes gentes*

EXAMPLE 4-11 (Cont.)

## BIBLIOGRAPHICAL NOTES

For a provocative discussion of the varying meanings of the word *concerto*, see David Boyden, "When is a Concerto not a Concerto?" in *MQ*, XLIII (1957), 220–32. The articles of Denis Arnold occupy what is otherwise a void in literature in English on the early sacred concerto: "Giovanni Croce and the

*Concertato* Style" in *MQ*, XXXIX (1953), 37–48; and "Alessandro Grandi, a Disciple of Monteverdi," *MQ*, XLIII (1957), 171–86. Needed reevaluations of the Monteverdi Vespers of 1610 are "Where are the Vespers of Yesteryear?" by Denis Stevens, *MQ*, XLVII (1961), 315–30; Stephen Bonta, "Liturgical Problems in Monteverdi's Marian Vespers," *JAMS*, XX (1967), 87–106; and Jeffrey Kurtzman, "Some Historical Perspectives on the Monteverdi Vespers," *Analecta Musicologica*, XV (1975), 29–86 and *Essays on the Monteverdi Mass and Vespers of 1610*, Rice University Studies, Vol. 69, no. 4, Fall 1978 (Houston; 1979). There are two book-length studies of Giovanni Gabrieli's life and works: Egon Kenton, *The Life and Works of Giovanni Gabrieli* (American Institute of Musicology, 1967), and Denis Arnold, *Giovanni Gabrieli* (London: Oxford University Press, 1979).

Malipiero's edition of the works of Monteverdi contains sacred music in volumes XIV, XV, and XVI. The *Opera omnia* of Giovanni Gabrieli, edited by Denis Arnold (American Institute of Musicology, 1956–  ) includes the *Concerti* of 1587 (Vol. I), the *Sacrae symphoniae* of 1597 (Vols. I, II), and the *Sacrae symphoniae* of 1615 (Vols. III–V). Six motets of Giovanni Gabrieli for seven and eight voices are in *CW*, Vols. 10 (1931) and 67 (1958), Motets of Grandi are in *CW*, Vol. 40 (1936) and in *Cantio sacra* (Cologne: E. Bieler), Vol. 18 (1960). There are two editions of the first cycle of the Cavalieri Lamentations, neither altogether reliable, one edited by Gianfranco Maselli (Zürich: Ars Viva, 1950), the other edited by Francesco Màntica (Padua: G. Zanibon, 1960). Viadana's *Cento concerti ecclesiastici* are edited by Claudio Gallico in Viadana's *Opere* (Kassel: Bärenreiter, 1964), Ser. 1, no. 1, of the series *Monumenti musicali Mantovani*.

# FIVE

# LUTE AND KEYBOARD MUSIC

The seventeenth century is rightfully viewed as that in which instrumental music acquired an important independent repertory, but its emancipation had taken place well before 1600. Instrumental music in the first decades thrived on already accumulated momentum. The different kinds of variations, such as the *partite*; the prelude-types, such as the *toccata, ricercare*, and *intonazione*; the learned essays, such as the *fantasia* and *capriccio*; as well as the genres inspired by or parodying vocal music, such as the *canzone*, verse, and organ-mass all had acquired their identities in the sixteenth century. Fashions in dance music and the grouping of dances also straddled the century mark. Indeed, there was no significant break in methods of instrumental composition around 1600. Any consideration of seventeenth-century instrumental style must therefore begin with its sources in the Renaissance.

# VARIATIONS ON DANCE TUNES

Dance music and dance-derived music made up a large part of the instrumental music of the baroque period. This is one reason for beginning with this category. Another is that the dance gave rise to the variations form, which reached an early maturity in that repertory. It is appropriate to consider the dance and the variation together.

If one studies a number of pavanes and galliards—the favorite European dances of the sixteenth century—such as those of the manuscript collection known as the Fitzwilliam Virginal Book, it becomes obvious that the main principle of musical expansion in these dances, aside from repetition, is variation. Variation as a musical technique in the baroque may be defined as the restatement of a melodic or harmonic period with ornamentation or diversification of one or both of these elements and of rhythm. Normally the duration of each basic melodic note or harmony remains fixed, but, as we have seen in Monteverdi's *Romanesca* for two sopranos, irregularities are possible. In music for dancing, the duration of each harmony had to be fixed not only because the formations and steps of the dancers depended upon this regularity but because this permitted several musicians to improvise simultaneously. The variation was a natural method for dance music, and it is still used today for this purpose. It allows a dance to be made short or long by reducing or increasing the number of variations, and it allows a heterogeneous and unrehearsed group to play together on common tunes and their chord patterns.

Most of the pavanes and galliards of the two great English harpsichord composers William Byrd (1542/3–1623) and John Bull (c. 1562–1628) use the method of varying immediately each "strain" or melodic-harmonic statement once, and then proceeding to another strain. Some of the dances vary a single tune many times, such as the Spanish Paven of John Bull (*GMB* 147), which contains seven varied statements of the same harmonic material. Often the first statement is itself a variation of a well-known tune or harmonic pattern.

Bull's Pavana for virginals (*TEM* 30) from *Parthenia*, a collection published in 1611, will serve to demonstrate several methods of variation. The pavane was a dance in slow duple meter. It was often followed in a set for dancing by a galliard, which was in faster triple meter. In the present Pavana there are three strains (A, B, C), each varied once immediately after the original statement, producing the form $A^1A^2\ B^1B^2\ C^1C^2$. Each strain is sixteen whole notes long, and the variations preserve these durations. $A^2$ preserves both the melodic outline and the harmony of $A^1$, as may be seen in the first measures of each given in Example 5-1, but the "divisions," or figurative realization of the harmony and its rhythms, are different. On the

82

other hand, $C^2$ in its first two measures does not keep the melody of $C^1$ but only the approximate harmonic content and the bass (Example 5-2). The keyboard technique of sections A and B is inspired by that of the lute, in which the notes of a chord are frequently split to make them more accessible to the fingers, and only one fast-running line is possible. The C section realizes most fully the possibilities of the harpsichord in that here there are many full chords and, during a long section of $C^1$, four-part writing.

    An example that will illustrate the beginnings of the variation procedure is a *Pavana alla venetiana* for lute by Joan Dalza from his *Intabulatura di lauto* (Venice, 1508). Here there are several successive variations of the same strain. The first statement and the first variation are given below (Example 5-3). If the composer had any underlying melody in mind he did not state it, but rather kept as the constant element a simple harmonic pat-

**EXAMPLE 5-1**  J. Bull, *Pavana*

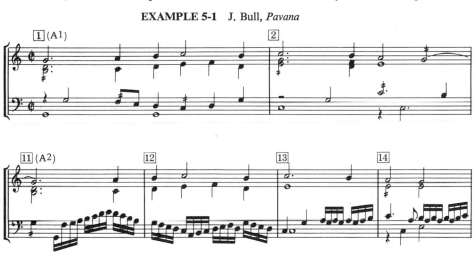

**EXAMPLE 5-2**  J. Bull, *Pavana*

tern, which the second time is somewhat enriched. The dance variation and the variation upon popular or standard tunes and harmonic patterns were cultivated by lute players throughout the century in Italy and by players of the lutelike vihuela in Spain. By the middle of the century the art of variation became one of high refinement and ample technical resources. Among the notable contributors to this development are the lutanists Pietro Paulo Borrono and Iacomo Gorzanis (c. 1525–1575), the vihuelists Luys de Milan, Luys de Narváez, and Enriquez de Valderrábano (c. 1500–1559), and the keyboard composer Antonio de Cabezón (1510–1566).

The most popular themes for variation in the latter part of the sixteenth and in the early seventeenth century were those associated with the *pass'e mezzo* (step and a half) or *passamezzo*. This apparently began as a Milanese form of the pavane but soon overtook the parent dance in popularity. It was characteristic of this dance that it consisted of a long series of choreographic patterns, each taking the time of an eight-measure period. To provide music for this, the players would improvise upon a musical period of that length. Whatever may have been the original tunes, two harmonic

**EXAMPLE 5-3**   J. A. Dalza, *Pavana alla venetiana*

patterns, one in minor mode, called *passamezzo antico*, and one of later origin in major, known as *passamezzo moderno*, are found to be the basis of most *passamezzi*. These harmonic patterns may be represented by the series shown in Example 5-4. Here the normal time values of the sixteenth century have been reduced by a fourth. If the bass of the passamezzo antico is compared to that of the Romanesca (Example 3-13), it is seen that they differ in only the first note and in meter—the passamezzo being duple, the Romanesca triple. This similarity has never been adequately explained. What is significant is that both show a wavering between a minor key and its relative major that was characteristic of many pieces oriented toward a minor tonality at this time. The passamezzo moderno, on the other hand, betrays a clear recognition of the constellation of chords that make up the major tonality: the chords on the first, fourth, and fifth degrees. Since the eighteenth century we have called these tonic, subdominant, and dominant.

**EXAMPLE 5-4** *Passamezzo* patterns

In the passamezzo the first statement is itself a variation of the harmonic pattern, but often it presents a melodic theme or a group of motives that will become the subjects for subsequent variations. This is the case in a passamezzo antico of around 1570 by Vincenzo Galilei, given in Example 5-5, where the second variation is set below the first. The basic harmony of the standard pattern is observed at the beginning of each measure. The playful short motives of measures 12–14, the breadth of the runs, alternately rocketing and plummeting, the headlong energy of the penultimate measure 15, to which brakes are applied by the syncopations of measure 16—all characterize the sophistication achieved in Italian lute variations at this time.

**EXAMPLE 5-5** V. Galilei, *Pass'e mezzo*

**EXAMPLE 5-5** (Cont.)

As the pavane was earlier paired with the galliard, the *passamezzo* was now often paired with the *saltarello*, a dance in quick triple time hardly distinguishable from the galliard. Gorzanis (1567) and Galilei (1584) both wrote cycles of dances including these two types in all twenty-four of the major and minor keys. Whereas Gorzanis's cycle contains a *passamezzo-saltarello* pair for each key, Galilei's sets consist in the twelve minor keys of a *passamezzo antico*, *Romanesca*, and a *saltarello* in the relative major. In the major keys, Galilei grouped a *passamezzo moderno* and a *Romanesca* (actually a *passamezzo moderno* in triple time) with a *saltarello* borrowed from the major cycle. In Galilei's cycle each *passamezzo* and *Romanesca* has at least four variations, sometimes as many as twenty.

## VARIATIONS ON SONGS

The Partite sopra l'aria della Romanesca (1637; *HAM* II, 192) of Girolamo Frescobaldi (1583–1643) is one of several sets of variations by this composer on standard airs and popular songs. The version of the theme used by Frescobaldi terminates, as did that of Monteverdi (Example 3-13), with the repeat, or *ripresa*, of the second four-measure phrase. The first statement is itself a variation of the melody, as may be seen by the asterisks above the melody's notes (Example 5-6). The standard succession of bass notes (encircled in the example) is similarly decorated. The treble tune is not prominent again until the fourth *parte*, and then again in the eleventh. Frescobaldi bestowed upon each variation a highly individual character. Each is unified by a limited number of motives or a particular style of figuration, and one, the fifth, is actually in a different meter and tempo, simple triple time. At the same time the whole set of variations is bound by a consistently contemplative and almost madrigalistic spirit. The opening statement, with its sharp dissonances and surprising syncopations, its fits and starts, evokes the spirit of the new monody. The third *parte* illustrates both the economy of motivic material and the rather special, almost rhetorical eloquence that Fresceobaldi achieved in this work.

The variation for harpsichord reached an early flowering in England, particularly in the work of William Byrd and John Bull. Virtuosity in keyboard technique and richness of invention are common to both composers. The variations on the popular song *John, Come Kiss Me Now* (Example 5-7a) by Byrd (Fitzwilliam Virginal Book, I, No. 10) illustrate well the lively tunefulness and the clever use of imitation characteristic of him. Here the melody appears in almost every variation, either in its simple or decorated form, sometimes on top, sometimes in an inner part, occasionally also in the bass, or wandering among the parts of the texture. This method has been compared to the cantus firmus technique in vocal polyphony. Although there is a certain parallel, the present melody is too dependent on its original harmony, which almost always accompanies it, to fit the concept of cantus firmus, in which a theme is surrounded by freely moving parts not tied to any harmonic scheme. Sometimes a single motive or style of figuration is pursued

**EXAMPLE 5-6**   G. Frescobaldi, *Partite sopra l'aria della Romanesca*

**EXAMPLE 5-7a**   Song, *John, Come Kiss Me Now*

John   come kisse   me      now;        John   come kisse   me      now;

John   come kisse me      by      and by,   And   make   no   more   a - dow.

throughout a variation, sometimes through only part of one. In Example 5-7b, variations 5 and 6 are paired by having the second part of 5 introduce the motive that lies at the basis of the first part of 6, while the second half of variation 6 returns to the first motive of the fifth. In variation 6 the melody is implied in the bare allusion to its harmonic scheme.

The thirty variations by Bull on *Walsingham,* a song (Example 5-8a) upon which Byrd had also written twenty-two variations, are a virtual compendium of variation techniques. This masterpiece deserves its place of honor as the first work in the Fitzwilliam Virginal Book (I, No. 1). Bull's achievement is all the more remarkable when it is recognized that his variations keep strictly to a melodic-harmonic subject and that they depend very little on voluntary ornaments. The melody is always discernible, and the harmony, although often enriched, maintains the basic scheme and usually also the bass line. More often than his predecessors, Bull tended to establish

**EXAMPLE 5-7b**   W. Byrd, Variations on *John, Come Kiss Me Now*

a pattern of figuration at the outset and to pursue it throughout a variation. The patterns are extraordinarily varied. There are crisp motives that are tossed from voice to voice (variations 6 and 19), broken-chord figures (variation 12), running figures using turns, scales, and broken chords (variations 15 and 16), repeated-note effects (variations 8, 25, and 28), and adaptations to the keyboard of the lute technique in which a harmony is distributed over several strings of the lute (here the fingers of the two hands) (variations 10 and 18). A few of these devices, which are the essence of the new harpsichord technique, are shown in Example 5-8b.

**EXAMPLE 5-8a**   Song, *As I Went to Walsingham*

As I went to    Wal - sing - ham,    To the shrine with    speed,    Met

I with a    jol - ly pal - mer,    In a pil - grim's    weed.

## IMPROVISATORY TYPES

Variations such as those just discussed—on popular songs, standard airs, and dance tunes—exemplify a style in which the improvisatory impulse was held under very strict control. Outgrowths of much freer improvisatory gestures are the toccata, prelude, ricercare, fantasia, and intonazione. These arose from a musician's need to test the tuning of his instrument, fix the tonality for a vocal performance, warm up his technique, set the stage briefly for some other music to come, or occasionally fill an interlude between songs and dances. That these types were originally linked by a common function is witnessed by a certain interchangeability of terms during the sixteenth century.

Although the etymology of some of the names is uncertain, they seem to contain vestiges of the early history of the music they describe. *Toccata* suggests a *touching* of the fingerboard of a lute or similar instrument, though *toccare* was also used for plucking with the fingers and for striking the keys of a keyboard manual. The verb *ricercare* was used to signify a *searching out* of strings to pluck. *Tiento*, the Spanish name for such a piece as the *ricercare*, means literally *trial*. Another term sometimes found for introductory sallies is *tastar de corde*, which even more clearly than *toccata* refers to the stopping of strings on the *tasto* or fingerboard. *Prelude*, *praeludium*, and *preambel* obviously refer to preliminary music. *Fantasia* is a free exercise of the musical *fancy* in an improvisation. An *intonazione* is literally an *intonation*—a giving of the pitch by the organ rather than by a cantor or precentor. The earliest examples of all of these genres, as might be expected from music so

**EXAMPLE 5-8b**  J. Bull, *Walsingham*

described, are brief, virtually frozen improvisations. Perhaps the most important fact that unites them is that they are almost always independent of the vocal or dance music that follows, though there are notable exceptions.

Despite this original community of method and function, a number of these musical types became quite clearly differentiated by the beginning of the seventeenth century. The ricercare and fantasia on the one hand and the toccata on the other will serve to illustrate this cleavage through evolution.

## The Ricercare

The earliest ricercari were published between 1507 and 1509 by the Venetian pioneer in music printing, Ottaviano Petrucci (1466–1539). They were by the lutanists Francesco Spinaccino (*HAM* I, 99b), Joan Ambrosio Dalza (*HAM* I, 99a), and Franciscus Bossinensis (i.e., of Bosnia) (*MR*, p.

163). Although they consist mainly of running passages mixed with strummed chords, in the examples of Spinaccino and Bossinensis there is already an attempt to achieve a polyphonic effect through alternation of low and high register (see Example 5-9, measures 15–25; the entire piece is in *HAM* I, 99b). This technique of simulating several voices while playing only one note at a time is called *style brisé*, or broken style, and is native to plucked instruments. Thus the ricercare at this stage exercised particularly the right or plucking hand, which must jump from one string to another deftly. The *tastar de corde*, which Dalza often put before the ricercare (as in *HAM* I, 99a), on the other hand, seems mainly to exercise the left hand, which must accurately and speedily find the proper frets on the lute's fingerboard, as in the later toccata.

**EXAMPLE 5-9**   F. Spinaccino, *Ricercar*

By 1523 Marc'Antonio Cavazzoni (c. 1490–1570) transferred the lute ricercare to the keyboard. The exchange of the material between high and low became an alternation of right and left hand, a device that lent structure to an otherwise free design of chords and runs and permitted a certain development of motives. With the *Musica nova* of 1540, containing twenty ricercari by, among others, Giulio Segni (1498–1561), Adrian Willaert, Girolamo Parabosco (1520/24–1557), and Marc'Antonio's son, Girolamo Cavazzoni (d. 1565), the ricercare invaded yet another medium—that of the ensemble of instruments, such as viols. In these pieces (*HAM* I, 115, and *GMB* 105 are somewhat later examples by Willaert), as well as those of G. Cavazzoni for organ of 1542–43 (*HAM* I, 116), the composer chose several different short subjects for imitation by all the "voices" in successive sections. In a few of the ricercari by the organists of the basilica of St. Mark's in Venice, Jacques Buus (d. 1565), Andrea Gabrieli, and Claudio Merulo (1533–1604), all of the material can be related to the subject first presented in the opening "point" of imitation. This also occurs in some Spanish fantasie. Eventually this became the standard procedure. Some of the devices used to vary the original material—augmentation, diminution, and inversion—will be observed also in the later works discussed below.

Girolamo Frescobaldi's *Ricercar dopo il Credo* of 1635 for organ (*MM* 34) illustrates the final stage of this genre's evolution. Its subject is highly colored by the chromatic progressions much favored by Frescobaldi because of their dynamic emotional quality. It is stated in all the voices either on the central tone, G, or its fifth degree, D, seven times, and twice more on A. After the initial statement it is always accompanied by the same short countersubject. After a close is made on G, a second section begins in which the subject is heard four more times on the first and fifth degrees, now in augmentation, that is, with the note values doubled. A second countersubject appears both in its original form (measure 24) and inverted form (measure 26) in various voices against the main subject. This method of using several countersubjects in successive sections against a single principal one achieved in the monothematic ricercare a unity and continuity that was missing in the polythematic motetlike ricercare of the mid-sixteenth century. It also drastically reduced the number of sections without sacrificing variety of material.

## The Fantasia

The term *fantasia*, applied frequently after 1540 to lute pieces that are indistinguishable from ricercari (see *GMB* 115 by Francesco da Milano), was rarely applied to organ music before the end of the sixteenth century. Keyboard pieces so named tended to be monothematic like the ricercari but often varied the subject itself progressively from one section to the next rather than adding new countersubjects. In the seventeenth century the keyboard fantasia more than the ricercare exploited learned contrapuntal devices and standard "school" subjects such as the hexachord *ut-re-mi-fa-sol-la*. Revealing of the nature of the fantasia is the fact that applicants for organ positions at St. Mark's in Venice were expected to improvise one on a given theme.

Jan Pieterszoon Sweelinck (1562–1621) left seventeen fantasias, among them one on the hexachord theme *ut-re-mi-fa-sol-la*. His *Fantasia chromatica* (*GMB* 158) on a theme descending chromatically a fourth is a brilliant tour de force. Except for a twenty-five-measure episode on a different subject (measures 61–85 in *GMB*), the chromatic theme permeates the whole work. The fantasia begins with two lengthy expositions in d minor, each with its own countersubject (Examples 5-10a, b). Then, after the episode, the theme is heard in double augmentation against two more countersubjects (measures 86–115; Example 5-10c), followed by a section in diminution (measures 116–38; Example 5-10d). A *stretto*, a passage in which the entrances of the theme are made to overlap (measures 138–50; Example 5-10e), and a section in

## EXAMPLE 5-10  J. Sweelinck, *Fantasia chromatica*

**EXAMPLE 5-10** (Cont.)

double diminution (note values quartered) over pedal points alternately on the fifth and final degrees of the mode bring the fantasia to a close. In the art of writing fantasias such as this now reposed the legacy of contrapuntal mastery gained in earlier centuries through the motet and mass. The learned devices disdained by the monodists found here their natural habitat.

The fantasies and fancies written in England during the seventeenth century, whether for keyboard or consort of viols, constitute a branch of the same tree that yielded the continental fantasia. Stemming directly from the mid-sixteenth-century Italian ricercare, the English form was almost untouched by later continental developments. Throughout the seventeenth century it preserved the polythematic, multisectional character of the early ricercare and motet. With the latter it shares the homophonic sections, often dancelike and in triple meter, that tend more and more to invade the imitative counterpoint. The mood of the century is felt, however, in the viol fantasies of John Cooper (Coperario) (c. 1570–1626), William Lawes (1602–1645). Matthew Locke (1632/3–1677), John Jenkins (1592–1678), and their contemporaries—not so much in their form as in their chromaticism, bold modulations, and soloistic and idiomatic lines (see *HAM* II, 230 by Locke).

## The Toccata

Of the types originating in the prelude function, the one whose development is most antithetical to the ricercare and fantasia is the toccata. Although some historians would trace its origin to the earliest prelude forms, the first dated composition designated a toccata (actually there spelled *tochata*) occurs in a collection of lute music issued by Castiglione in Milan in 1536.

Eventually keyboard composers made the toccata their own. Three organists of St. Mark's basilica in Venice led this development: Annibale Padovano (1527–1575), who was second organist until 1564; Andrea Gabrieli, who succeeded him; and Claudio Merulo, who took over the first organ the same year. The characteristic idiom of the toccata consists of scale-type passages, turns, trills, and short figures; these pass from hand to hand, while the hand not busy with them has sustained chords that often trace a descending or ascending diatonic line in the key of the piece. The narrow range of chord changes and the limited sphere of modulation also betray a preoccupation with establishing the central tone or mode. The toccata shares this manner of writing with the intonazione, which, however, tends to be shorter and more primitive in its chord progressions. Both Annibale and Merulo, and sometimes Andrea too, broke up the rapid finger work with quieter sections using short subjects in a three- or four-voice, freely imitative texture. These moments of concentrated energy usually explode into renewed paroxysms of digital fury. Usually there is one central imitative section (as in *HAM* I, 153, and *TEM* 29—both by Merulo), but often there are two or more (as in *GMB* 149 by Merulo, which has two). These sections have been compared to the ricercare, but they are far less strict in maintaining a given number of parts; the themes lack length and distinction, and are usually not sounded in an exposed single voice. Typical passages from one figurative and one imitative section are shown in Example 5-11 (from *GMB* 149).

This alternation of sections remained the favored procedure for the toccata throughout the baroque period, with some exceptions. Among the exceptions are the toccatas of Frescobaldi. Most of those in the *Fiori musicali* (1635) are short, meditative pieces, quite continuous in their texture, intended for different moments in the Mass, such as the Elevation, or just before the Mass. Those of his 1627 collection are generally longer and tend toward a looser juxtaposition of short sections, each exploring a key related to the main tonality and some type of figuration, in some cases even different meters and tempos, as in Toccata IX (*HAM* II, 193; Pidoux edition IV, 34). If despite this almost improvisatory method Frescobaldi's numerous and stirring toccatas suffer little slackening of momentum, it is partly because the figurative and imitative methods interpenetrate. Sweelinck is much truer to Merulo's form, but his figures are notably more varied and striking, possibly reflecting the influence of the English virginal school.

**EXAMPLE 5-11**   C. Merulo, *Toccata*

**EXAMPLE 5-11** (Cont.)

## BIBLIOGRAPHICAL NOTES

*The History of Keyboard Music to 1700* by Willi Apel, translated and revised by Hans Tischler (Bloomington, London: Indiana University Press, 1972), is a comprehensive, detailed and richly illustrated survey that is now the student's first resource in its field. A product of the author's lifelong study of the music and its sources, it is unfailingly illuminating and stimulating. A dependable shorter survey is Frank E. Kirby, *A Short History of Keyboard Music* (New York: Free Press, 1966).

On the ricercare and some of its sixteenth-century exponents, see H. Colin Slim's introduction to his edition of *Musica nova* (Venice, 1540) (Chicago: The University of Chicago Press, 1964). A sympathetic review of the music of one of the composers in this chapter is Wilfrid Mellers, "John Bull and English Keyboard Music," *MQ*, XL (1954), 364–83; 548–71.

The Fitzwilliam Virginal Book is a large, comprehensive manuscript in Cambridge complied by Francis Tregian (d. 1619) that contains keyboard music written between about 1562 and 1612. It was edited in 1894–1899 by J. A. Fuller Maitaland and W. Barclay Squire and reprinted in two paperbound volumes (New York: Dover, 1963). *Parthenia*, containing 21 compositions for keyboard by Byrd, Bull, and Orlando Gibbons, first published in 1611, was reprinted in 1951 in an edition by Kurt Stone (New York: Broude Brothers).

Among the earliest keyboard ricercari are those published in *I Classici musicali italiani*, Vol. I: *M. A. Cavazzoni, J. Fogliano, J. Segni ed Anonimi: Composizioni per organo*, ed. Giacomo Benvenuti (Milan, 1941). Vol. VI of the same series has the ricercari of G. Cavazzoni (1941), which are also published in an edition by Oscar Mischiati (Mainz: Schott, 1959).

The organ works of Andrea Gabrieli, including ricercari, toccate, and intonazioni, are available in five volumes (Kassel: Bärenreiter, 1953). Merulo's toccatas have been edited by Sandro Dalla Libera (3 volumes; Milan: G. Ricordi, 1959). Some of Galilei's lute compositions and transcriptions are in *IMAMI*, Vol. 4.

The keyboard works of Frescobaldi have been collected in an edition by P. Pidoux (5 volumes; Kassel: Bärenreiter, 1949–1954); nine toccatas from MS sources previously unpublished are in Frescobaldi, *Nove toccate inedite*, ed. S. Dalla Libera (Brescia, *L'Organo*; Kassel: Bärenreiter, 1962).

Sweelinck's works for organ and harpsichord have been published by the Vereeniging voor Nederlandse Muziekgeschiedenis in an edition by Max Seiffert (second edition; Amsterdam: G. Alsbach, 1943). A new edition of the keyboard works is in *Opera omnia*, Vol. I, The Instrumental Works, ed. Gustav Leonhardt, Alfons Annegarn, and Frits Noske (Amsterdam: Vereeniging voor Nederlandse Muziekgeschiedenis, 1968). Concerning the English influence on continental keyboard music, see Alan Curtis, *Sweelinck's Keyboard Music: A Study of English Elements in Seventeenth-century Dutch Composition* (Leyden: University Press; London: Oxford University Press, 1969).

For a sampling of English fancies and fantasies, see John Jenkins, *Fancies and Ayres*, edited by Helen Joy Sleeper (Wellesley, Mass.: Wellesley College, 1950), and William Lawes, *Select Consort Music*, edited by Murray Lefkowits, *Musica Britannica*, Vol. 21 (Stainer & Bell, 1963).

# SIX

# THE SACRED CONCERTO IN GERMANY

The Italian ambivalence toward musical styles, hospitable to both the ancient and modern manners, had its parallel in Germany, but here an important ingredient absent in Italy contributed to the staying power of the ancient style: the Lutheran hymn or chorale.[1] Composers in Italy early abandoned attempts to combine the concerted and recitative styles with plainsong themes; it took a Monteverdi to bring off such an experiment in the Vespers and Magnificat of 1610. By contrast, German composers found that the chorale and traditional ways of elaborating upon it could be made compatible with the most modern idioms.

---

[1] The term *chorale* comes from the German *Choral*, which is applied equally to the plainsong of the Catholic church and to the Reformation hymn. Both were conceived originally as unison choral music; hence the name.

# PRAETORIUS, SCHEIN, AND SCHEIDT

Michael Praetorius (1571–1621) is the supreme example. Son of a minister who had been a pupil of Luther and Melanchthon in theology, he published more than 1200 works based on chorales between 1605 and 1610 under the title *Musae Sionae* (The Muses of Zion), a series in nine parts. Praetorius, highly receptive to Italian innovations, set Parts 1 to 4 (1605–1607) in the Venetian polychoral style, which had already been popularized in Germany by Hans Leo Hassler (1564–1612; see *TEM* 28). Like his Italian contemporaries, Praetorius allowed instruments to take the place of voices when the latter were scarce.

The hybrid technique that the chorale engendered may be studied in the work of Johann Hermann Schein (1586–1630), from 1616 Cantor of the Thomasschule at Leipzig, a post that Bach was eventually to hold. Schein's *geistliche Konzerte* (sacred concerti), as he called them, were published in two parts under the title *Opella nova* (A Little New Opus) in 1618 and 1626. These concerti were undoubtedly intended to be performed at the chief or morning service after the Gospel or sermon and at Vespers. All but one piece in Part I are settings of first stanzas of Lutheran chorale texts, while in Part II only about a third are on chorale texts, the remainder on biblical texts. Along with the chorale texts, the melody of the chorale is almost always present. The two manners of reworking the chorale melody described below account for most of these compositions.

Schein's favorite technique was to use the phrases of the chorale melody as subject matter for a duet of two sopranos with basso continuo, the bass part being played by a bassoon, trombone, or string bass along with the organ. This is illustrated in the concerto on the Easter chorale *Erschienen ist der herrliche Tag* (The glorious day has dawned) in the collection of 1626 (*Sämtliche Werke* VI, 115; *TEM* 38). The first forty measures are based on the music of the first two lines of the chorale. Example 6-1 shows Schein's opening elaboration of the chorale melody against Nicolaus Herman's original version. At measure 6, the second soprano, which has been silent until now, begins the same line. A little later imitation is applied at a closer interval of time. A further point of imitation on the same words builds on the rhythm of the opening of the hymn in a rising series of exchanges between the two sopranos and the basso continuo to evoke the dawning of the glorious day.

Particularly apt is Schein's paraphrase of the third line (Example 6-2). The gamboling rhythms of Herman are converted into a confident gushing of eighth notes that fittingly conveys the excitement of the words "Christ our Lord today triumphs." *Erschienen ist* was modeled upon the sixteenth-century motets that paraphrased hymns or plainsong melodies (See *TEM* 24: Johann Walther's [1496–1570] *Komm, Gott Schöpfer, heiliger Geist*).

However, the medium of two treble voices and basso continuo calls forth from the composer not the rather abstract fuguing of the motet but an animated, beguiling, and concrete personal expression.

**EXAMPLE 6-1**   J. H. Schein, *Erschienen ist der herrliche Tag*

**EXAMPLE 6-2**   J. H. Schein, *Erschienen ist der herrliche Tag*

Schein's other manner is based on an even more archaic model. This is the fifteenth-century practice of quoting a plainsong in the tenor voice in equal long notes as a cantus firmus while the other parts weave counterpoints around it. The sacred concerto *Gelobet seist du, Jesu Christ* (*GMB* 188) from the 1627 collection illustrates this approach. As in the other example, there are two sopranos and basso continuo. To these is added a tenor voice, which sings the chorale in long notes over the thorough bass between sections of the duet, joining the duet only at the end. This method frees the two sopranos from having to rework all the material of the chorale melody, though the composer chose to utilize motives from it throughout most of the concerto. The juxtaposition of simple statement and gloss is somewhat archaic, yet Schein suited the duet sections to the mood and rhythm of the text in a way unknown to writers of sixteenth-century chorale motets.

Schein stood midway between two other masters of the first half of the seventeenth century in Germany: Samuel Scheidt (1587–1654) and Heinrich Schütz (1585–1672). The former almost always wrote his concertos on chorale tunes, whereas the latter almost never used them. Scheidt, though conservative in this respect, pointed in the direction of the eighteenth-century chorale cantata by frequently setting to music all the stanzas of a chorale, varying in the several stanzas the combination of voices and instruments and the manner of reworking the given melody.

## *SCHÜTZ*

The only one of the three composers who had the opportunity to become intimately acquainted with the Italian musical scene was Schütz. His thorough assimilation of this experience as a composer sets him off from most of his German contemporaries. He sojourned in Venice on two occasions, first between 1609 and 1612, when he was a disciple of Giovanni Gabrieli, and again between 1628 and 1629, when he had contacts with Grandi and Monteverdi. Despite the foreign influence and his neglect of the chorale, Schütz was very much imbued with the German and Lutheran tradition. Thus his music presents not only the two faces of ancient and modern, but like a prism reflects by turns many aspects of the musical world around him: the polychrome splendor of Gabrieli, the subtle sonorities of the Venetian concerto for few voices, the dramatic accents of Florentine monody, the fanciful imagery and emotionalism of the concertato madrigal, the spinal strength and seriousness of the German motet and Passion, and the naive simplicity and earthy glee of the German secular song.

The first collection of sacred works published by Schütz was the *Psalmen Davids* (Psalms of David, 1619), grand concertos for two or more choirs. Unlike the collections of Praetorius in similar format, this contains only one chorale composition. The spirit of the Reformation is represented nevertheless in the translations by Luther. The inherent antiphonal structure of the psalms invited the alternation of choirs or of soloists and chorus. Schütz paid only token tribute to the antiphony of the half-verses, preferring to apply the alternation between soloist with basso continuo and chorus with basso seguente in a free and ever-changing scheme. Here is an outline of the setting of Psalm 121 (*Sämtliche Werke*, edited by Spitta, II, pp. 130–42):

| | | |
|---|---|---|
| 1 | Soprano solo | I will lift up mine eyes unto the hills, |
| | Polychoral answer | from whence cometh my help. |
| 2 | Alto solo | {My help cometh from the Lord, {Which made heaven and earth. |

| | | |
|---|---|---|
| | Polychoral answer | Same text |
| 3 | Tenor solo | {He will not suffer thy foot to be moved: <br> {he that keepeth thee will not slumber. |
| | Polychoral answer | Same text |
| 4 | Bass solo | {Behold, he that keepeth Israel <br> {shall neither slumber nor sleep. |
| | Polychoral answer | Same text |
| 5} <br> 6} | Quartet of soloists | {The Lord is thy keeper: <br> {the Lord is thy shade upon thy right hand. <br> {The sun shall not smite thee by day, <br> {nor the moon by night. |
| 7} <br> 8} | Polychoral finale | {The Lord shall preserve thee from all evil: <br> He shall preserve thy soul. <br> The Lord shall preserve thy going out <br> {             and coming in <br> from this time forth, and even for <br> {             evermore. |

Schütz here seems to have wanted to seize the best of both worlds—the resounding block harmonies of the older polychoral style and the sensuous coloratura of the new solo idiom. The opening dialogue illustrates this contrast (Example 6-3).

As the fruit of his second trip to Venice, Schütz published there the *Symphoniae sacrae* (Sacred Symphonies), Part I, in 1629. In the letter of dedication to his patron in Dresden, the Elector Johann Georg of Saxony, the composer reported that he found the method of composing melody quite changed since his earlier visit: "the ancient rhythms had been set aside in favor of teasing the ears with new devices." Since the days of the Gabrielis, musical taste had indeed changed radically in Venice. Monteverdi had brought into the church the vocabulary of the concertato madrigal and operatic recitative, though always reverently transformed. The emphasis was now on music for one or a few solo voices accompanied by thorough bass and often two violins.

Schütz's collection contains sacred concertos or motets for the Catholic service. Several of the texts from the *Song of Songs* popular with Italian composers are prominent here. One of the most beautiful is a setting of *O quam tu pulchra es* (How fair you are; *NAWM* 84) that outdoes those of Grandi and Monteverdi (*Sämtliche Werke*, edited by Spitta, V. p. 42; *Neue Ausgabe sämtliche Werke*, XIII, p. 80). It is for tenor, baritone, two violins, and basso continuo (lute and chitarrone, as well as organ, are indicated as possibilities). Its sequel, *Veni de Libano*, is intended to complete the composition.

The composer seemed preoccupied with achieving a single reigning mood of wonder and adoration. He extended this mood much beyond what

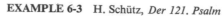

**EXAMPLE 6-3** H. Schütz, *Der 121. Psalm*

Ich he - be mei - ne Au - gen auf, ich

he - be mei - ne Au - gen auf zu den Ber - - - -

**EXAMPLE 6-4** H. Schütz, *O quam tu pulchra es*

O quam tu pul - chra, tu pul - chra es, a - mi - ca me - a,

the earlier motet technique was capable of doing. The music of the opening lines, "How fair you are, my love, my dove, my beautiful spotless love!," permeates the work. This music is stated three times at the outset, first by the baritone (Example 6-4), then by both voices in a quasicanonic duet, then by the two violins. Subsequently sections of it are reworked as vocal or instrumental ritornelli. The remainder of the poem is set either in arioso or recitative styles, alternating with the ritornello. At the end the music of the opening lines is heard in a new guise. As in the later instrumental concerto, the ritornello serves to assert new key areas or to modulate. Comparison with *Song of Songs*, 4, 1–5, will reveal that the repetition of the opening line is the composer's doing and that he skipped many of the lines of the biblical source. The entire work may be outlined as follows.

| | | |
|---|---|---|
| *O quam tu pulchra es!* etc. | Ritornello | d |
| How fair you are etc. | (three times) | |
| *Oculi tui columbarum.* | Recitative—tenor | d to A |
| Your eyes, like eyes of doves | | |
| *O quam tu pulchra es!* | Ritornello | A to d |
| *Capilli tui sicut greges caprarum.* | Arioso—baritone | d to D |
| | (See Example 6-5) | |
| Your hair, like a flock of goats | | |
| *O quam tu pulchra es!* | Ritornello | D to G |
| *Dentos tui sicut greges tonsarum.* | Recitative—tenor | G to A |
| | (See Example 6-6a) | |
| Your teeth like a flock of sheep newly shorn | | |
| *O quam tu pulchra es!* | Ritornello | A to A |
| *Sicut vita coccinea labia tua.* | Arioso duet | A to G |
| Like a strand of scarlet, your lips. | | |
| *O quam tu pulchra es!* | Ritornello | G to E |
| *Sicut turris David collum tuum.* | Arioso duet | C to C |
| Like the tower of David, your neck. | (See Example 6-6b) | |
| *O quam tu pulchra es!* | Ritornello | C to D |
| *Duo ubera tua sicut duo hinnuli capreae gemelli.* | Madrigal style duet with vlns. | d to a |
| Your two breasts, like twin roes. | | |
| *O quam tu pulchra es!* | Ritornello | a to A |

It is remarkable how thoroughly Schütz absorbed the "new devices" he noted in his letter. The free treatment of dissonance, the "accented" singing, the art of diminution as practiced in Italy for expression and embellishment—all these pervade the *Symphoniae sacrae*. Many of these devices were named and classified by a composer who was vice-chapelmaster for the Elector of Saxony between 1655 and 1664, when Schütz was chapelmaster: Christoph Bernhard (1627–1692). In the *Tractatus compositions augmentatus*

(An Augmented Treatise on Composition)[2] written about 1660 he developed a nomenclature for them based on the figures of classical rhetoric. Bernhard claimed he found examples of his "melopoetic figures" in works of a large number of composers, including Monteverdi, Cavalli, Carissimi, Scacchi, Schütz, and a number of Italians working in Germany. Some of these figures may be pointed out in *O quam tu pulchra es*.

For example, the downward leap of a diminished fourth, which is almost a motto in this composition (Example 6-4), Bernhard classified as a *saltus duriusculus*—"a somewhat harsh leap." This figure represents a license—a departure from ordinary vocal writing—as many of the figures of oratory are departures from correct everyday speech.

EXAMPLE 6-5    H. Schütz, *O quam tu pulchra es*

Most of Bernhard's figures were ways of introducing dissonance. Some were suitable for the grave style, some for the *stylus luxurians communis* (common luxuriant style)—concerted music for church and chamber. Some were reserved for the *stylus luxurians comicus* or *theatralis*, that is, the recitative style. Bernhard showed that most of the dissonant patterns used in the two latter styles were the result of embroidering upon passages that followed the correct ancient style. Thus they were analogous to certain rhetorical figures that were ornaments to straightforward speech.

The *arioso* passage of Example 6-5 contains several of the figures. The second G in measure 64 is a *quasi-transitus* (relatively accented passing note), a grave-style ornament rendered emphatic here by two other figures belonging to the luxuriant style: an *anticipatio notae* (anticipation of a note) and a *prolongatio* (prolongation). B in the same measure is treated likewise. The

---

[2]The treatise, left by the author in manuscript, is printed in Joseph Müller-Blattau, *Die Kompositionslehre Heinrich Schützens in der Fassung eines Schülers Christoph Bernhard*, 2nd ed. (Kassel: Bärenreiter, 1963), translated into English in Walter Hilse, "The Treatises of Christoph Bernhard," *The Music Forum*, III (1973), 31–196.

**EXAMPLE 6-6**  H. Schütz, *O quam tu pulchra es*

(a)

Subsumptio

Den - tos tu - i

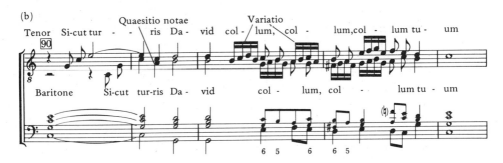

(b)

Tenor Si-cut tur - - ris Da - vid  col - lum, col - lum, col - lum tu - um

Quaesitio notae          Variatio

Baritone  Si-cut tur-ris Da - vid   col - lum, col - lum tu - um

6  5       6      6  5

(c) Cadentia duriuscula

Vl.I
Vl.II

pul - chra es!

Ten.
Bar.

rising minor sixth in measure 64 is another *saltus duriusculus*. The final measure uses a *mora* (delay)—a suspension that rises rather than falls to the next consonance. This is followed by a *superjectio*, usually used to embellish a downward step by going up a step and leaping down a third, though here it is applied to a larger interval. Both of these also belong to the luxuriant style, the *mora* being limited to the recitative. How much the expressive force of this passage owes to the figures may be judged by comparing Schütz's version to a hypothetical plain model (Example 6-5).

Bernhard recognized many more figures, of which a few further examples from the same concerto are given in Example 6-6a-c. A *subsumptio* is the opposite of *superjectio*. A *quaesitio notae* is literally a searching for a note, reaching for it from a dissonance immediately below it. A *variatio* is a florid diminution of a simple melodic step or skip. The *cadentia duriuscula* (harsh cadence) is normally used in triple-time arias and is marked by an unprepared dissonance (under asterisk) on the antepenultimate chord of a cadence. All of these belong to the common luxuriant style.

Although Bernhard was himself a composer, his theory of figures probably does not tell us much about the process of musical creation, because this is rarely fully conscious. Also, the theory should not be linked too exclusively with Schütz, as most writers have done, for it applies even more cogently to the music of Carissimi, whom Bernhard knew in Rome in 1656. The figures are worth studying, nevertheless, because they point up the degree to which the baroque style was a result of the urge to embellish and render rhetorically forceful an essentially simpler Renaissance style. The figures also show how much the modern style depended on the relation of melody to a bass upon which chords were built. The older linear method of composition was not abandoned, but the number of parts controlled by the rules of counterpoint was reduced to two. It is also significant that Bernhard ignored most of the figures earlier expounded by Joachim Burmeister,[3] which were either purely technical, such as various ways to make a fugal exposition, or pictorial, such as *hypotyposis*, through which a text is made to come to life in music through spatial imagery.

Schütz's next two collections continued the trend toward reduced means. The *Kleine geistliche Konzerte* (Small Sacred Concertos) in two parts, published in 1636 and 1639, are for one or a few voices with basso continuo. They reflect not only musical fashion but the shortage of musical personnel in Dresden during the Thirty Years' War. Beginning as a holy war between German Catholics and Protestants in 1618, it widened into a general European conflict in which Catholics fought Catholics and Protestants fought Protestants before it was over in 1648. Schütz managed to find some relief from the problems of keeping up a musical establishment in the midst of discouraging wartime austerity in his sojourns in Denmark. There he served as an interim choirmaster for King Christian IV, one of the leaders of the Protestant cause, from 1633 to 1635, again in 1637, and between 1642 and 1644.

Schütz's monodies of this period are particularly interesting because they are based on the theatrical recitative style, or *stylus oratorius* (oratorical style), as Schütz called it. It departs from the typical theatrical recitative of this time, though, in its more consistently active bass and in the greater fluency and structural continuity of the solo voice. As in the Italian cantatas of this period, the recitative, in common time, is broken by occasional airy passages in triple time. Sometimes Schütz abstained from this contrast for the sake of a concentrated and unrelenting mood of pathos, as in *Was hast*

---

[3] *Musica poetica* (Rostock: Stephan Myliander, 1606; facsimile ed. Kassel: Bärenreiter, 1955), caput 12, pp. 55–70.

**EXAMPLE 6-7**   H. Schütz, *Was hast du verwirket?*

die Angst dei - ner Pei - ni - gung die Angst dei - ner Pei - - ni - gung,
*(the anguish of your torments)*

**EXAMPLE 6-8a**   H. Schütz, *Saul, Saul, was verfolgst du mich?*

Saul,      Saul,      Saul,    Saul    was   ver - forgst  du mich?

*du verwirket, o du allerboldseligster Knab, Jesu Christe* (What have you lost, o most gracious child, Jesus Christ?) in the 1639 volume on a text from the *Meditations* of St. Augustine (*Sämtliche Werke*, edited by Spitta, VI, p. 94; *Neue Ausgabe* X, p. 16; *GMB* 190). The melody is often built up through sequences, as in Example 6-7. Here the composer put to advantageous use two figures of Bernhard: the *syncopatio catachrestica* (misused syncopation)— a suspension improperly prepared by a dissonance instead of a consonance— and a *consonantia impropria*, in this case the fourth used as if it were a consonance.

With the war over and the prospect that the musical forces of court chapels would soon be regrouped, Schütz found it expedient to publish some of the works for massed voices and instruments he had composed for Copenhagen; this he did in the *Symphoniae sacrae*, Part III, 1650. Among the grandest of the concertos of this collection is *Saul, was verfolgst du mich?* (Saul, why do you persecute me?; *Sämtliche Werke*, edited by Spitta, XI, p. 99; *HAM* II, 202). It is for six solo voices or *favoriti*, two violins, two four-voice choirs, and—one assumes—a complementary orchestra to double the voices of the choruses. The subject is taken from the New Testament, Acts 9: 1–31, which is used as a lection, or reading, on the day of the Feast of the Conversion of St. Paul. The hero of this miniature drama is Paul when he was a militant Jewish anti-Christian named Saul. On the way to Damascus

Heinrich Schütz directing the choristers, surrounding him, and instrumentalists, in the organ loft, at the chapel of the Elector of Saxony, where after the thirty-years war the musical forces were restored to their full strength. (Christoph Bernhard, *Geistreichen Gesang-Buch*, 1676.)

**EXAMPLE 6-8b**   C. Monteverdi, *Hor che'l ciel e la terra*

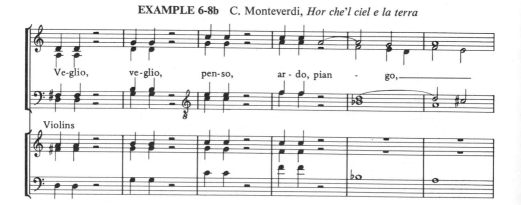

to bring back Christian disciples in bondage, Saul is startled by a sudden light around him and a voice that calls "Saul, Saul why do you persecute me?" It is the voice of Jesus, who tells Saul to rise, and, though he has been blinded by the light, to go to the city, where Ananias will restore his sight. Saul's vision leads to his conversion to Christianity, for which under the name of Paul he becomes a celebrated and eloquent crusader.

Schütz limited his setting to the words of Jesus. Christ's question is given first to the *favoriti*, then to the double chorus, which takes possession of the refrain "Saul, Saul" as a ritornello. Christ's warning, "It is hard for you to kick against the pricks," on the other hand, is sung first by two solo tenors, then by another pair of voices, finally by the entire solo ensemble in madrigal style, but it is never conceded to the choruses.

In the ascending sequences built on the opening two-measure motive (Example 6-8a) Schütz captured with one master stroke the mystery of the voice rising from the depths and echoed by the hills, the sudden light kindling into a vibrant incandescence, and the anguish of Christ, abandoned by Saul. This opening was probably modeled on the setting of the words "veglio, penso, ardo, piango" in Monteverdi's concertato madrigal, *Hor che'l ciel e la terra*, in his Eighth Book of 1638 (Example 6-8b).

Schütz next gave the motive quoted in Example 6-8a to the tenors in a minor, then to the sopranos in F Major, returning to d minor in the violins. The work reaches its highest point in a bright D Major, in which all the instruments and voices join in the call. Each of the statements closes with the same IV–V–I pattern. Note that the second measure of the motive is a cluster of figures, among which a dissonance (A) resolves not by falling a step but leaping down (to E).

Schütz now set the warning of Jesus as a dialogue between two tenors, underlining the word *löcken* (kick) with the downward skip of a sixth and a swift turn. After an interruption by the ritornello this motive is developed further. Eventually all six solo parts enter and now Schütz described the word *schwer* (hard, difficult) with what Bernhard called a *quasi-transitus*. The violins also join in this development, and at the height of tension the ritornello imposes itself upon the others and gains ascendancy. The motive of *was verfolgst du mich* climbs higher in a series of echoes, *forte, mezzo piano, pianissimo*,[4] as a lonely tenor voice cries "Saul, Saul." The sounds die down until nothing but an octave and unison D are heard.

Schütz here attained a synthesis of some earlier phases in his work: the proclivity for grand polychoral canvases, which was a product of his first exposure to Venetian music; the exploration of the possibilities of the small

[4]Viadana also used echoes in a setting of this text published in 1622.

concerto, which was stimulated by his second visit, as was the absorption of recitative into the sacred concerto. Like Monteverdi, Schütz never abandoned the word images and the free dissonance of the late polyphonic madrigal. The contrast structure of *Saul* is reminiscent too of the works of Gabrieli. But the intensity of focus, the unity of conception, and the realism signal a new style come of age.

## BIBLIOGRAPHICAL NOTES

Fundamental to the study of any chorale compositions are Johannes Zahn, *Die Melodien der deutschen evangelischen Kirchenlieder*, 6 vols. (Gütersloh: C. Bertelsmann, 1889–1893), which gives the melodies in their original forms (index in Volume 5); and Philipp Wackernagel, *Das deutsche evangel-ische Kirchenlied von den ältesten Zeiten bis zu Anfang des 17. Jahrhunderts*, 5 vols. (Leipzig: B. G. Teubner, 1864–1877), which contains the texts.

The complete works of Michael Praetorius are gathered in a *Gesamtausgabe* (Collected Edition) of which Friedrich Blume was general editor (Wolfen-büttel: Kallmeyer Verlag; Möseler Verlag, 1928–1960). *Musae Sionae* occu-pies Volumes I–IX (1928–1939).

The *Sämtliche Werke* (Collected Works) of Johann Hermann Schein occupy seven volumes under the general editorship of Arthur Prüfer (Leipzig: Breit-kopf und Härtel, 1901–1923). The *Opella nova* was edited by Karl Hesse and Bernhard Engleke in Volumes 5 (1914) and 6 (1919).

Samuel Scheidt's collected works are found in the thirteen-volume series of *Werke* edited by Gottlieb Harms and Christhard Mahrenholz (Hamburg: Ugrino Verlag, 1923–1962). The sacred concertos are in Volumes 9–11.

The older *Sämtliche Werke* of Heinrich Schütz edited by Philipp Spitta, Arnold Schering, and Heinrich Spitta (18 vols.; Leipzig: Breitkopf und Härtel, 1885–1927) is being superseded by the *Neue Ausgabe sämtlicher Werke* (Kassel: Bärenreiter, 1955– ). Individual works, such as *O quan tu pulchra es*, are available singly from this publisher.

The standard German work *Heinrich Schütz, His Life and Work* by Hans Joachim Moser (lst ed. 1936; 2nd ed., 1954) is one of the few such studies we possess in English translation, thanks to Carl F. Pfatteicher, the translator (Saint Louis: Concordia Publishing House, 1959). Exhaustive and scholarly, it is also readable and well provided with musical examples.

# SEVEN

# ITALIAN CANTATA, ORATORIO, AND OPERA IN MID-CENTURY

## THE CANTATA

As, earlier, the proving ground for new styles in Italy had been the pastoral, between 1620 and 1640 it was the cantata. Demand for the kind of vocal music popularized by the monodic movement continued, but opportunities for composing stage works were rare. So an extended aria or a group of them around a single subject, sometimes with recitative passages interspersed, fulfilled with simpler means the desire for music in the new style. Some of the labels by which compositions of this kind were designated in titles of printed collections were *arie, musiche, lamenti, madrigali, scherzi*, and *concerti*. Occasionally also the terms *cantata* or *cantade* appeared, usually for pieces in strophic variation form. The term *cantata* was used little for the kind of composite work historians now comprehend by it.

By *cantata* we mean a piece for one or two voices, occasionally three, composed of several discrete sections exploiting diverse styles, usually accompanied by no instruments other than the basso continuo group. In the most common type, portions of an extended poem are sung in recitative, while other portions are set in a flowing line that can best be described as aria style. Sometimes there is a sequence of several such aria movements without recitative intervening. Often one of the arias returns as a refrain at the end or along the way. Another type uses instrumental ritornelli to separate strophes of poetry set to variations of the same, or to different, music. Or there may be a combination of these approaches. The texts are not unlike those of the earlier madrigal, but there is a tendency toward dramatization through monologue or dialogue, or through narrative out of which these emerge. The subject matter is almost always amorous, though there are other themes, occasionally a sacred one.[1]

Between 1620 and 1640 a great many works that fit this general definition were printed in Italy. Subsequently publication became less and less customary. A cantata was usually composed for a particular patron or singer and often for a special occasion. Thus it became attached to that person, who might favor a few friends with manuscript copies. The cantatas of the 1620s and 1630s show progressively longer and more clearly separated sections. There is a growing differentiation between recitative and aria. After 1640 the number of pieces strung together increased and the longer aria sections were subjected to various formal schemes through calculated repetitions of musical material. The poetry was mainly by anonymous authors, who showed an awareness of the composers' needs. They usually provided madrigal-type verse of mixed seven- and eleven-syllable lines to be set as recitative, whereas strophic poems, canzonets, and the like, with uniform syllable count and closed rhyme schemes, were intended for lyrical settings. Composers, however, did not always respect the poet's layout.

Of the numerous composers who contributed to the emergence of the cantata from the shorter lyric pieces, Luigi Rossi (1597–1653) stands out for the artistic quality and variety of his production as well as its quantity. As against two stage works, *Il Palazzo incantato* (1642) and *Orfeo* (1647). he is credited with 375 extant cantatas.[2] Two of the most lavish patrons of his age assured him a cultivated public and the most talented singers and instrumentalists: for twenty years he was with Marc' Antonio Borghese, who kept the largest musical staff in Rome, and after 1641 with Cardinal Antonio

---

[1]The sacred "cantatas" of J. S. Bach belong to the category being discussed here only by extension, since they in effect are a cross between the cantata proper and the sacred concerto.

[2]This is the number of cantatas in the thematic index in Alberto Ghislanzoni, *Luigi Rossi* (Milan, Rome: Fratelli Bocca, 1954), if we omit the Latin motets and compositions for four voices.

Barberini, whose palace contained the largest theater of the city. Rossi's chamber works range from extended arias, such as the bipartite song with da capo, "Io lo vedo, ò luci belle," (*HAM* II, 203), to multisectional cantatas, such as *Alla ruota, alla benda* (unpublished). This consists of six recitative-aria pairs, the second aria having six strophes on one melody, which also serves for the closing aria.

Rossi's *Del silentio il giogo algente* (last six sections in *HMS* VI, 14) illustrates an intermediate stage in the development of the mid-century cantata. It contains eleven sections, of which three are recitatives, the rest in aria style. Letting R and A represent these two types of numbers, respectively, we have the sequence AARAAAARRAA.

The arias are so short that the use of this term for these brief moments of lyricism needs justification. The term *aria* was still applied at this time mainly to strophic songs, as it had been in Caccini's *Le nuove musiche*. Later the term was extended to nonstrophic pieces having usually a definite formal repetition scheme, which is lacking in these arias. Often the short triple-time sections such as that of Example 7-1 are referred to as *arioso*. This term is better reserved, however, for *recitativo arioso*, for which there is a contemporaneous precedent: Giovanni Battista Doni, in a treatise written in the early 1630s and probably read publicly while he lived in the Barberini household, exhorted composers to make their recitatives more pleasing by "using a vocal line that imitates ordinary speech but that is nevertheless varied and arioso."[3] This same author used the term *aria* to evoke the notion of melodiousness, as when he invited composers to imitate the "bell'aria del canto"[4] of certain polyphonic madrigalists and to cultivate a style that in the nineteenth century was to become known simply as *bel canto*. Domenico Mazzocchi (1592–1665), who was also in the Barberini circle, similarly referred to short nonstrophic lyrical pieces inserted to relieve the "tedium of the recitative" as "near-arias" (*mezz'arie*) in the preface to his opera *La catena d'Adone* (1626).

"Ardo, agghiaccio," the fourth number of Rossi's *Del silentio* (Example 7-1) illustrates some of the features of these aria passages: an active, rhythmically structured bass; a smoothly molded melody, mainly consonant with the underlying harmony, unified through parallel and symmetrical phrases and rounded off by a good closure.

This passage exemplifies both dependence upon a poem's form and a certain disregard for it. From the poet's stanza Rossi cut off the first line, which rhymes with the last, to dramatize it as recitative. Otherwise he followed the poetic form. The two eight-syllable lines are given parallel treat-

---

[3] "Trattato della musica scenica" in *Lyra Barberina*, ed. A. F. Gori (Florence: Typis caesareis, 1763), II, 25: "usare un canto, che imiti gli accenti del'ordinaria loquela, e tuttavia sia variato e arioso."

[4] *Ibid.*, p. 32.

**EXAMPLE 7-1**  L. Rossi, "Ardo, agghiaccio," *Del silentio*

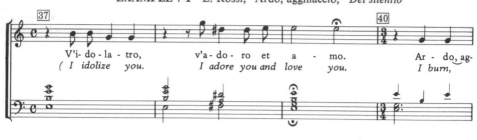

V'i- do- la- tro,        v'a- do- ro et a -        mo.        Ar - do, ag-
*( I idolize you.        I adore you and love        you.        I burn,*

ghiac - cio,    av - vam- po    e    tre - mo,        Spe - ro, ohi -
*I freeze,    I blaze        and    tremble.        I hope,*

6    7    6

mè!    di - spe - ro    e    te - mo,        Non
*alas.    I    despair,    and    I fear,        I do not*

#    7

so        quel    che mi    vo - glia    e il    tut - to    io
*know        what    I    wish.    Everything is what I*

bra -    mo,    Non    so    Non    so        quel che mi
*long for.)*

#    7    6

EXAMPLE 7-1 (Cont.)

vo - glia e il tut - to io____ bra - mo.

ment in four-measure phrases, each over a descending fourth in the bass, and the rhyme is underlined through identical cadences. But the final eleven-syllable line is sung twice to different melodies, the first wandering from the main key of a minor, the second returning to it. Eschewing the free melodic dissonances of Florentine recitative, the composer achieved expressive intensification through a delicate mingling of dissonance in the chords—for example, the sevenths in measures 42, 46, and 57.

Modulation is often used expressively, as in the aria "Occhi belli," the sixth number of this cantata (Example 7-2). The words "E v'adoro" (and I adore you) are emphasized by a striking detour into c minor by way of B-flat Major. Just as suddenly the harmony veers back home through the dominant of the main key (Example 7-2, measure 94). The tonal adventures of the madrigalists are not far behind!

EXAMPLE 7-2   L. Rossi, "Occhi belli," *Del silentio*

V'a - mo quan - to a - mar si puo, E v'a -
( I love you as much    as love one can.    And

do - ro,    E v'a - do - ro    quan - to so.
adore you,    E v'a - do - ro    as much as I know how.

Tal' hor    che    non vi mi - ro,    all'
When    I    cannot gaze upon you,    then

7    6

EXAMPLE 7-2 (Cont.)

ho - ra io - mo - ro.
I die. )

In the recitatives, too, the burden of expression is upon the chords and chordal progressions. The superposition of a dominant seventh chord over a static tonic bass is a typical device, as in measures 126–27 of the eighth number of the cantata (Example 7-3). Melodic dissonance, by contrast to the freedom of the first decades of the century, has been subjected to the strict control of the bass-driven harmony. Aside from the anticipated F in measure 132, the notes of the recitative are either implied in the chords or are short passing notes. Cantatas, deprived of stage effects, relied upon clear declamation and the subtle touches just described to put across their miniature dramas.

After Rossi, whose cantatas were written mostly before 1650, the leading composer of vocal chamber music in Rome was Giacomo Carissimi (1605–1674). He is credited with 145 extant cantatas. Making an opening aria return between recitative or arioso sections is a frequent scheme with Carissimi. In this way the keynote aria lends its identity to the whole composition. Carissimi's arias are often extensive and patterned in ABB, ABA, or AABB forms. Beautiful flowing melody takes precedence over the demands of the text. A middle ground between aria and recitative emerges as an important component of his writing. This is the *recitativo arioso*. Arioso sections may take over an entire recitative section or merely portions.

Example 7-4, from a cantata mainly in recitative style, shows how Carissimi passed from one style to another without harming the continuity of the text. The example is taken from the *Lamento di Maria Stuarda*, a monologue representing the speech of Mary, Queen of Scots, as she is led to her execution. Her words occupy the entire cantata except for the concluding lines, in which a narrator, sung by the same voice, tells of Mary's beheading. The passage that I have labeled "arioso," in contrast to the surrounding recitative, uses text repetition or melodic sequences or both, but does not break the flow of the plastic, rapid, declamatory rhythm. The last few measures of the arioso (39–41) are in a style that Monteverdi dubbed *concitato* (agitated), because he found it useful for expressions of anger and disdain.[5]

[5]See below, p. 131.

**EXAMPLE 7-3** L. Rossi, *Del silentio*

Quin-di nel vos-tro co - re   Scin-til -la di pie-ta - de al - me - no, oh   Di - o!
*(Thus   in your heart   a spark of mercy   at least,   o   God:*

De - sti l'af - fet - to   mi   o,   Già che de - star non
*let   my affection   arouse,   since it cannot arouse*

può ___ fuo - - - co d'a - mo - - re.
*fire   of love. )*

**EXAMPLE 7-4** G. Carissimi, *Lamento di Maria Stuarda*

(Arioso)
Vi - li-pe - sa,   vi - li-pe - sa in-no -
*(Scorned   inno-*

cen - za! ___ Vi - li - pe - sa,   vi - li -
*cence,*

EXAMPLE 7-4 (Cont.)

pe - sa in-no-cen - za! ___ Vat - - te-ne, vat - te-ne, pur da
*(leave me alone,*

(Recitative)

me, tor - - na tor-na al - le stel - le, Ch'io con
*return           to the    heavens,          that I, with*

a - ni - ma in - tre - pi - da e se - re - - na,.....
*fearless    spirit          and serene,(may be both spectator and actress in my tragedy.])*

The arioso style may be contrasted to the section that begins in Example 7-5. This is clearly set off as an aria; the marking *Adagio* nullifies the usual speeding-up effect of the proportional sign 3, which, rather than $\frac{3}{4}$, is usually used in manuscripts of the time. Several techniques contribute to the cohesiveness of this aria. It relies upon one of the many formal patterns common at this time: Refrain—Strophe 1—Refrain—Strophe 2—Refrain. As is typical of aria style, not only are words repeated, but a unit of two lines of text and their music is repeated a fourth lower in measures 64–77. The rhythm of the motive for "a morire" is another important unifying device that pervades the aria. The second strophe, not shown in the example, uses the same harmony as the first but varies the melody. The harmonic movement, clearly oriented around a key center, as is characteristic of Carissimi and other mid-century composers, helps to fence in the aria.

The utmost refinement of cantata writing is reached in the work of Antonio Cesti (1623–1669). An ordained priest and Franciscan friar for most of his life, he nevertheless carried on an active career that took him to, among other places, Venice, Florence, Rome, Innsbruck, and Vienna. In

**EXAMPLE 7-5**  G. Carissimi, *Lamento di Maria Stuarda*

EXAMPLE 7-5 (Cont.)

these cities, and particularly as director of chamber and choral music for Archduke Ferdinand Carl of Innsbruck and as vice-music director at the Imperial Court in Vienna, he had the opportunity of staging at least eleven operas. Fifty-five extant cantatas are attributed to him, among which nine are for two voices. The alternation of recitative and aria styles becomes quite standard in these works. Often several arias are grouped together, or one aria serves as a refrain, as in the beautiful *Alpi nevose e dure* (Wellesley Edition, No. 5, p. 10), which has the form:

|                | R  | A1 | R | A2 | A3 | A4 | R | A5 | A3 |
|----------------|----|----|---|----|----|----|---|----|----|
| Keys           | e  | e  | G | a  | e  | e  | a | a  | e  |
| Time           | C  |    | 3 | C  | 3  | 3  | C | 3  | 3  |
| signatures     |    |    | 2 |    | 2  | 2  |   | 2  | 2  |

The second aria (Example 7-6) is based in its first half on the descending-fourth bass pattern popular at this time. The suave vocality is typical of Cesti. His musical style in the cantatas is so similar to that of his operas that a closer look at some samples of it will be postponed until later in this chapter.

## THE ORATORIO

The musical performances that most impressed the French traveler André Maugars, who reported on the state of music in Italy in 1639, were those he heard at the lay gatherings in the *oratorio*, or meeting hall, of the

**EXAMPLE 7-6** A. Cesti, *Alpi nevose e dure*

Fer - ma - te, oh Di - o, fer - ma - te! Trop - po,
( *Stop,*      *oh God!*

trop - po, trop - po vi - lu - sin - ga - - -
*Too much*     *do you deceice yourself.* )

- - - - - - - - - te

Arciconfraternità del SS. Crocifisso (Archconfraternity of the Most Holy Crucifix) attached to the Church of San Marcello. Some of the leading citizens and diplomats in Rome would go there for devotions that included prayers, sermons, and music. After describing a spacious gallery that contained an organ and a choir, he related:

> On two sides of the church there were two other little galleries, in which were placed some of the most excellent instrumentalists. The voices would begin with a psalm in the form of a motet, and then all the instruments would play a very good symphony. The voices then would sing a story from the Old Testament, a form of spiritual play, for example that of Susanna, of Judith and Holofernes, or of David and Goliath. Each singer represented one person of the story and expressed perfectly the force of the words.[6]

Such musical dramatizations of the Bible began to be known around this time as oratorios, from the halls (oratories) in which they were performed.

[6] *Reponse faite à un curieux sur le sentiment de la musique en Italie, escrite à Rome le 1er Octobre 1639* (n.d., n.p.), p. 11.

Laymen had been uniting for devotions and singing since the Middle Ages, and the spirit of the Counter-Reformation helped spread the movement. The Arciconfraternità del SS. Crocifisso was founded in 1522. It boasted a brilliant tradition of Lenten and Holy Week music. During these periods of fasting, abstinence, and mourning, when public entertainments were discouraged by the church, such illustrious composers as Palestrina, Emilio de' Cavalieri, and Luca Marenzio (1553–1599) had led the music at the oratory.

The trend toward dramatizing religious themes can also be traced quite far back to the devotional songs called *laude*, often sung in dialogue form. Cavalieri's *Rappresentatione di Anima et di Corpo* is a musical setting of one such extended dialogue, between the Soul and the Body, by Padre Agostino Manni. It was performed in February 1600 at the Oratorio della Vallicella, where the group founded by Filippo Neri met. Various other allegorical persons also enter, such as Time, Intellect, Good Counsel, Pleasure and her Companions, a chorus of damned souls and one of blessed souls. The fact that this was staged with scenery, dancing, and costumes, albeit very modestly, takes it out of the mainstream of oratorio development. It did have successors, though, such as Agostino Agazzari's *Eumelio* (1606).

More in direct line with the oratorios Maugars must have heard are the dialogues of Giovanni Francesco Anerio (c. 1567–1630) published in the *Teatro armonico spirituale di madrigali* (Rome, 1619), among which is *La conversione di S. Paolo* (The Conversion of St. Paul), a subject later treated, as we have seen, by Schütz. Whereas Anerio's dialogues pointed to the so-called *oratorio volgare*—the vernacular oratorio—numerous motets in dialogue form published in the early seventeenth century led to the Latin oratorio. One such dialogue is *Abraham, Abraham* (*GMB* 180) by Giovanni Francesco Capello, in which Abraham, Isaac, an angel, and a narrative chorus develop the story of Abraham's sacrifice of his son, Isaac. This piece happens to belong to the Venetian orbit and quite typically relies for the solo roles upon the few-voice polyphonic style fashionable there rather than Florentine monody. The Latin dialogues, whether in the form of short motets or fully developed dramas, were particularly favored during Lent at the SS. Crocifisso oratory.

Who may have composed the dramatizations heard by Maugars? One composer who probably figured in that season is Marco Marazzoli (c. 1602 or c. 1608–1662). He is credited with eleven extant oratorios, both Latin and Italian, and when his music is better known he may well be recognized as the most important composer of oratorios before Carissimi. Others who were active around this time were Domenico Mazzocchi and his brother Virgilio (1597–1646).

With the works of Carissimi the Latin oratorio reached at once its full bloom and its high point. A native Roman, Carissimi worked in and around this city throughout his life. From 1630 until his death he was chapelmaster at the Church of San Apollinare attached to the German-Hungarian College. His oratorios, however, were destined primarily for the oratory of the SS. Crocifisso. One, the *Historia de Abraham et Isaac*, is known to have been performed in 1656 at the German College. Otherwise his one Italian and fifteen Latin oratorios are not presently datable. *Jephte* is known to have been composed before 1649, because Athanasius Kircher wrote of it in his *Musurgia universalis* (The Universal Science of Music; Rome, 1650). Carissimi's reputation was by then already well established, for Kircher wrote:

> Giacomo Carissimi, a very excellent and famous composer . . . through his genius and the felicity of his compositions, surpasses all others in moving the minds of listeners to whatever affection he wishes. His compositions are truly imbued with the essence and life of the spirit. Among numerous works of great worth, he has composed the dialogue of *Jephte*. In this, after victories, triumphs, and ceremonies, Jephte's daughter approaches him with instruments and dances of all sorts to congratulate him. In a musical style called recitative, Carissimi gives expression to the bewildered father with singular genius and piercing tones. Jephte is suddenly transported from joy to sadness and lamentation as his daughter unexpectedly runs toward him, because the irrevocable decree of the vow must fall on her for this fateful greeting [in thanks for victory he vowed to sacrifice the first person he met on returning home]. Carissimi achieves this transition to the opposite affection beautifully with a mutation of mode. To this he adds later a lament for six voices by the daughter's virgin companions, in which they intensely bewail her misfortune. This is composed with such skill that you would swear that you hear the sobs and moans of the weeping girls.[7]

The mutation of mode or change of tonality to which Kircher alludes is indeed striking. The keys of G Major and C Major dominate the happy scenes in which the daughter and her companions, playing drums and psalteries, go dancing and singing to meet Jephthah. This portion of the score is organized, in the manner of some cantatas, out of several short arias and a duet, with one of the melodies (Example 7-7c) functioning as a refrain. The initial phrase of each of these sections is given in Example 7-7. The jubilant chorus that follows is also in G Major, but at the words of the Historicus (narrator), "Cum vidisset Jephte. . . ." ("When Jephthah, who vowed a vow unto the Lord, saw his duaghter coming to meet him . . ."), the key shifts to a minor. This key, with its dominant, prevails during the succeeding dialogue up to the plaintive final chorus for six voices. The entire section up to the chorus, except for a few arioso passages, is entirely in recitative style. (The entire scene is in *NAWM* 83; see the biblical account in Judges 11: 29–38.)

[7]Kircher, *Musurgia universalis* (Rome: Haeredes F. Corbelletti, 1650), Vol. I (Bk. I, Part 3, ch. 6), p. 603. On the succeeding pages Kircher printed the chorus *Plorate, filii Israel*, with which Carissimi's oratorio concludes.

EXAMPLE 7-7   G. Carissimi, *Jephte*

(a) In - ci - pi - te in tym - pa-nis, et psal - li - te in cym - ba -lis.
*(Strike up the timbrels, and pluck the psaltery.*

(b) Hym-num can-te - - - - - - - - mus Do - mi - no,
*( Hymns let us sing to the Lord,)*

(c) Lau - de - mus re - gem coe - li - tum, lau - de - mus bel - li prin - ci - pem,
*(Let us praise the heavenly king, the prince of war,)*

(d) Hym-num can - te - - - - - mus Do - mi - no
*(Hymns let us sing to the Lord)*

The lament of Jephthah, "Heu, heu mihi," in this section is one of the most moving pages of the whole century. Carissimi attains this height within the new idiom of chordally controlled dissonance. His principal means are augmented and diminished melodic skips, cross-relations, suspensions, and the ubiquitous dominant chord over a tonic pedal. Subtle repetitions, refrains, sequences, and carefully planned modulations weave a thread through the declamation. This lament may be put in Doni's class of "expressive recitative." It is set in relief by Carissimi's normal narrative style, which is diatonic, consonant, full of triadic skips, and extremely slow in its chordal changes—in short, a parlando style, decorated only occasionally with short runs. In *Jephte* the opening speeches of the Historicus and of Jephthah are good examples. Doni had foreseen the advent of this style, when he said that speeches of dramatic characters should use many skips of thirds, fourths, fifths, and octaves, tempered with graceful, rapid runs.[8]

The chorus has an ambivalent role in the oratorios of Carissimi, as in Greek tragedy. It is sometimes a protagonist, as in the chorus of the daughter's companions in *Jephte* or of the sailors in *Jonas*. At other times it reflects upon the action, as in the final chorus of *Jephte*, which, contrary to what Kircher stated, does not represent the daughter's companions. Another

[8]"Trattato della musica scenica," p. 33.

important function of the chorus is to take up the biblical narrative along with the Historicus; this occurs in both *Jephte* and *Jonas*. In the *Diluvium universale* (Genesis 6–9), the chorus preempts most of the unfolding of the panorama of the flood. The faithful presentation in the oratorios of Carissimi of the biblical account by the narrating chorus and the Historicus, free from the commentary, sentimentalizing, and moralizing of librettists, endows these works with an objectivity that later composers found difficult to maintain.

## OPERA IN ROME

The generous Roman patrons who fostered the cantata also left an important mark on the history of opera. The musical theater's principal supporters after its beginnings in Florence were the Barberini. The fortunes of opera in Rome waxed and waned with those of this one powerful family. Maffeo Barberini (1568–1644) enjoyed as Pope Urban VIII one of the longest reigns—21 years, having been elected in 1623. His nephews, Don Taddeo, Lieutenant-General of the Church, later Prefect of Rome, and Cardinals Antonio and Francesco, were all patrons of music. The two cardinals built the Teatro delle Quattro Fontane, which seated more than 3,000 persons and whose stage gave scope to the brilliant machinery and magical scenic effects of the architect Gian Lorenzo Bernini.

The theater opened in 1632 with the opera *Sant'Alessio* (Saint Alexis; first performed in 1631), composed by Stefano Landi on a libretto by Giulio Rospigliosi (1600–1669), a protegé of the Pope (and himself elected Pope Clement IX in 1667). Another of Rospigliosi's opera librettos, *Erminia sul Giordano* (Erminia at the Jordan), based on Tasso's *Jerusalem Delivered*, was produced with music by Michelangelo Rossi under the sponsorship of Taddeo Barberini in 1633. Among Rospigliosi's later librettos are the first two comic operas: *Chi soffre speri* (Let Him Who Suffers Hope), 1639 (first version 1637), and *Dal male il bene* (From Evil Comes Good), 1653, Other composers of opera patronized by the Barberini were Marco Marazzoli, Loreto Vittori (c. 1590–1670), and Luigi Rossi. The latter's *Palazzo incantato d'Atlante* (The Enchanted Palace of Atlantis), another of Rospigliosi's librettos, closed the first period of the Barberini theater in 1642. At this time the Papacy's disastrous war with the Duke of Parma and the enmity of Pope Urban's successor, Innocent X, caused the family to seek refuge in France. During this exile the Barberini and their musical entourage exerted a strong influence on the musical theater in Paris, particularly through the production of Luigi Rossi's *Orfeo* in 1647.

Through the Roman experience the Florentine pastoral matured into the full-blown spectacle that is opera. The pastoral atmosphere was still the mainstay, but the participation of numerous divinities, lowered and raised in cloud machines and woven in and out of subplots, the entries of dancing choruses of tritons, satyrs, and naiads in intermezzo-like revels, and the luxurious costuming and settings added substance and wonder, if not clarity, to the spectacle.

The conversion from the simple play of passions to this bazaar of attractions shifted the distribution of weights among the musical ingredients of recitative, aria, chorus, and orchestra. The recitative became a consonant, rapid, speechlike delivery of the exposition necessary to the presentation of the next attraction, be it lyrical aria, chorus, machine transformation, or dance. It is cut and dried to an extreme in *Chi soffre speri*, for example, which contains music by Virgilio Mazzocchi and Marco Marazzoli. A single chord often lasts through several lines of poetry. Instead of the enhanced emotional speech envisioned by the Florentines, recitative became a mere vehicle for traversing the dialogue.

The dryness of the recitative lent prominence to the arias. These took the forms that are found in the cantatas of the period: strophic airs, both simple and with variations; through-composed arias organized in various simple patterns, such as ABA; arias with instrumental ritornelli; arias on ostinato bass patterns. Euridice's aria, "Mio ben," in Rossi's *Orfeo* is a fine example of the later. It uses the ostinato of the descending fourth ten times before proceeding to a free second section. Comic characters, whether introduced into serious operas or in comic operas, often received delightful *ariette*, such as that of the two pages, "Poca voglia di far bene," in *Sant' Alessio* (*HAM* II, 209) or that of Tabacco in *Dal male il bene*, "Il più bello dell'età." Both are caricatures of procrastinating servants.

The large part given to ensembles, from a few soloists to plural concerted choruses, harked back to the court intermezzi. Closing an act with a chorus or ensemble became a standard practice in Rome. The five-voice chorus of shepherds, "Alla barca pescatori" (To the boat, fishermen!), in Vittori's *Galatea*, with its pavane rhythm and strophic variations for soloists, is an end-of-act ballet entertainment. *Sant' Alessio* ends with a brilliant double chorus accompanied by three violin parts and continuo instruments. Rospigliosi united all the principal characters of *Dal male il bene* in a sextet in the final scene.

When the chorus reflects on some fateful or sorrowful event, it is often in the style of a polyphonic madrigal with continuo. The tritons in *Galatea* express their outrage over the murder of Acis by Polyphemus—rivals for the love of Galatea—in a three-voice madrigal full of intense harmonies. Bare interludes for single unison voices over an instrumental bass are an unusual feature of this chorus. The tritons are then joined by the naiads in the lamenting five-part chorus, "Lagrimam, sospiram, compagni fidi" (Let us weep, let us sigh, faithful companions). Another fine lamenting chorus, for four sopranos and continuo, is Rossi's over the death of Euridice in *Orfeo*.

The grandest of the Venetian opera houses, built in the parish of S. Giovanni Chrisostomo in 1678 for Giovanni Carlo and Vincenzo Grimani by the architect Tomaso Bezzi on the site of the house in which Marco Polo had lived centuries before. There are five tiers of boxes, 30 in each tier. (Venice, Museo Civico Correr.)

## OPERA IN VENICE

An oligarchy, Venice lacked the ruling families that sponsored grand court entertainments. Instead, patrician families that had acquired their wealth through trade were the principal patrons. Musical productions tended to be, more than elsewhere, cooperative enterprises. Religious confraternities called *scuole*, for example, sponsored concerted music on certain church holidays or to celebrate patron saints. The opera theaters, built and sometimes partly subsidized by individual families, were maintained through the leasing of boxes to other families and the sale of admissions. Although the audiences were as aristocratic as they were elsewhere, the repertory did not reflect the taste of a prince, nor was opera any longer an occasional entertainment put on for a wedding, an important visitor, or other state reception by a host for his guests. A manager of a traveling or resident company contracted to supply performances during a season, and it was his responsibility to satisfy the public. This system worked so well that by 1700 there were sixteen such theaters, and 388 operas had been produced. For the first time composers, librettists, designers, and stage managers were assured opportunities to repeat a work many times and to try out ever new approaches.

The first opera theater opened in 1637. Named San Cassiano after the parish in which it was situated, it had previously been used for spoken plays and was rebuilt that year by the Tron family. The inaugural opera was *Andromeda*, produced by the poet, composer, and theorbo-player Benedetto Ferrari (1597–1681) and the singer and composer Francesco Manelli (1595–1667). Manelli and his wife both sang in it. The troupe had set out from Rome and played in Padua the year before. It consisted of six singers and an orchestra of two harpsichords, two trumpets, and twelve other instruments. Much labor was lavished on the scenic effects. The first scene was a seascape in which Dawn, dressed in silver, appeared in a cloud. Later Juno appeared in a golden chariot drawn by peacocks, and Mercury leaped from the sky in an invisible machine. Then suddenly the scene changed to a wooded pasture with snowy mountains in the background, and shortly after switched back to the maritime scene. Here Neptune entered in a silver seashell drawn by four sea horses. The first act ended with a madrigal for several voices concerted with instruments, and by way of an intermezzo there followed a dance by three cupids. The other acts disclosed similar marvels. Nothing survives of the music, but in other respects this production set the pace for the succeeding ones.

Monteverdi contributed four operas to the Venetian theaters: *Adone* (1639), *Le Nozze d'Enea con Lavinia* (1641), *Il Ritorno d'Ulisse in patria* (The Return of Ulysses to his Country, 1641), and *L'Incoronazione di Poppea* (The Coronation of Poppea, 1642). Only the music of the last two has survived. *Poppea* is Monteverdi's masterpiece for the stage. It is outstanding among the early Venetian works that survive, for the excellence of its libretto by Francesco Busenello as well as its music.

In *Poppea* Monteverdi gave evidence of being affected by some contemporary trends in dramatic music. The chorus has all but disappeared, and arias and arioso passages, madrigallike duets, and comic ariettes share a large proportion of the vocal music with the recitative. In other ways Monteverdi asserted his independence, particularly in avoiding the closed structures of the Roman cantata composers. In his choice of librettos he showed that he was not interested in purely decorative spectacles but insisted upon dramas of passion.

The interactions of the characters in *Poppea* are of a deeply human nature. Poppea is consumed not only by her love for Nero but also by her craving for the title of empress still held by Nero's wife, Ottavia. Nero, enamored of Poppea, is more than any of the rest a slave of his desires. Ottavia is torn between her love for Nero and her lust for vengeance. Ottone longs to recapture the love of Poppea; nevertheless he welcomes Drusilla's attention and only with great effort forces himself to seek revenge. Seneca risks death to stand up to Nero and voice his fears about the public's disapproval of Poppea. Such conflicts come to life in Monteverdi's music as vividly as in any opera ever written, partly because he never bowed to convention but dealt with each situation according to its own demands.

Rather than use the recitative as a passageway to more melodious utterances, Monteverdi continued to fill it with the loftiest moments of drama and emotion. It not only prepares for lyricism; in dramatic scenes it becomes lyrical itself and mounts to an emotional pitch that the aria serves to sustain. The music moves effortlessly and without ceremony from recitative to aria-like passages and back to recitative. The following excerpt (Example 7-8; the entire scene is in *NAWM* 70) from the tender scene of parting of the illicit lovers at Poppea's house shows his mastery of this mixed medium. The flow of emotion is never sacrificed in such scenes to some preconceived formal scheme.

Some of the most dramatic scenes pass up the aria style altogether. In Ottavia's long speech of self-questioning and self-pity (Act I, scene 5), triple-time melody is reserved for the few poignant lines in which she evokes the hateful image of Nero in Poppea's arms. Ottavia's powerfully moving farewell to Rome is composed entirely in recitative style (Act III, scene 7). The altercation between Nero and Seneca over Poppea's aspiration to the imperial crown derives its fury from a free use of recitative. Nero's angry speech culminates with a passage in concitato style (Example 7-9). Monteverdi claimed to have invented this style under the influence of ancient philosophy and poetics. In a preface of 1638[9] he stated that composers had not yet found a suitable way to express anger, although the other principal passions recognized by the ancient philosophers—temperance and humility or supplication—had found adequate vehicles. Since the ancient poets had solved the problem of expressing anger by using the pyrrhic meter of three short syllables to the foot, Monteverdi reasoned that a continuous series of short notes, sixteen sixteenth notes to the measure, would be an apt rhythm to express texts containing anger and disdain. He first tried out the new style, which he called the *stile concitato*, in the *Combattimento di Tancredi e Clorinda*, performed in 1624, and he used it many times after that.

In *Poppea* Monteverdi realized a true meeting of the demands of poetry, the stage, and music. In the operas of his principal successors in Venice, Pier Francesco Bruni, known as Cavalli (1602–1676), and Antonio Cesti, this synthesis suffered a gradual breakdown. Instead of poetry, spectacle, and music cooperating to produce a joint impact, each was given its turn, as later each principal singer was given an equal share of public exposure. Thus dialogue, narration, and action took the forefront in the recitative sections;

[9] *Madrigali guerrieri, et amorosi* (Venice: A. Vincenti), translated in Strunk, *Source Readings*, p. 413.

EXAMPLE 7-8  C. Monteverdi, *L'Incoronazione di Poppea*, Act I, scene 3

132

EXAMPLE 7-9  C. Monteverdi, *L'Incoronazione di Poppea*, Act I, scene 9

the eye was beguiled during the symphonies, ritornelli, and *balli*, when the machinist and dancing masters took over; and the ear received its due during the arias for one and more persons, sometimes with instrumental accompaniments and interludes.

Librettos were expected to provide for visual attractions, and poets often blamed the weaknesses of their dramas on this convention. Giacomo Badoaro, in the preface to his *L'Ulisse errante* (1644) wrote: "At present, to satisfy the sense of sight, what was once prohibited seems to have become a precept, and every day more numerous changes of scene are contrived."[10] Giovanni Faustini, in publishing his *favola dramatica musicale* (dramatic musical tale) of *Egisto* in 1643, asked the reader's indulgence, because "the theaters want machines to evoke marvels and delight; and frequently adornments, gold and purple vestments so deceive the eyes they make objects seem beautiful that are not. If you are a critic, do not condemn the madness of my *Egisto* . . . because authoritative pleas from an important person coerced me . . . to satisfy the talent of the stage director."[11]

Yet, Cavalli relied upon the recitative, as Monteverdi had done, to carry the burden of the drama. More often than Monteverdi, however, Cavalli tended to slip into passages of arioso in common time in which the bass moves rapidly and rhythmically. The triple-time aria passages are longer and more developed, and occasionally they are unified by recurrent rhythmic or melodic motives. The aria is often placed prominently—for example, at the beginning or conclusion of a scene. In Cavalli's most memorable arias the

[10]Quoted in Simon T. Worsthorne, *Venetian Opera* (Oxford: Clarendon Press, 1954), p. 41, n. 4.
[11]Quoted in Andrea della Corte, *Drammi per musica* (Turin: Unione tipografico editrice, 1958), II, p. 513.

musical material is highly concentrated in a few rhythmic and melodic
motives. Some good examples are Ormindo's lament on the death of Erisbe
in *Ormindo* (*GMB* 200), Climene's lament, "Piangete occhi dolenti" in *Egisto*
(*NAWM* 71), and "Tremulo spirito," Hecuba's lament in *Didone* (Mac-
Clintock, *The Solo Song*, no. 18).

Types of aria construction are similar to those found in the contemporary cantata. They show a subtle interplay between the demands of poetry
and music. A particularly fine example of a form in grand proportions is the
dialogue between Lidio and Clori in *Egisto* (facsimile of manuscript score in
Worsthorne, *Venetian Opera*, pp. 110–13). Each of the two characters has
almost identical musical strophes consisting of an extened aria accompanied
by two violins, a recitative, and ritornels. (Monteverdi had used such a grand
strophic form in *Poppea*, Act I, scene 11.) Each of the strophes has the following form, here shown beside the text sung by Lidio:

|  | Rhyme | Syllable Count |  | Music | Measures | Cadences |
|---|---|---|---|---|---|---|
| Musici, della selva | A | 7 |  | A | 4 | (d) |
| Augeletti canori | B | 7 |  |  | 9 | F |
| Su cantate, | C | 4 | Aria | B + Rit. | 6 + 6 | d V |
| Festeggiate. | C | 4 |  | C + Rit. | 6 + 6 | d V |
| Ecco l'alba, ecco Clori. | B | 7 |  | C extended | 6 | A |
| Quella che sorse già | D | 6 |  | Continuo only |  |  |
| Fù di questa beltà | D | 6 | Reci-tative |  | 5 |  |
| Un luminoso albore. | E | 7 |  |  |  | C |
| O dolce fiamma, ò spirto del mio core | E | 11 |  | 2 vlns. arioso | 9 | d |
|  |  |  |  | Ritornello | 6 |  |

The poet seems to have intended the closed form of the first five lines for an
aria and the paired lines of varying lengths for recitative. The most progressive feature of this strophic aria-recitative complex is the use of the two
violins to accompany the voice and to play ritornels that echo the music of
the vocal sections. Here we have a virtual short cantata, but one unified by a
single mood. It is easy to see why such beautifully conceived structures should
occupy the foreground in these productions which, after all, were conceived

mostly to please and gently move the public, and arouse its admiration. The strong trend seen in this last example toward melodic expansiveness and the integration of voice and instruments is consummated in the work of Cesti.

## A SYNTHESIS OF ROMAN
## AND VENETIAN OPERA: CESTI

From his very first opera, *Orontea*, Cesti drew together with remarkable skill the new musical resources of his age for the enhancement of a new kind of music drama. Though he was undoubtedly acquainted with the work for the Venetian theaters of his immediate predecessors, he revealed even more kinship with the composers of Roman opera and cantata, in whose orbit he was trained.

*Orontea* was first performed with great success at the Teatro Santissimi Apostoli in Venice during its first carnival season of 1649. It was repeated during the next forty years with minor adaptations to current and local taste in Lucca, Rome, Naples, Innsbruck, Florence, Genoa, Turin, Milan, Macerata, Bologna, Chantilly, and other places. Its exceptional durability for this age proves the timeliness and validity of Cesti's solution to the problem of uniting poetry, music, and drama. His was the solution that in its essence dominated the next half-century. Briefly stated, it was to set narrations, dialogue, and the truly dramatic exchanges among the characters in recitative style, whereas generalized expressions of emotion or point of view and comic positions were set as arias. This obviously required close collaboration between Cesti and the librettist, Giacinto Andrea Cicognini, for this formalization is evident in the text as well as the music.

*Orontea* is a completely realistic opera. The action is plausible and devoid of supernatural interventions, which had not been altogether dispensed with even in *Poppea*. Although *Orontea* deals with historical personages, and Orontea herself is a serious, dignified heroine, the play is a comedy.

Orontea, Queen of Egypt, begins the first act by proclaiming in an aria that her heart is immune to the conquest of love. Her refrain "Libertà, libertà" and its ritornello still echo at the end of the following scene, in which her adviser, Creon, tries to persuade her to find a proper consort because the people want to see her married. She succumbs soon to the lowly if handsome painter Alidoro, who has sought refuge in her court from his enemies in Phoenicia. Orontea's sense of honor, reinforced by Creon's disapproval of Alidoro's modest station, prevails at first. By the third act, though, she has stopped fighting her passion and has decided to make the painter her husband. Meanwhile, the fickle Alidoro, attracted to Orontea at first, has found in Silandra a more responsive partner.

At the end of the third act the situation is resolved through a medal belonging to an old nurse, Aristea, who raised Alidoro from the time he was snatched as an infant from his lawful guardians by her pirate husband. Creon recognizes the medal as the one given to the infant son of King Sidonio and Queen Irene of Phoenicia by Ptolemy, King of Egypt. Alidoro is therefore their son, Prince Floridan, fully worthy to marry a queen. Silandra goes back to her neglected Corindo, and the four sing a happy final quartet.

A number of minor characters fill out the small cast. There are two comic servants: Tibrino, who always dreams of love, and Gelone, who thinks of nothing but wine. Another servant, Giacinta, is disguised as a man, this being her means of escape from the unwanted embraces of the Duke of Cyrene. She is coupled in several farcical scenes with Aristea, who, believing Giacinta to be young "Ismero," tries her fading charms upon "him."

Some scenes are entirely in recitative style, such as that in which Giacinta recounts the adventures of her escape (II, 3). It is in a static, though lively, Roman style. Almost the whole scene is centered in C Major, with short excursions to the neighboring keys of G, D, and F. Similarly handled are the long expositions in the third act during which Alidoro's true identity is gradually revealed. Most of the other scenes are dominated by one or several long arias.

The monologue of Orontea, in which she decides to communicate her love to Alidoro by letter, progresses through several stages of lyric expression. This entire scene is a good example of how Cesti could turn simple resources to great advantage. In the few opening measures, as the harmony passes from C Major to a minor, Orontea beautifully sums up her predicament (Example 7-10).

**EXAMPLE 7-10**   A. Cesti, *Orontea*, Act II, scene 17

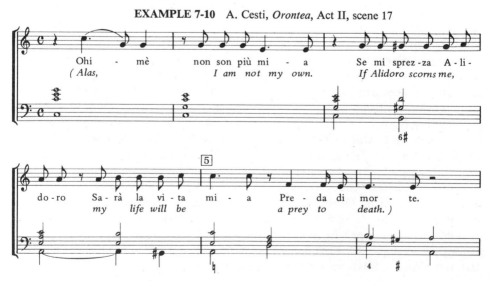

A little later, sighing, she conjures up a vision of Alidoro as her beautiful partner on the throne. A rapid progression from e minor to the dominant of its dominant renders her sense of wonder (Example 7-11). A few measures later (Example 7-12) she breaks into an extended arioso accompanied by a walking bass figure, saying that she cannot keep her gnawing feelings imprisoned in her heart. At the close of this, as she sits down to write, the plain recitative style returns.

The scene culminates with a formal aria. This begins with a device called a "motto," in which the voice sings the principal motive, or motto, and is interrupted by an echo in the violins before it starts again and this time finishes the phrase (Example 7-13). This sort of beginning remained a standard one well into the eighteenth century.

The economy of melodic and harmonic means in this gently rocking lullaby and the sureness of tonal destination reached without any false turns epitomize the masterly simplicity of Cesti's style, purged of the excesses of the past. It is typical also that the voice and instruments alternate rather than merge into a single texture, a vestige of the practice of confining the written-

**EXAMPLE 7-11**   A. Cesti, *Orontea*, Act II, scene 17

**EXAMPLE 7-12**   A. Cesti, *Orontea*, Act II, scene 17

**EXAMPLE 7-13**  A. Cesti, *Orontea*, Act II, scene 17

Dor - mi, dor - mi ben mi - o,
*(Sleep, sleep, my dear,*

Violins

Dor - mi, dor - mi ben mi - o, Per te ve - glia O - ron -
*Sleep, sleep, my dear, for you lies awake Orontea.*

te - a. Mia vi - ta, mia vi - ta a di - o.
*My life, my life, farewell. )*

out instrumental parts to the ritornels. That Cesti was aware of the possibilities of concerted writing is evident in the lush four-part counterpoint at the end of Silandra's aria, "Vieni, vieni Alidoro." Alone on the stage, Silandra fancies herself inviting the painter's love. The aria is built on seventeen statements of the descending-fourth ostinato, followed by a free section, which culminates in Example 7-14. Enhancing the seductiveness of Silandra's imagined appeal

**EXAMPLE 7-14**  A. Cesti, *Orontea*, Act II, scene 8

to Alidoro, the parts move in chains of suspensions similar to those frequently found in trio sonatas. As Silandra finishes her aria, Corindo approaches; taking her invitation to be addressed to him, he answers in an aria, "Vengo, vengo cor mio" (I come, I come, my heart), which could not have failed to fill the theater with uproarious laughter. An animated quarrel ensues that leaves Corindo only too aware of Silandra's rebuff.

Some of the most brilliant melodic invention is found in the comic arias, of which there are a large number. A fine example is the aria in which Gelone mocks Silandra's tears after she has been disappointed by Alidoro. Gelone would laugh at the sorrows of lovers to the weeping of a wine barrel, he sings. Two musically identical strophes are each made up of three discrete sections. The first (Example 7-15a) is characterized by much text repetition and syncopation, two perennial components of the *buffo* (comic) style. The third section (Example 7-15b) calls for exaggerated accents on the first of each of four sixteenth notes to imitate laughter.

**EXAMPLE 7-15** A. Cesti, *Orontea*, Act III, scene 7

EXAMPLE 7-15 (Cont.)

Though *Orontea* seems satisfactory to us today and was successful in its own day, a repertory of operas like it would have lacked one ingredient demanded by the public: the "marvelous." With this word the operatic theorists of the seventeenth century summed up the magical transformations and stage effects worked by complicated concealed machinery: the fires, the dawns, the sunlit, twilit, and moonlit scenes that were controlled by hundreds of candles; the splendid array of gods and goddesses; the sea and land battles engaging scores of supernumeraries; and the dancing nymphs and naiads. Cesti's own operas rarely lacked this element, and one of them, *Il pomo d'oro* (The Golden Apple, Vienna, 1667), is the most notorious example of excess in this department. The taste for these baubles was not to last, however. *Orontea* is typical not so much of the times as of what outlasted them.

## BIBLIOGRAPHICAL NOTES

Long neglect of the cantata by publishers is being remedied under the leadership of Owen Jander, editor of a series of volumes of selected cantatas by several composers: *The Wellesley Edition: The Italian Cantata*. The first number contains seven cantatas by Antonio Cesti edited by David Burrows (Wellesley College, 1963). Other volumes will include cantatas by Luigi Rossi, Antonio Stradella, and Carissimi. Also edited by Burrows are duet-cantatas by Cesti in *Four Chamber Duets* (New Haven: Department of Music, Yale University, 1969) in the *Yale Collegium Musicum Series*, New Series, Vol. I. Numerous short cantatas by various composers are in Jeppesen's *La Flora*. Rossi's *Del silentio il giogo algente* is printed in Edward J. Dent, "Italian Chamber Cantatas," in *The Musical Antiquary*, II (1910–11), 195–99.

A fine survey of Carissimi's cantatas is "The Cantatas of Giacomo Carissimi" by Gloria Rose in *MQ*, XLVIII (1962), 204–15; and a companion anthology of *Six Solo Cantatas* by him (London: Faber, 1969), edited by Rose, presents a representative selection. Both cantatas and oratorios are being collected in the series edited by Lino Bianchi in *Monumenti* (Rome: Instituto per la storia della musica, Accademia nazionale di S.Cecilia, 1960–). A good edition of *Jephte* is that by Gottfried Wolters, with continuo realized by Mathias Siedel (Wolfenbüttel, Zurich: Möseler Verlag, 1969).

The superb first two volumes of *A History of the Oratorio* by Howard E. Smither (Chapel Hill: The University of North Carolina Press, 1977) sum up what is known of this genre in the baroque period.

A comprehensive history of seventeenth-century Italian opera needs still to be written. The period is covered briefly in Donald Grout's *SHO*. The Venetian phase is treated in a selective topical manner by Simon T. Worsthorne in *Venetian Opera in the 17th Century* (Oxford: Clarendon Press, 1954).

Full scores of the operas of the mid-seventeenth century abound in manuscript copies, but few have been published. Monteverdi's *L'Incoronazione di Poppea* is available in numerous editions, most of them overly revised for performance purposes. The only authentic versions are Malipiero's in the complete works, Vol. 13 (1931), and the facsimile of the autograph manuscript, edited by Giacomo Benvenuti (Milan: Fratelli Bocca, 1938). Monteverdi's *Il Ritorno d'Ulisse in patria* is in Vol. 12 (1930) of the complete works, edited by Malipiero, and in *DTOe*, XXIX (1922), in an edition by Robert Haas. Cesti's *Orontea* is edited by William Homes in *The Wellesley Edition*, no. 11 (Wellesley College, 1973). Two operas of Cavalli have appeared in piano-vocal "realizations" by Raymond Leppard, which, though adapted for modern performance, are faithful enough to give us a good idea of the original: *L'Ormindo* (1969) and *La Calisto* (1975), both published by Faber in London and G. Schirmer in New York. A number of manuscripts of seventeenth-century operas are published in facsimile, under the direction of Howard Mayer Brown, by Garland Publishing, Inc.

The Prologue and Act I of Cavalli's *Giasone* are in Robert Eitner, ed., *Publikationen älterer praktischer und theoretischer Musikwerke* (Berlin: Gesellschaft für Musikforschung), XII (1883), 3–85. The same volume contains the Prologue, Act I, and scenes from Acts II and III of Cesti's *La Dori* (pp. 86–177), and scenes from his *Le Disgrazie d'amore, La Magnanimità d'Alessandro*, and *La Semirami* (pp. 178–206). All of the extant music of Cesti's *Il Pomo d'oro*, namely the Prologue, Acts I, II, and IV are edited by Guido Adler in *DTOe*, III/2 and IV/2 (1896).

# EIGHT

# SONATA, CONCERTO, AND SINFONIA

The music of the mid-seventeenth century seems to us to strike a happy balance between freshness and maturity. It exudes confidence without self-consciousness and enjoys a certain homogeneity without conformity. After decades of experimentation, the monodic idiom and the thorough-bass technique are seen to join in an effective partnership. Melody and bass line proceed with purpose and structural clarity. The bass part, now typically active and linear, occasionally competes with or enters into dialogue with the upper parts. Sequences, imitations, and repetitions give to the expansion of motives a logical and flowing continuity. Harmony is varied, but its digressions are curbed by a unified tonal scheme. At last a consistent and distinct style has been achieved that may be called, for lack of a better name, baroque.

These characteristics, already observed in cantata and opera, grew as much out of instrumental as out of vocal practice. More than at any other time in the history of music the capabilities of instruments and the aspirations of their players were having a deep effect on musical style. At the same time

The violin family that emerged in the sixteenth century came to dominate ensemble music in the seventeenth. The earliest known representation of the new family of instruments is this fresco from the 1530's on the cupola of the church of Santa Maria delle Grazie in Saronno, Piedmont, Italy. Left center is the violin, lower middle the 'cello, and right the viola. Such instruments were first manufactured in this region.

adaptations of vocal procedures made up a strong component of the instrumental idiom. The basso continuo, the texture of two treble voices against a bass, the recitative style, and the triple-meter aria style were points of departure for the composers of sonatas and concertos.

The instrument par excellence of the baroque era was the violin. The violin and its family of bowed, unfretted instruments appeared mysteriously about 1520 in northern Italy in the region around Milan. Regardless of size, they were called at first interchangeably *violini, viole, viole da braccio, violons* (French), and *violoni*. At the outset they had only three strings tuned in fifths, like the rebec, but by the middle of the sixteenth century the three principal members of the family all had four strings and were tuned like the modern violin, viola, and violoncello. The lowest member of the family, playing an octave lower than written (hence now called double bass), became known as the violone. Unlike the *viole da gamba* (leg viols), usually called in English simply viols, and most often played with the instrument between or on the knees, the violins, or *viole da braccio* (arm viols), were held against the body by the left hand, except for the larger instruments, which were played like the leg viols. By contrast to the leg viols, the violins were not fretted and were bowed with an overhand instead of an underhand grip. The resultant pressure and the tighter strings needed to resist it produced a louder and cleaner tone, and the technique of bowing encouraged sharper attacks, more emphatic rhythms, and less flowing and less vocal lines.

Besides those of the violin family, the favorite instruments for sonatas were the cornett, a curved wood instrument with conical bore and cup-shaped mouthpiece, and the trumpet, to which toward the end of the century were added the transverse flute and the oboe.

## THE SONATA

Both the meeting and parting of the vocal and instrumental idioms were already evident in Monteverdi's aria "Possente spirto" in *Orfeo* and in the short songs with ritornelli of the *Scherzi musicali* (1607; *Opere*, Vol. 10). In the latter, two sopranos and a bass voice alternated with two treble viole da braccio and a bass instrument. The two ensembles exerted a subtle influence over each other, but the style of writing for the violins was obviously more vigorous, more square in its rhythms, and faster in its runs. The same year, Salomone Rossi (1570–c. 1630) published the first of his two collections of *sinfonie* and *gagliarde*, of which the *sinfonie* are mostly for two treble viole da braccio (violins) or cornetts with a chitarrone or other instrument playing the basso continuo. As in the vocal duets of Monteverdi and their ritornelli, the two upper parts exchange motives or play in parallel motion, while the bass has a supporting role. From a later collection by Rossi of 1613, the *Sonata prima detta la moderna* (*HM* 110) shows a debt to the vocal concerto on other counts. The two violins attack in imitation a drawn-out vocal ornamental figure called an *accento*, and the common meter is broken by triple-meter passages, after which the violins join in madrigalistic runs of sixteenth notes.

Biagio Marini (1597–1665), a violinist and violin composer who also left many concertato madrigals and sacred concertos, combined a conscious absorption of vocal methods and ideals in his violin music with a full realization of the instrument's potential. The title of his Opus 1 of 1617, *Affetti musicali* (Musical Affections), suggests that the goal of moving the affections could now be fulfilled by purely instrumental music: sonatas, canzoni, sinfonie, and dances for one or two violins or cornetts and a bass played by both a trombone or bassoon and a chordal instrument. The main constructive method in the nondance pieces for more than one treble part is imitation, but the medium of the single treble instrument and bass, less amenable to this method, challenged Marini to invent a new idiom. The sinfonia entitled *La Gardana* (*GMB* 182) fluctuates between a rhetorical posture analogous to recitative and melodious passages winding through sequences. Like the closing aria of a cantata, the last part of this short sinfonia consists of two varied strophes of the same music.

The resemblance to vocal music is most striking in the *Sonata per sonar con due corde* (Op. 8, 1629; *GMB* 183), which opens with some rhythmic mannerisms and free dissonances reminiscent of solo madrigals. Vocal ornaments such as *groppo* (trill) and *trillo* (tremolo), dynamic gradations of *piano* and *forte*, and instructions to the player to insert *affetti* (perhaps diminutions or vocal *accenti*) all contribute to the human, passionate effect of this music. At the same time the sonata is full of violinistic sallies, such as wide leaps, double stops, and rapid scales. Some of the sections are labeled *tardo* (slow) or *presto* (fast).

EXAMPLE 8-1    B. Marini, *Sonata quarta per il violino per sonar con due corde*

Writing imitative of monodic vocal music constituted only a minor if important part of the collections of Rossi, Marini, and their contemporaries. The mainstream of instrumental music continued the currents of the *canzone francese*, sinfonia, and sonata for four and more parts of the late sixteenth century. An earlier wave of imitation of vocal procedures had left upon these the marks of the polyphonic chanson, madrigal, and motet. All of these vocal types and their instrumental derivatives consisted of loosely connected sections in which imitation was the basic procedure, relieved by occasional homophonic writing, often in triple meter. The smooth lines of vocal music were transformed, partly through diminutions, into the square-cut, angular rhythms of instrumental music. (See *MM* 20–21, which shows how a chanson by Crecquillon was converted into a canzona for keyboard by Andrea Gabrieli.) Modernization of this idiom in the seventeenth century assumed at first the guise of a reduction for fewer parts. One or two trebles and a bass could simulate with the help of a continuo player the effect of many-voice polyphonic and polychoral pieces. Thus the reduced vocal polyphony of Viadana had its counterpart in such works as A. Gabrieli's *Canzone alla francese* for violin, cornett, and bass instruments (1602; Riemann, *Old Chamber Music*), or Giovanni Paolo Cima's *Sonata a 3 per violino, cornetto, e violone* (1610; *DM, Die italienische Triosonate*, p. 17).

Tarquinio Merula's canzone *La Strada* for two violins, violone, and basso continuo, from *Canzoni overo Sonate concertate per chiesa e camera,*

Op. 12, 1637 (*GMB* 184), is in this same tradition. All the parts are involved in imitation of a series of contrasting subjects, which are developed at greater length than they would be in a chanson, but the return of the first section at the end recalls the Parisian chanson. There is one change to a triple meter for a homophonic section. The canzone begins with the long-short-short rhythm of the sixteenth-century narrative chanson. This opening subject is distinctly instrumental in character and, in common with many of this period, lends itself to expansion by means of sequence. Over the bass entrance of the subject the upper parts become entwined in a chain of suspensions, a technique that is one of the most marked features of the two-violin sonata throughout its later history (Example 8-2).

**EXAMPLE 8-2**   T. Merula, *Canzone, La Strada*

The terms *canzona, sonata,* and *sinfonia,* as labels for the pieces discussed so far, had no precise signification. The distinction made by Praetorius[1] that the sonata was more severe than the canzona is generally valid. The term *canzona* was used little in the second part of the century and was eventually dropped. *Sonata* was the preferred name for an independent piece of several movements for few parts with basso continuo. *Sinfonia,* at first synonymous with *sonata,* was retained in the second half of the century particularly for the first number of a suite of dances or for pieces with fuller texture, and for those inserted in vocal works such as operas or sacred concertos.

Compositions published under these titles seem to have been destined until around the 1660s for both church and chamber—"per chiesa e camera." In the church they helped fill with sound silent intervals of the Mass and Vespers, such as, in the Mass, after the Epistle, during the Offertory, during the Elevation of the Host, and during the Post-Communion. Sometimes instrumental pieces replaced the chanting of the Gradual and Alleluia, particularly when an organ Mass took the place of a sung Ordinary. Exactly how the sonatas or portions of them fitted into these points in the Mass is not clear.

[1]*Syntagma musicum,* III, 22.

The printed collections that contained sonatas usually also included numerous dances for either dancing or listening. The order of dances in the collections was often guided by ballroom practice. A company or group dance such as the *branle* or *allemande* would be followed by a couple dance such as the *corrente*. For example, Giovanni Maria Bononcini (1642–1678) in his Op. 1 (1666) presented as numbers 13 to 15 three branles of different types followed by a gavotte and courante, all in the order prescribed for French court balls. Often all the dances of one type were placed together and the choice of dances for a set was left to the players. The makings of dance sets were available from the 1620s, as for example in S. Rossi's *Il quarto libro de varie sonate, sinfonie, gagliarde, brandi, e corrente per sonar due violini, et un chittarrone o altro stromento simile*, 1622. Eventually Italian and German composers themselves formed sets or suites of dances, sometimes, as in those of Schein, related by a common theme. Corelli entitled such suites *sonate da camera*, to distinguish them from the *sonate da chiesa*, from which dances—at least such as were plainly labeled—were excluded for reasons of propriety. These suites usually began with an introductory slow movement, often derived from the allemande, followed by a selection of dances, dance airs, and occasional nondance movements, such as transitional adagios.

The basic ingredients of what Corelli and his contemporaries called the *sonata da chiesa* are evident in the sonatas of Giovanni Legrenzi (1626–1690). The four or five sections are clearly separated and usually labeled with tempo markings. The outer movements are chiefly fast fugues on one or more subjects. In his sonatas *a 3* (generally called trio sonatas) the bass tends to take a passive role. In the sonatas *a 2* (which we shall call duosonatas) the violin and violone tend to be two equally important parts. When the violone is a part separate from the basso continuo, it is sometimes called *violone concertante*. Legrenzi's carefully wrought, highly concentrated subjects are self-sufficient individualities possessing strong tonal direction. A theme may proceed from tonic to dominant, like Examples 8-3a and b from *La Cornara*; from tonic to dominant and back, like 3c from *La Raspona* (*HM* 31 and *NAWM* 90; both sonatas from Op. 2 of 1655); or from dominant to tonic, like 3d from *La Rosetta* (Op. 8, 1671).

A good though late example of Legrenzi's fugal method is the first allegro of Op. 10, No. 4 (1673; *HM* 84), a sonata for violin, bass viola da braccio (i.e., cello), and basso continuo in g minor. After the opening exposition, imitations upon fragments of the subject effect a modulation to the principal destination, B♭, in which the subject is restated. Cadences are carefully avoided except at important way stations to this key, namely d and g, and for the return at the subdominant. The reaffirmation of the principal tonality is marked by a thickening of the counterpoint through overlapping imitations of a theme derived from the subject. The sequences in Example 8-4 drive the harmony powerfully toward the final cadence while tracing an

**EXAMPLE 8-3**   G. Legrenzi, fugal subjects

**EXAMPLE 8-4**   G. Legrenzi, *Sonata Op. 10, No. 4,* Allegro

unmistakable g minor through the skips of the various parts. The sequence has by now become the indispensable essence of instrumental writing. Its stubborn harmonies proclaim and delimit the frontiers of a key.

The flowing triple-meter Adagio in sarabande rhythm that follows applies the chain-of-suspensions technique in its most characteristic context, a slow canonic duet (Example 8-5). It is a sort of piece frequently encountered in the operas and cantatas of the period.

**EXAMPLE 8-5**  G. Legrenzi, *Sonata Op. 10, No. 4*, Adagio

The leadership in violin composition remained for the first part of the century with men who originated and worked in the region in which the violin itself was born. Marini, a native of Brescia, worked in Mantua, Venice, Neuberg in Germany, and Ferrara. Merula, born in Cremona, worked there and in Bergamo and Poland. Cima was active in his home city of Milan. Legrenzi, from Clusone near Bergamo, settled in Venice after a period in Bergamo and Ferrara. With the next generation, the center shifted to Bologna and neighboring Modena. Maurizio Cazzati (c. 1620–1677) was the link between the northern cities and Bologna. Born in Mantua, he early established his reputation in Ferrara and Bergamo and in 1657 founded a school of violin playing in Bologna.

Bologna boasted two institutions that fostered instrumental composition and performance, the vast church of San Petronio and the Accademia dei Filarmonici. San Petronio had long been a center of concerted music. The roll of salaried musicians in 1595 listed twenty-eight singers, four trombonists, a cornettist, and a violinist. In 1670, thirteen years after Cazzati took over as choirmaster, there were among the salaried musicians a nucleus of string players: three violinists, one violist, two tenor violists (i.e., cellists), and one each on the theorbo and violone. To these were added others, hired as needed for large concertos.

The Academy, to which compositions were submitted for criticism, both encouraged musical life and exercised a scholastic influence upon it. The contrapuntal rules of the sixteenth-century theorists, modified to suit the thorough-bass style, were now being taught and applied with renewed vigor. Cazzati, accused of lapses from these rules by Giulio Cesare Arresti, an officer of the Academy, was dismissed from his post at San Petronio in 1673 because of the ensuing controversy. Composers vied with one another to produce learned compositions full of canons and fugues by contrary motion, inversion, and in double counterpoint. Cazzati's pupil, Giovanni Battista Vitali (c. 1644–1692), filled a book, his Op. 13, *Artificii musicali* (1689), with contrapuntal tours de force. Another composer in the circle, Giovanni Maria Bononcini (1642–1678), who worked in Modena, had earlier offered a series of sonatas in canon, Op. 3 (1669).

Cazzati's sonatas are notable for the wide range of their bold violinistic themes, such as the opening gigue of the *Sonata La Pellicana* (*HAM* II, 219 from Op. 55, 1670). Particularly effective are the slow movements with tremolo (*HM* 34) characterized by acerbic augmented and diminished intervals. Cazzati was one of the first to use the tonal answer. The typical imitation of a subject up to now had been by exact transposition at the fifth or fourth, producing what had been known since the sixteenth century as the *fuga realis,* or real answer. The new consciousness of tonal center led composers to sacrifice exact imitation for unity of key, which is preserved through the tonal answer. For instance, when a subject moves from the dominant to the tonic, as in Example 8-6, the tonal answer goes from the tonic to the dominant instead of from the dominant to its dominant, as would a real answer. Tonal answers appear in the first books of sonatas of both Bononcini (Op. 1, 1666) and Vitali (Op. 2, 1667) and frequently from this point on in sonatas generally. Other refinements of counterpoint are strettos and countersubjects that appear both below and above the subject, that is, composed in double or invertible counterpoint.

**EXAMPLE 8-6**  M. Cazzati, *Sonata La Pellicana*, Presto

No other prominent composer so drastically limited his output to a single medium as did Corelli (1653–1713), for he left only string sonatas and concertos. Born in Fusignano, not far from Bologna, he spent four years of study in the latter center of violin music before settling in Rome about 1671. His five books of sonatas, published in 1681, 1685, 1689, 1694, and 1700, are built on the advances of his predecessors. They constitute a corpus of works that in its consistency of high artistic achievement has few equals. Corelli clearly separated church and chamber sonatas, grouping them in dozens or half-dozens. The content of the two types of sonatas shows, nevertheless, an interpenetration of the two manners of writing.

Corelli's diversity of approaches, too numerous to permit a description of each, is mitigated by the recurrence of certain musical stereotypes. Behind these characteristic poses seems to lie an awareness of several static moods or affections that are linked to particular complexes of meter, tempo, and harmonic density. Very often Corelli found these musical types in the French dance music cultivated by his predecessors and still in vogue in Italian society.[2] He usually began his church sonatas with a severe, majestic, solemn, or proud mood, passed on to a resolute and contented one, then to a tenderly melancholic affection, and finally to a light and carefree one. The types that best answered to these moods were the slow allemande and its kin the French-overture *grave* for the first; a bright fast fugue for the second; an operatic arioso, perhaps in sarabande rhythm, for the third; and usually a fast allemande or gigue, occasionally a gavotte or balletto, for the last. The order of movements in a chamber sonata was less predictable.

The opening *Grave* of Op. 3, No. 11 illustrates the French-overture type of beginning. Jean-Baptiste Lully (1632–1687) established this kind of overture as the opening music for ballets and operas, starting with his *Ballet d'Alcidiane* in 1658. It consists of a slow, solemn section in common time with many dotted rhythms, followed by a fast triple or compound meter in fugal style, after which the slow music sometimes returns (see *MM* 36). It is a stylization of the processional allemande, during which dancers used to enter, and the ensuing courante. Example 8-7 illustrates several of the characteristics of the overture-like *grave*—upbeat motives, dotted rhythms, many first-inversion chords and suspensions, and close imitations in a prevailingly homophonic style. Corelli usually followed this sort of movement with a fast fugue or, in a chamber suite, a corrente. Related to this grave style is the opening slow movement employing the *andante*, or walking bass (see, for example, Op. 3, No. 2), which in the chamber suites is unmasked as an allemande.

Corelli's typical second church-sonata movement is a well-worked-out

---

[2]Johann Mattheson years later characterized the various dances in terms of the affections in *Der vollkommene Capellmeister* (Hamburg, 1739), Part II, chap. 13. See the trans. by Hans Lenneberg in *Journal of Music Theory*, II (1958), 57–69.

**EXAMPLE 8-7**  A. Corelli, *Sonata da chiesa, Op. 3, No. 11,* Grave

fugue. As in the late works of Bononcini and Vitali, the bass shuttles between foundation work and taking its turn in expositions. Often a strettolike texture is achieved by closely spaced fragmentary statements of a subject, as in Op. 3, No. 7 (*MM* 39). Some of the fugues are as learned as those of the Bolognese masters. The second movement of Op. 3, No. 4 (Vivace) has a countersubject contrived in invertible counterpoint and is particularly rich in true strettos. The medium of solo violin and bass is made to yield a brilliant fugal movement in three voices through double stops in Op. 5, No. 3 (*HAM* II, 252).

The slow triple-meter aria continued to find a place in Corelli's scheme, usually in the third-movement position, though sometimes also in the first. Opus. 3, No. 7, has such a third movement (*MM* 39). Like the parallel cantata duets, this type is fugal, its melodies full of affective intervals like rising minor sixths, its harmony dominated by the suspension dissonance on the first beat, its rhythms often marked by hemiola and the sarabande's reinforced second beat.

Corelli rarely used the bipartite dance form in his church sonatas outside the last movement. In the chamber sonatas however, it is the form of most of the dances and even of some of the preludes. These types of movements are most often composed of two sections, each immediately repeated. The first makes a cadence on the dominant or relative major, whereas the second moves from this key, usually through the subdominant, back to the tonic. Unlabeled gigues, fast allemandes, and gavottes account for many of the fast movements, and these same dances, usually more homophonically conceived, tend to be the closing numbers of the suites (e.g., *GMB* 240; *HAM* II, 253). A rarer capping movement for a church-sonata set is the balletto of Op. 3, No. 7 (*MM* 39).

Adagio, from Corelli's Sonata Op. 5, no. 3, as printed in *Sonata's or Solo's for a Violin a Bass Violin or Harpsicord Compos'd by Arcangelo Corelli His fifth Opera*, J. Walsh, London (1711). Walsh claimed that the embellished version in the upper treble staff stemmed from Corelli himself. (New Haven, Yale University Music Library.)

Virtuoso display is not a central feature of the trio sonatas, except in a few movements inspired by the multisectional keyboard toccata, as in Op. 3, No. 12. However, the church sonatas 1, 3, and 6 of Op. 5 for violin and bass are clearly written with a virtuoso in mind. The fugues, with their double

**EXAMPLE 8-8**   A. Corelli, *Sonata for Violin, Op. 5, No. 3*, first Allegro

and triple stops and bravura episodes, contain some of the most violinistic writing conceived up to that time. Example 8-8a shows the final measures of the second movement of No. 3. This cadenza over a single bass note ("tasto solo" indicates that the right hand is silent) requires the player to bow rapidly across two, three, and four strings. Measures 46–49 are played as in Example 8b. In the slow movements of these sonatas the virtuosity is implied rather than explicit, since it was customary to add embellishments to the simple lines of an Adagio such as that of Op. 5, No. 3. Estienne Roger of Amsterdam published ornamented versions of this opus, claiming that they were sent to him by Corelli. These can be approximately dated through the fact that John Walsh and J. Hare of London put out a similar edition in 1711, eleven years after the original unornamented versions (both versions of Op. 5, No. 3, Adagio, in *HAM* II, 252). Cadenzas provided further opportunities for display, as at the end of the Allegro of this same sonata (*HAM* II, 252).

The two sets of sonatas for two violins, bass, and basso continuo by Henry Purcell (1659–1695), published in 1683 and 1697 (the last posthumously by the successors of John Playford), show a strongly independent direction. Although in his preface to the first set Purcell acknowledged that he had "faithfully endeavour'd a just imitation of the most fam'd Italian Masters; principally, to bring the seriousness and gravity of that sort of Musick into vogue, and reputation among our Country-men," it is difficult to pinpoint the models imitated, particularly in the sonatas of 1683. The music is studious, earnest, and sober, revealing little of the dance influence that dominated Italian violin music. The fast movements are permeated by fugal

procedure, with the bass—distinct from the basso continuo—participating
fully in the expositions. One of the fugal movements is usually labeled
"Canzona" and, indeed, often has more of the character of a canzona for
viols than a sonata for violins. Nevertheless, the subjects of these movements

**EXAMPLE 8-9**   H. Purcell, *Sonata II,* [Allegro]

**EXAMPLE 8-10**   H. Purcell, *Sonata II,* Adagio-Vivace

possess incisive intervallic and rhythmic profiles, reminding one of those of Legrenzi—for example, that of Sonata 2 in B♭ (Zimmerman no. 791; Example 8-9). There is an abstractness and busyness in the counterpoint that links these fugal movements to the English fantasies for viols. Clear triadic themes become suddenly gnarled in chromatic involutions that are intensely moving and at the same time exhibit the native predilection toward augmented intervals, cross relations and so-called "simultaneous false relations," as in the Vivace, the next-to-last movement of the same sonata (Example 8-10).

Even when Purcell struck a veritable Italian pose, as in the Chaconne-Sonata No. 6 of the second set (Zimmerman no. 807), the many repercussed and double suspensions and others resolved by leap, the sudden chromatic turns, syncopations, and other rhythmic quirks, and most of all the abstract unviolinistic lines set him apart. More than one movement, though, betrays admiration for Corelli's moving *grave* style. The opening of the third sonata of the 1697 collection (Zimmerman no. 804; Example 8-11a), perhaps a late work, captures the mood and manner of the Corelli model (Example 8-11b) in its suave passionateness, the Phrygian cadence that ends the first phrase, the crisscrossing of the two violins over the subordinated bass, the wry dissonances, and the striving toward harmonic goals.

**EXAMPLE 8-11a**  H. Purcell, *Sonata III*, [Grave]

EXAMPLE 8-11a (Cont.)

EXAMPLE 8-11b  A. Corelli, *Op. 3, No. 7*, Grave

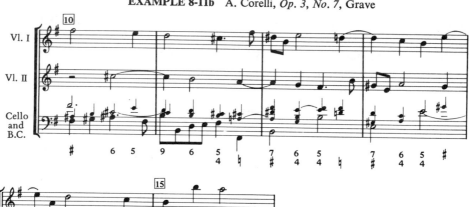

   The outstanding composer of sonatas in the German-speaking countries was Heinrich Ignaz Franz Biber (1644–1704), a violin virtuoso who served the Archbishop of Salzburg from around 1676, eventually becoming director of his music in 1684. Building as much on the work of his teacher Johann Heinrich Schmelzer (c. 1623–1680) as on the Italians, Biber achieved a personal idiom that is expressive as well as polished and brilliant. His most famous sonatas, the sixteen "Rosary" or "Mystery" sonatas for violin and basso continuo of around 1674, remained in manuscript (Munich, Bayerische Staatsbibliothek Mus. Mss. 4123) and are comparatively early works. Each

The drawing accompanying Sonata XI in the manuscript of "Rosary" or "Mystery" sonatas for violin and bass by Heinrich Biber. The sonata represents the resurrection. (Munich, Bayerische Staatsbibliothek, Mus. Ms. 4123.)

of the sonatas in the cycle except the final Passacaglia is accompanied in the manuscript by a picture from the life of Mary and Jesus, but the music is not programmatic in any specific way. All but the first and last sonatas require the violinist to retune his instrument to a special tuning, such as g–g'–d'–d in the eleventh sonata (instead of the normal g–d'–a'–e''), a process called *scordatura*, literally "mistuning," to permit easier fingering of double and triple stops and arpeggios in a particular key. In the second movement of this sonata, Adagio (*HAM* II, 238), the resurrection hymn "Surrexit Christus hodie" is converted into a passacaglia bass, and at the end the violin states the theme in octaves, which are played in double stops with one finger moving up and down the adjacent top strings (retuned). The melody is further doubled by the basso continuo, creating a unique climax.

Despite the obvious devotional intention of the Biber sonatas, most of them contain dance movements, among them allemandes, sarabandes, courantes, correnti, gigues, and ciaconas, as well as arias with variations. The latter are among the most interesting of the pieces, because they provide occasions for virtuoso display as brilliant and idiomatic as anything seen so early in the century. In the tenth sonata, on the subject of the Crucifixion, which consists of a Praeludium and an Aria con Variazioni, the variations demand a variety of advanced technical resources: bowing across several strings (Var. 1, Example 8-12a), rapid exchange between double stops and

**EXAMPLE 8-12**  H. Biber, *"Mystery" Sonata 10*, Aria con Variazioni

runs (Var. 2, Example 12b), wide leaps and cascading runs (Var. 2, Example 12c), and bariolage and repeated notes (Var. 5, Example 12d).

The sonata and suite for one or two instruments and bass retained the attention of composers throughout the baroque period and sometime afterwards. The sonata spread quickly to instruments other than the strings, particularly the flute, oboe, solo organ, and solo harpsichord. In the sonatas of the Italian successors of Corelli we find his model adjusted to the currents of late baroque music. The most important were Tommaso Albinoni (1671–1750), Antonio Vivaldi (1669?–1741), and Francesco Maria Veracini (1690–1768). Their works are characterized by an expansion and roundedness of

**EXAMPLE 8-12**   (Cont.)

form, an intensification of fugal writing in the allegros balanced by an increasing homophony in other movements, and many written-out embellishments formerly left to the player. Several Frenchmen, notably François Couperin (1668–1733) and Jean-Marie Leclair (1697–1764), combined the Corelli style with a native flair for simple melody, ever nourished by the *air de danse* and tastefully laced with trills and turns. The supreme eclectic was Johann Sebastian Bach (1685–1750), who in his many sonatas drew together the techniques of an international host of predecessors and contemporaries. In his sonatas and suites for unaccompanied violin and cello, the familiar and aging categories burn with a twilight glow as every difficulty of counterpoint and mechanical limitation of the instruments is pushed aside. Curiously, Bach neglected the true trio sonata, of which the only significant authentic example by him is that of *The Musical Offering* for transverse flute, violin, and bass.

## THE CONCERTO AND THE SINFONIA

The personnel structure of the large musical chapels, where players were divided into ripienists and soloists, inevitably gave rise to an instrumental form that took advantage of this division. The ripienists (from *ripieno*, meaning full choir, or tutti) were usually players of average ability who accompanied the full chorus in grand sacred concertos by doubling the choral parts on instruments of the violin family. The instrumental soloists, on the other hand, were usually highly skilled violinists or cornettists who played in dialogue with the vocal soloists in concertos for few voices or during solo sections of grand concertos. This contrast also occurred in dramatic music. In Monteverdi's aria "Possente spirto," in *Orfeo*, various duets of instrumental soloists alternate, as we have seen, with the solo voice in the first strophes, while in the last an ensemble of viole da braccio, obviously a ripieno group, plays a sustained chordal accompaniment.

A somewhat different kind of contrast was enjoyed in Venetian ensemble music composed for several choirs of instruments. The choirs played separately and jointly, opposing different colors and large and small sounds. The first work to designate precisely the instrumentation of the choirs was Gabrieli's *Sonata pian' e forte* (*HAM* I, 173): a cornett and three trombones form one group, a viola da braccio and three trombones, the other. When both groups are to play together, the music is marked *forte*; when only one plays, *piano*. Similar works were written throughout the seventeenth century, and this kind of orchestration persisted in the following century in sinfonie and sinfonie concertanti.

A composer who divided the orchestra in many of his vocal compositions was Alessandro Stradella (1644–1682). His Serenata *Qual prodigio è ch'io miri*, for three voices and instruments of around 1675, uses in two of its short sinfonie and in several of its arias distinct groups of instrumental players designated as concertino and concerto grosso. The concertino consists of two treble parts and bass, evidently for two solo violins and continuo, while the concerto grosso is in four parts and is at one point described as an ensemble with the parts "doubled," that is with more than one player to a part. In the third aria, for bass, "Basilisco allor," the concerto grosso plays the opening and closing ritornels and reinforces several cadential passages, but otherwise only the concertino plays with the voice. Although in the work

EXAMPLE 8-13 A. Stradella, Serenata, *Qual prodigio è ch'io miri*

as a whole there is little difference in style between music of the concertino and concerto grosso, in this aria the concertino parts are definitely soloistic, as in Example 8-13.

This same kind of orchestration occurs in arias of Stradella's famous oratorio *San Giovanni Battista* and in the second of a set of twelve unpublished sinfonie. This sinfonia appears in two different manuscripts with variant titles that reveal the work's special characteristics: *Sinfonia a violini e bassi a concertino e concerto grosso distinti* ("with distinct concertino and concerto grosso"; Modena, Mus. F. 1129, No. 2), and *Sonata di viole cioè concerto grosso di viole concertino di 2 violini e leuto* ("Sonata for viols [da braccio], that is, concerto grosso of viols and concertino of two violins and lute"; Turin, Foà 11, F 69). In an age when composers generally neglected to write out any but the obbligato instrumental parts and the basso continuo, leaving the rest to improvisation, Stradella was one of the first to specify carefully exactly what the ripieno group was to play and to cultivate a polite rivalry and sociability between it and the soloists.

In Rome, where Stradella worked mainly until 1677, another composer began to use the divided orchestra around this time: Arcangelo Corelli. His practices were described by Georg Muffat in a preface to a collection of sonatas, *Armonico tributo* (1682; revised version of 1701 in Strunk, p. 449). However, none of Corelli's compositions for such ensembles was printed until after his death. Meanwhile Muffat and others had published similar works. One of these composers, Lorenzo Gregori, in the preface to his *Concerti grossi* (1698), shows that the practice consisted essentially of augmenting the sound of certain passages in sonatas written for the typical trio ensemble. "So as not to multiply the number of partbooks, I have written down in this opus as best I could the concertini. Those who play in the concerto grosso will please be careful to remain silent and to count whenever is written Soli, and to reenter immediately where is written Tutti. . . ." Thus all of the music is played by the concertino, which is joined in tutti sections by a larger body of players. Muffat suggested that such concertos might be played either as trio sonatas or as concertos. This same situation holds for the Corelli *Concerti grossi*, Op. 6 (1714), though Corelli, unlike Gregori, issued the tutti parts separately.

The effect of these concertos of Corelli is often that of trio sonatas played with novel terraced dynamics, but the intended manner of performance significantly influenced Corelli's conception of the form. Static and symmetrical phrase groups result from the echoing by the concertino of tutti statements (e.g., the Vivace of No. 3), or the converse (first Largo of No. 1). Mainly, though, the tutti's function is to underscore the cadences. Figurative display of technique usually excludes the tutti (as in the first Allegros of Nos. 2 and 12, the final Allegros of Nos. 1, 3, 8), but not always (see first Allegros of Nos. 1 and 7).

With the collection, Op. 8, of Giuseppe Torelli (1658–1709), the concerto acquired a distinctive style. Published after his death in 1709 by his brother Felice, the twelve concertos of Op. 8 constitute one of the great achievements of the baroque period. The principal traits that mark the mature concerto are here displayed: the fast-slow-fast sequence of movements, the ritornello form, and the virtuoso flights of the soloists. In six of the concertos there is only one concertante violin; in the other six, two such violins.

The ritornello form is an application of the vocal refrain structure to instrumental music. The music of the opening tutti recurs as a whole or part in different keys between solo sections and again at the end. It is the form of most fast movements of concertos with soloists until approximately 1760, when this form became modified by the classic sonata and sinfonia. Torelli apparently did not arrive at the ritornello structure until the end of his career, which he spent almost entirely in Bologna as violinist at San Petronio. The numerous concertos—with trumpets and oboes and written for this church—that have not been dated undoubtedly contributed to the crystallization of the form in Op. 8. The fast-slow-fast pattern with occasional introductory adagio movements became established in Torelli's Op. 6 (1698), containing twelve concertos for church use. Some of these contain also solo passages for one or two violins (e.g., Op. 6, No. 10; in "Nagels Musik-Archiv," No. 70).

Torelli's fast movements of Op. 8 are generally based on the fugal method. The opening tutti usually engages the first and second violin sections and sometimes the violas in a fugal exposition over a basso continuo foundation. The three to five further tutti may contain further expositions or single statements of the subject. Between these tutti, the violin soloist or soloists, accompanied by the bass, launch into figurative work usually unrelated to the fugal subject. Both the tutti and solos tend to be modulatory and to close with a cadence. The pattern of cadences is often tonic; dominant; tonic; relative minor or major or other related key; subdominant or dominant; and, finally, tonic. Some good examples of this structure are the first and last movements of Nos. 3 and 7 (*GMB* 257), and the first movement of No. 9. Occasionally the roles of the tutti and solos in the fugal structure are reversed, as in the first movements of Nos. 1 and 2, in which the solos are expository and the tutti episodic.

Framed by the two fast movements is usually a complex of slow-fast-slow sections. The outstanding set of this type is the Largo-Allegro-Largo of No. 9. This begins with an intense operatic arioso in triple time, followed by a courante-derived fast section with brilliant broken-chord figures in the solo violin, after which the conclusion of the first Largo is recalled.

More than Torelli, Tommaso Albinoni (1671–1750) seems to have felt the influence of Corelli, for often he resorted to the reinforced trio-sonata texture, sometimes side by side with a more modern movement. Such a one is the first movement of Op. 5, No. 5 (1707), whose first ritornello has the thematic multiplicity that became an almost standard feature of the late baroque concerto. The opening ritornello consists of three sections, the first fugal, of four measures, then two homophonic sections of three and six measures, each with its own theme. Only the head-theme is used for the internal tutti. Torelli's Op. 8, No. 8 (*HAM* II, 246), it should be noted, is similarly constructed. A further development of this technique is exemplified by Op. 9 (c. 1721–1722), No. 9. This concerto for two oboes exploits a manifold contrast of instrumental groups: the full orchestra with oboes, the same without oboes, the ripieno violins and violas without continuo, and the oboes with this ripieno group. The opening tutti announces three ideas, a ın the concerto grosso, b in the violin-viola group, and c in the concerto grosso. Then the oboes state a fourth idea, which they will keep as their own, while the tutti return with a and c and the violin-viola group with b. Thus the thematic contrast is tied to instrumental byplay as in the later sinfonia concertante.

The greatest and most prolific writer of concertos was Antonio Vivaldi (c. 1669–1741). Of the more than 450 of various types extant, some are for a single solo instrument, chiefly the violin, and others are for several solo instruments. Some 50 do not employ solo instruments but, like the approximately 20 sinfonie, are for full orchestra. Vivaldi sometimes labeled these *concerto a 4* or *concerto ripieno* (full concerto). The quantity and variety of Vivaldi's instrumental music reflect his professional activity as a virtuoso violinist, sought-out teacher of violin, musical director, and composer of many operas and sacred works. From 1703 to 1740, with interruptions for trips and service elsewhere, he was a teacher of violin, director of concerts, and choirmaster at the Seminario musicale dell'Ospitale della Pietà in Venice, a combination of musical conservatory for girls, orphanage, nunnery, and convent-school. Many of Vivaldi's concertos and symphonies were written for faculty associates and student ensembles in this school. As was to be expected in a man so immersed in the musical life of his times, Vivaldi's style felt the currents of musical fashion, from the high baroque of his earliest published works to the preclassical and *galant* style of some of the fruits of his old age.

The collection of concertos that established his European reputation, *L'Estro armonico* (The Harmonic Fancy, Op. 3, Amsterdam, 1712), presents the concerto form at its most balanced and typical moment. All but three of the twelve are in the fast-slow-fast sequence, the others having an extra slow movement at the beginning. Numbers 3, 6, 9, and 12 are for solo violin; the others, for more than one string instrument, may be called, as they sometimes were in Vivaldi's day, concerti grossi. Op. 3, No. 8, for two "violini obbligati" (first movement in *HAM* II, 270) illustrates many of the characteristics of Vivaldi's approach. In the first Allegro he strung together several thematic

Women singers and string players entertain guests with a concert in a convent in Venice. The performers are arranged on three balconies, at the left. Painting by Francesco Guardi. (Munich, Alte Pinacothek.)

ideas at the outset, like Albinoni, and from these he drew the material of the internal and closing ritornelli. These ideas may be labeled with the letters from a to e, as in Example 8-14. Of the seven tutti (T), T2 (measures 23–25) uses theme e; T3 (measures 37–47), mixed with soli, uses c and a; T4 (measures 51–54), a; T5 (measures 62–65), d; T6 (measures 68–71), a; and T7 (measures 78–93), mixed with soli, themes b, c, e, b, and e, in that order. Theme b also appears in several of the soli. The first two soli (at measures 16 and 25) are linked by a common theme exclusive to the concertino (x in Example 8-14). Surpassing Albinoni in thematic diversity and multiplicity, this mosaic of homophonically conceived melodic subjects departs radically from the single-minded fugal approach of Corelli or Torelli. Yet the subtle motivic links between the themes and the continuous drive of the rhythm permit the listener to grasp the movement as a unity. The clear and simplified tonal routing (i-III-iv-i or a–C–d–a) subjects this riot of inventiveness to a commanding form.

Two traits revealed in this example—additive construction, as opposed to the spinning out of a single subject, and interpenetration of solo and tutti material—are hallmarks of Vivaldi's early style. But he preferred no one structural frame for the Allegro, such as the five tonally stable tutti and four

**EXAMPLE 8-14**   A. Vivaldi, *Concerto, Op. 3, No. 8,* Allegro

modulatory soli that some composers of this period favored. There have been few composers, indeed, who have so avoided casting their works into ready molds as Vivaldi. The slow movements also take many shapes; if there is any general tendency in them, it is to reduce the scoring to a trio or duo and to imitate the operatic aria of affections. The final Allegros are mainly in triple or compound meter, often based on a dance type. They usually follow the procedures of the first Allegro but in a casual and whimsical way. They also tend to be less complex thematically, though there are exceptions, such as Op. 3, No. 10, for four violins, which has extended polythematic ritornelli.

In contrast to these early works, Vivaldi's concertos of the 1720s show new approaches to melodic construction and expression and a simplification of structure. The composer seems torn between writing extended monothematic ritornelli like those of the first Allegro of Op. 9 (*La Cetra,* Amsterdam, 1728) and No. 10 (F. I, 49; P. 103, Vol. 124)[3] and ritornelli with an even greater profusion of subjects than before. Melody tends to be constructed in static groups of two or four measures, often immediately repeated or symmetrically counterposed. The Largo of Op. 9, No. 2 (F. I, 51; P. 214, Vol. 126), offers many examples of the new *galant* style with its frequent cadences, trills, and triplets (Example 8-15; the entire movement is in *NAWM* 93).

---

[3]The numbers preceded by F are those of the classification of Antonio Fanna, the founder of the Istituto italiano Antonio Vivaldi, the sponsor of the complete edition. The Roman numeral stands for the class, such as I, concertos for violin, and the Arabic number for the nonchronological numbering within this class. Numbers preceded by P are those assigned by Marc Pincherle in his thematic index in Vol. II of *Antonio Vivaldi et la musique instrumentale* (Paris: Librairie Floury, 1948). The volume numbers refer to the complete edition published by Edizioni Ricordi.

EXAMPLE 8-15  Vivaldi, *Concerto for Violin, Op. 9, No. 2*, Largo

Violino Pricipale

Vc. B.C.

These tendencies became most pronounced in Vivaldi's last published collection, Op. 12 for solo violin (Amsterdam, c. 1729–1730). Number 5 of this group (F. I, 86; P. 344, Vol. 183) shows clearly that the new operatic style emanating from the Neapolitan and Venetian composers (and in which Vivaldi participated as an operatic composer) thoroughly impregnated his instrumental style. In the first Allegro the repetitious closing theme of the ritornello has a decided comic opera flavor (Example 8-16). The solo figura-

EXAMPLE 8-16  A. Vivaldi *Concerto for Violin, Op. 12, No. 5*, Allegro

Violino principale
Violino I
Violino II

Viole
Violonecelli

Contrabassi
Basso continuo

tion, full of graces and triplets, avoids the bold violinistic leaps of earlier works in favor of diatonic vocal coloratura. Also notable are the moments of delicate chromaticism in the manner of the sensitive or sentimental style, later known in Germany as *empfindsamer Stil* (Example 8-17).

**EXAMPLE 8-17**  A. Vivaldi, *Concerto for Violin, Op. 12, No. 5*, Allegro

Johann Philipp Kirnberger (1721–1783), the noted pupil of J. S. Bach, was to size up these developments with acumen when he wrote the article "Musik" about 1760 for J. G. Sulzer's encyclopedia of the arts:

In the past century, through the introduction of the opera and concerto, music has received a new impetus. The arts of harmony are beginning to be pushed forward, and more melismatic ornaments are being introduced into singing. Thereby the so-called *galant* or free and light style and much greater variety of beat and movement have gradually appeared. It cannot be denied that the melodic language of the emotions has gained extraordinarily thereby. . . . Certainly much has been gained in fire and liveliness and other manifold shades of feeling through the multiplicity of the new melodic invention and even through clever transgressions of the strict harmonic rules. But only great masters know how to take advantage of them.

That music in recent times has the nice and very supple genius and the fine sensibility (*Empfindsamkeit*) of the Italians to thank is beyond doubt. But also most of what has spoiled the true taste has also come out of Italy, particularly the dominance of melodies that say nothing and merely tickle the ear.[4]

[4]J. G. Sulzer, *Allgemeine Theorie der schönen Künste* (Biel: Heilmannischer Buchhandlung, 1777), III, pp. 438–39.

One is inclined to agree with Kirnberger's mixed reactions to this music, for despite its charm and tender emotion it lacks the craftsmanship, vigor, and depth of Vivaldi's earlier works.

The symphonies and ripieno concertos of Vivaldi's late period are the most steeped in the preclassic style. The Concerto for Strings and Harpsichord in A Major (F. XI, 4; P. 235, Vol. 8), though not one of the few works in this category that can be dated precisely, obviously belongs with the late works. The first movement may be described as a telescoping of the normal form by eliminating the soli. The first ritornello, eighteen measures long, modulates from the tonic to the dominant, stating no less than eight different themes, each of which is either immediately repeated or briefly developed by sequences. The next, of twenty-one measures, restates the same material while modulating to c♯ minor. A ten-measure transition in which the opening motive is stated in c♯ and f♯ leads to the return of the main key. The material of the first section is then presented without modulation. This tri-strophic form is found in many early classical sonatas, concertos, and symphonies.

The final movement of this concerto is built on the same plan but within the bipartite dance form. Here the opening section of thirty-four measures can be divided into a tonic group of ten measures (Example 8-18), a modulatory group of twelve measures, and a closing dominant group of twelve measures. After the repeat sign the same material somewhat abridged is heard twice more on the dominant and the dominant of the dominant, after which the opening section is recapitulated entirely in the tonic. A typical

**EXAMPLE 8-18**  A. Vivaldi, *Concerto F. XI, 4,* Allegro

method of melodic construction is illustrated below. A short segment, open-ended melodically, harmonically, and rhythmically, is followed by another short segment that completes the thought. This symmetrical phraseology operates on several levels. A number of eighteenth-century theorists compared the effect of this process to subject and predicate in a sentence (abbreviated S and P in the example).[5] The slow rate of harmonic change, owed partly to the probable folk-dance origin of the subject, is quite characteristic of Vivaldi's late style.

From the synthesizer of the high baroque concerto style that he was in his youth, Vivaldi thus turned in his old age to experiment with classical procedures. Stirred by the rapid changes in the musical practices of the theater, he continually adapted the older forms to new content.

The first wave of Italian influence on concerto writing in Germany came on the heels of the well-traveled Georg Muffat, who made a profession of uniting the Italian and French styles. The twelve chamber concerti grossi of his *Auserlesene Instrumentalmusik* (Selected Instrumental Music, 1701) follow Corelli in their augmented sonata texture. Six of them, in fact, are reworkings of sonatas *a 5* published in Muffat's *Armonico tributo* (1682). The inclusion of minuets and rondeaux, the fuller ripieno writing, the simpler melodic idiom, and the frequency of dotted rhythms betray a strong French influence. Also based on the Corelli design and texture are the concerti grossi of Handel, written in England and reflecting conservative tastes there (Op. 3, c. 1734; Op. 6, c. 1739), but they are filled with woodwind colors unknown to Corelli and the strong contrasts of mood of the high baroque, from the pompous and majestic opening movements to the graceful melodies, verging on the *galant,* of some of the others.

A second wave of influence came from the direction of Torelli, Albinoni, and Vivaldi. Johann Gottfried Walther (1684–1748), Weimar town organist and a good friend and distant relative of J. S. Bach, arranged for solo organ several concertos by Torelli and Albinoni. Bach himself, during his tenure as court organist, composer, and music director in the same city between 1714 and 1717, arranged nine of Vivaldi's concertos from Op. 3, 4, and 7 for solo organ or for one and more harpsichords with orchestra. In his original works in the concerto medium, Bach leaned greatly upon Vivaldi for the forms and types of opening and slow movements, while he enlarged upon the fugal allegro of earlier Italians for his last movement. There are three concerti grossi in the set of six dedicated to Christian Ludwig, Margrave of Brandenburg, in 1721–Nos. 2, 4, and 5–and three ripieno concertos. In vastness of conception and complexity of thematic and contrapuntal relationships they surpass the work of any of the Italians.

The first movements of Nos. 2 and 5 follow the Vivaldi model. As in

[5] See Leonard Ratner, "Eighteenth Century Theorists of Musical Period Structure," *MQ,* XLII (1956), 438–54.

Vivaldi's Op. 3, No. 8, which Bach transcribed for solo organ (BWV 593), the opening tutti presents a series of thematic segments from which subsequent tutti are drawn, while the first soli announces an idea that will remain the exclusive property of the soli. In No. 5 Bach draws three variants from the soli theme.

EXAMPLE 8-19   J. S. Bach, *Brandenburg* Concerto, No. 5, Allegro

The concertino of No. 2, consisting of trumpet, recorder, oboe, and violin, does not merely double the ripieno parts in the tutti but bears its share of thematic content. This follows the procedure in Vivaldi's Op. 3, No. 10, for four violins, which Bach arranged for four harpsichords (BWV 1065). In *Brandenburg* No. 5, on the other hand, Bach followed the more common practice of letting the concertino of flute, violin, and harpsichord be submerged in the ripieno group during the tutti, the flute remaining silent, the violin joining the first violins, and the harpsichord returning to its normal chordal filling.

Bach's perennial quest for fully integrated designs is everywhere in evidence. The patchy effect risked by having many disparate thematic segments is avoided by keeping a steady rhythmic figure in the bass or by having the parts interchange rhythmic motives. In both Nos. 2 and 5, the ripieno instruments occasionally play the head theme from the ritornello softly as an accompaniment to the soli. In No. 5, two of the three tutti themes appear in the soli as well. A desire for symmetry governs the design of the outstanding feature of the first movement of No. 5, the extended cadenza for unaccompanied harpsichord that caps the long final soli. In a shorter early version of this cadenza,[6] Bach carried forward the momentum of thirty-second notes of the harpsichord's part in the concertino for a spectacular and startling finish. In the final version of this cadenza, he interrupted the rapid motion to recapitulate and develop the exclusive soli theme before returning to the rapid figuration. Thus he counterbalanced the tutti recapitulation with reminiscences by the harpsichord.

As Vivaldi was accustomed to do, Bach reduced the orchestra for the slow movements. Whereas No. 2 lacks tutti-solo contrast, this is ingeniously

[6]Heinrich Besseler, ed. J. S. Bach, *Neue Ausgabe sämtlicher Werke*, Serie VII, Bd. 2, *Revisionsbericht* (Kassel & Basel: Bärenreiter-Verlag, 1956), pp. 120–22.

preserved in No. 5. Here a trio ensemble with harpsichord continuo playing *forte* alternates with sections *a 4*, played softly, in which the fourth part is the right hand of the keyboard. Another antithesis results from the fact that the trio sections are fugal while the *a 4* sections are episodic.

The final movements of *Brandenburg* Nos. 2, 4, and 5 are fugues. The studious approach to counterpoint, still strong in Albinoni's concertos but generally fading in Italy at this time, was revived in these concertos by Bach. As was common in Italy, the tutti plays the expositions while the soli are mainly active in the episodes. The most unusual of the fugues is that of No. 5, for it is a composite of fugal method, gigue rhythms, concerto contrast, and da capo-aria form. Rather than rely upon the bipartite scheme of the gigues of Corelli, Bach introduced a long middle section based on a cantabile version (Example 8-20b) of the fugue subject (Example 8-20a). After the cadence at measure 232 Bach wrote "da capo," signifying a repeat of the first seventy-eight measures, after which is written in the autograph "Fine," meaning the piece comes to an end here. The contrast of affection strongly resembles that of the da capo aria, and, as in the aria, the form permits a leisurely exploitation of every potential of the subject matter.

**EXAMPLE 8-20**   J. S. Bach, *Brandenburg* Concerto No. 5, Allegro

## BIBLIOGRAPHICAL NOTES

Neglected subjects, until recently the baroque sonata and concerto are now covered by a number of excellent books. William S. Newman's *The Sonata in the Baroque Era*, 3rd ed. (New York: W. W. Norton & Co., Inc., 1972) surveys the topic with exhaustive bibliographic detail and great insight into the development of forms and styles. Arthur Hutchings' *The Baroque Concerto* (New York: W. W. Norton & Co., Inc., 1965) is a useful survey and guide to the music. Studies of the leading composers are also recommended reading: *Corelli* (New York: W. W. Norton & Co., Inc., 1956) and *Vivaldi* (same publisher, 1957), both by Marc Pincherle; *Giovanni Maria Bononcini of Modena* by William Klenz (Durham, N. C.: Duke University Press, 1962), which has valuable accounts of the dance types and contains many complete sonatas by Bononcini and Cazzati; *Antonio Vivaldi: His Life and Work* (London: Faber and Faber; Berkeley: University of California Press, 1970) by Walter Kolneder, translated by Bill Hopkins; and *François Couperin and the French Classical Tradition* (London: Denis Dobson, 1950; New York: Dover, 1968) by Wilfrid Mellers. Concerning Purcell, see the bibliography at the end of Chapter Ten.

An essential related field has received at last a definitive and readable study: David D. Boyden's *The History of Violin Playing from its Origins to 1761 and its Relationship to the Violin and Violin Music* (London: Oxford University Press, 1965).

The best bibliography of original sources, though confined to Italy, is Claudio Sartori's *Bibliografia della musica strumentale italiana stampata in Italia fino al 1700* (Florence: Leo S. Olschki, 1952). It contains prefaces, letters of dedication, and tables of contents of published collections up to 1700.

There is much about the economic, social, and professional background of music making as well as about stylistic development in Eleanor Selfridge-Field's *Venetian Instrumental Music from Gabrieli to Vivaldi* (Oxford: Blackwell, 1975).

Three specialized anthologies with extended introductions in German (but also available in English) are in the series *Das Musikwerk*: *Die italienische Triosonate*, edited by Erich Schenk, and *Das Concerto Grosso* and *Das Solokonzert*, edited by Hans Engel (Cologne: Arno Volk Verlag Hans Gerig K. G., 1954, 1962, 1964).

The standard edition of Corelli is *Les Oeuvres de Arcangelo Corelli*, edited by J. Joachim and F. Chrysander (5 vols.; London: Augener, 1888–1891), and some of the sonatas are available also edited by Walter Kolneder (Mainz: Schott & Co.). A new complete edition of the works of Corelli, *Historisch-kritische Gesamtausgabe der musikalischen Werke* (Cologne: Arno Volk Verlag Hans Gerig KG) began to appear in 1976 under the leadership of Hans Joachim Marx. Purcell's sonatas are in his *Works*, V (London, New York: Novello, Ewen and Co., 1893), and in a new edition by Karl Schleifer (Leipzig: Peters, 1958). Biber's sonatas are in *DTOe* XII/2. Stradella's *Sonata di viole* is edited by Edward H. Tarr (Paris: Editions Costallat, 1968).

A large number of Vivaldi's instrumental works have been published in his *Opere* (Milan: Ricordi, 1947–), which is a continuing series. One opera, *La Fida Ninfa* (1732), has been edited by Raffaello Monterosso in "Istituta e Monumenta," Series 1, No. 3 (Cremona: Athenaeum Cremonense, 1964). Georg Muffat's concertos are in *DTOe* XI (1904) and LXXXIX (1953), edited by Erwin Luntz and Erich Schenk. Handel's concertos are in the *Hallische Händel-Ausgabe*, Series IV, Vols. 11 (1959), edited by Frederick Hudson, and 14 (1961), edited by Adolf Hoffman and Hans F. Redlich (Kassel and Basel: Bärenreiter-Verlag).

# NINE

# LUTE AND HARPSICHORD MUSIC
# IN FRANCE

Of the nations of Europe, France managed best to resist foreign musical influences through the baroque period. French musicians in the seventeenth century enjoyed a long period of relatively undisturbed cultivation of their own soil. Even instrumental idioms—which, lacking a close tie to language habits, tend to be homogenized by border-crossing musicians, printed editions, and instruments—preserved in France a distinct character. It is doubtful whether the categories and characteristics of baroque music that have emerged in preceding chapters, or the term *baroque* itself, can be applied with meaning to the most personal expressions of French composers.

The reasons for this independence were several. King Louis XIV during his long reign—from 1643 to 1715—concentrated on building up an image of France as the leader of Europe and a unified state. Even the arts were subject to national policy. Although, during Louis's minority and youth when Cardinal Mazarin (d. 1661) was the effective ruler, troupes of musicians were brought in from the Cardinal's native Rome (most notably a production of Luigi Rossi's *Orfeo* in 1647), the net result was not Italianization of theatrical music but the setting up of an operatic monopoly by royal privilege that effectively excluded foreign composers. Another factor was the strong guild of musicians, the *menestriers*, whose strict rules of apprenticeship and accreditation made it difficult for outsiders to enter the musical profession. The central social function performed by music in France was to accompany court dancing and ballet entertainments, and this also tended to concentrate creative effort in a special direction.

The native traits of French music at this age may be recognized in a short but typical example by François Couperin (1668–1733), who summed up in his work the musical tradition of the age of Louis XIV (Example 9-1). *La Persévérance* (Perseverance) is the sixth *couplet* (i.e., strophe, or variation) of a chaconne entitled *Les Folies françoises, ou les Dominos*, which, in turn, forms the last half of a suite of pieces for harpsichord that makes up the thirteenth *ordre* of Couperin's *Pièces de clavecin* (Book III, 1722). This chaconne is a predecessor of Schumann's *Carnaval* in that its strophes represent masqueraders in a French carnival, each costumed in a different cloak, or domino, whose color reflects the affection or virtue personified by the mask. "Perseverance" wears a cloak of linen gray. Some of the other dominoes are *La Virginité* (Virginity), *La Pudeur* (Modesty), *L'ardeur* (Ardor), *L'espérance* (Hope), *La Fidélité* (Fidelity), *La Langueur* (Indolence), *La Coquéterie* (Flirtatiousness), *La Jalousie Taciturne* (Silent Jealousy), and *La Frénesie, ou le Désespoir* (Frenzy, or Despair). The titles seem intended more to mock the affections than to achieve concreteness of expression; they represent postures rather than passions. They tell us less about the music than about the intended effect of Couperin's books of pieces on the amateur harpsichordist, who is to be both enticed and amused by the innocent play with masks of real emotions. The music is conceived not in the thorough-bass texture of melody-plus-bass-plus-filler-chords but in three distinct lines, which are somewhat obscured by the lutelike breaking of the melodic continuity in the left hand.

The chaconne is one of the dances frequently found in the ballet music of Lully and his predecessors, having made its debut in the *Ballet des Fées de la Forêt de Saint-Germain* (1625) in an "Entrée des Chaconistes espagnoles." Originally known as a *chacona*, it was a harmonic pattern used by Spanish guitarists to accompany the refrains of romances and similar lengthy sung poems: I–V–VI–V. The chaconne of which *La Persévérance* is the sixth couplet has the pattern i–V–i–V–V/iv–iv–V–i. Each eight-measure pattern consists of two halves, the first ending in the dominant, the second proceeding from the dominant of the subdominant to the tonic. This spare frame is dressed up with *agréments*, as the ornaments were called.

The principal ornaments were those illustrated here, the *pincé* (mordent; literally "plucked" or "pinched"), the *tremblement* (trill), and the *port de voix* (upward-resolving approggiatura), which came, as may be seen in the example, in several forms. The ornaments had an expressive function, intensifying dissonance, creating suspense, marking climaxes or closes. But they also underlined the rhythm, as drums do in a dance orchestra. For example, the pincé in the first measure puts a stress on the second beat, reinforcing the prolongation of that melodic note characteristic of the chaconne. The tremblements in the second measure, on the other hand, intensify the harmonic motion through dissonance and are a source of continuity. The port de voix in the third measure underplays the normal stress of the first beat, accumulating rhythmic energy for the downbeat of the fourth measure. The *coulés* (appoggiaturas) in measure 14 are another means of achieving continuity. In measure 3 the coulés, which were written out by the composer, contribute to the anacrusis effect of the penultimate measure of the phrase. These are only a few of the ornaments used in Couperin's music, but they illustrate the main function of French ornamentation, which is to achieve momentum and articulate temporal and harmonic events in the structure.

It should be emphasized that the agréments were not developed to make up for the lack of sustaining power of the harpsichord, as is often said. The same ornaments are to be found in music for string and wind instruments; indeed, some of them originated in the voice. In the lute, the instrument in which ornaments first appeared in quantity, they did serve to prolong the sound and to fill the silences between the notes of a plucked melody. It is also true that in instruments such as the lute, harpsichord, and organ, in which the player cannot control the volume or attack of individual notes, ornaments can create the illusion of sharp, soft, strong, or weak attacks. The ornaments make the music more subtle by obscuring the melody while making it more obvious by marking the rhythm.

From this analysis it is evident that Couperin's little piece departs in several significant ways from the typical Italian music of the period around 1700. It is not conceived in thorough-bass texture; it is not spun out by

**EXAMPLE 9-1** F. Couperin, Ordre 13, *La Persévérance, sous le Domino Gris du lin*. The realization of the ornamentation given is one of the many possible interpretations.

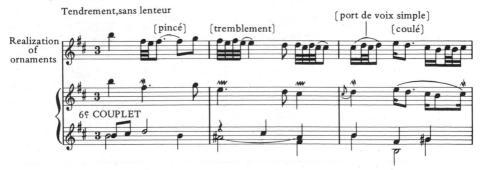

**EXAMPLE 9-1** (Cont.)

178

motivic development; it is not really concerned with the expression of the affections, although it plays with them. It is broken up into little phrases which are combined to form balanced periods; it is overladen with ornaments that, unlike those of Italian music, are not there mainly to express the passions or to display virtuosity; it is not primarily written for the professional musician and virtuoso but for the amateur with limited technique and short span of attention.

The French harpsichord style as it flowered in Couperin's work was the final bloom of a hundred years' growth of French instrumental music. Its ancestry goes back to the lute transcriptions of favorite dances at the beginning of the seventeenth century. The French lute repertory of the preceding century, like the Italian, consisted largely of transcriptions of polyphonic chansons and arrangements of dance tunes. The popularity of the chansons declined after 1600, while the songs and dances from the court ballet gained favor.

## BALLET DE COUR

The *ballet de cour* was a French adaptation of a type of entertainment used in Italy to honor important visitors or events such as weddings and baptisms. It took root in France with the entertainments for the marriage of Catherine de' Medici and King Henry II in 1533. The ingredients of these festivals—unconnected intermezzos between acts of plays, entries of masked dancers in both indoor and outdoor feasts, pantomimes, processions of decorated floats in public parades, dances in which the courtiers participated—were blended into a new union of the arts in the ballet de cour.

The first ballet with a grand unifying design and a central theme was *Circe*, commissioned by Catherine de Medici for the marriage of her sister, Mademoiselle de Vaudémont with the Duc de Joyeuse in 1581. Known as the *Ballet comique de la reine*, it was created by the violinist and ballet dancing master from Piedmont, Italy, Baltazarini di Belgioioso (Balthasar de Beaujoyeulx). Dancing masters were accustomed to play tunes, often of their own making, on a small pocket fiddle as they instructed their noble pupils, and it is therefore not a coincidence that many of them were violinists. Lully was famous as a violinist and composer of dance airs before he began composing operas.

Baltazarini conceived of himself as reviving in *Circe* the long abandoned ancient drama: "I have blended together poetry, music and dancing, in a manner which, if ever done before, must have been in such remote antiquity that it may now well be called new. . . . I have, however, given the first place to dancing, and assigned the second and third to poetry and music, in order to gratify at once the eye, ear and understanding."[1] The libretto was by the King's Chaplain, Nicole de La Chesnaye; the principal music was by Girard de Beaulieu, one of the Queen's musicians, and Jacques Salmon, a singer and *valet de chambre* of the King.[2] Besides instrumental music for the dances there were solo and choral verses set to music in a style approximating the *vers mesuré à l'antique*, in which the theoretical length of vowels rather than their stress was observed in setting words to music. The show ended with a grand ballet, in which only noblemen took part, wearing black masks with a crest of feathers, and tunics enriched with gold and tinsel that left the legs bare except for stockings. The grand ballet was a figured dance in Italian style; that is, the dancers traced various geometric patterns on the floor, circular, square, or triangular.

Eventually the ballet de cour acquired a conventional sequence of events: a grand chorus, addressed to the King and ladies, followed by a set of entries of dancers illustrating the main theme. Each entry was preceded by a *récit*—a song, often strophic—that narrated the situation, accompanied by a lute. The dances were grouped in sets, or *suites*, in which slow alternated with fast. The entertainment closed with the *grand ballet*. The orchestra that accompanied the dances was dominated by strings—members of the violin family, approximately twenty-four in number—augmented by cornetts, lutes, oboes, flutes, and bagpipes. The music was usually scored in five parts, without thorough bass. Not all the instrumental music was simply dance music; often it accompanied pantomime and delineated a mood, a nationality, or a grotesque character, or it imitated sounds of birds, battles, hunting calls, storms, and the like.

## DANCE MUSIC ARRANGED FOR THE LUTE

It was music such as this that the lutanists arranged and collected. Robert Ballard (c. 1575–after 1650), son of the music printer of the same name, published in 1611 a collection of pieces arranged for the lute drawn largely from ballets de cour. The *second chant* of the Ballet de la Reyne (also used in the *Ballet du Roy Henry IV* of 1601) was arranged by Ballard as in Example 9-2. It consists of two strains. Each one, of four measures, is immediately varied. To vary a musical statement in the way that measures 5–8 vary 1–4 and 13–16 vary 9–12 was to "double" it—*doubler*—and the product was called a *double*. This doubling was applied traditionally to the French court song, or *air de cour*, which was sung in its plain setting, or *simple*, the first

---

[1] Trans. by H. Sutherland Edwards in "A Forgotten Centenary," *The Lute*, October 1, 1884, pp. 218–20.

[2] A reprint of the libretto has been issued by G. A. Caula (Turin, 1962).

time, then varied with embellishments. In Example 9-2 the doubles preserve both the harmony and melodic outline of the melody. The free mixture of chordal and linear texture is typical of the lute. The linear motion has to be reconstructed by the modern transcriber, for the duration of any one note is only as long as vibration continues or until another note is fingered on the same string. Except for chords that are plucked with several fingers at once or strummed, the player sounds only one note at a time, alternating thumb and other fingers. In measures 12–15 an illusion of two parts is created by alternating higher and lower strings. A free texture, called *style brisé*, results, in which inner voices enter at will and soon evaporate. This is a texture native to the lute. Keyboard composers appropriated it because they liked the aerated, loose mixture of polyphony and chords, particularly its richness of rhythmic nuance and its animation.

**EXAMPLE 9-2** R. Ballard, *Ballet de la Reyne*, second *chant*, arranged for lute; transcribed by André Souris and Sylvie Spycket

A generation later, Ennemond Gautier (c. 1575–1651; known as Le vieux Gautier to distinguish him from his cousin Denis) adopted a more linear, less chordal manner, in which ornaments, mainly tremblements and appoggiaturas, help to define the rhythmic stresses previously marked by chords. We are fortunate to be able to observe the transfer of the lute idiom to the keyboard in an anonymous double for harpsichord of a gigue by Gautier, *La Poste* (both are in *NAWM* 101), for lute. Most of the ornaments in the Gautier piece were indicated in the tablature by means of the symbols that appear in the transcription. However, some of the ornaments were written out—for example, the endings of the tremblements in measures 3 and 8 and the broken third in measure 9, called *arpegé*. In the harpsichord version even more of the ornaments were written out, or written-out endings were combined with ornaments represented by signs. Eventually various compound signs, such as that on E in measure 4, were developed to include these endings. A rather exhaustive table of these as well as the simple ornaments was included by Jean-Henry d'Anglebert in his *Pièces de clavecin* in 1689.

Example 9-3 gives the first half of the gigue. The duple meter was quite common for gigues at this time; later they were almost all in 6/4, 9/8, or 12/8. But the form of this gigue is the familiar one encountered in Corelli—that of two repeated sections, the first ending on the dominant, the second on the tonic. The linear character of the lute version is reinforced by the imitation in measure 4 of the motive in measure 3, which in turn is a transposition of the opening motive. The same motive is heard again in two parallel voices in measure 6. This contrapuntal and motivic development removes this gigue from the category of functional ballet music of earlier days and places it in the more sophisticated solo repertory of the private chamber and academy. The harpsichord version reaches a height of preciosity with its rather overwhelming chain of embellishments.

The lute was the most common instrument of the amateur in France before the harpsichord assumed that role in the last half of the seventeenth century. A contemporary, Tallemant des Réaux, bore witness to the prestige of the lute among the nobility in a story about the regent Queen mother, Marie de' Medici and her minister Cardinal Richelieu: ". . . although quite old, she decided to learn to play the lute. . . . She sent for [Ennemond] Gautier. Here everyone plays the lute. The Cardinal learned it also; and it was the most comical thing you can imagine to see him taking lessons from Gautier."[3]

The instrument then in use had, in addition to the traditional six courses of strings, five courses of bass strings that did not pass over the fingerboard but were tuned diatonically to suit the key of a piece. (One refers to "courses" rather than strings, because lutes had all but the highest string

[3] M. Monmerque, ed., *Les historiettes de Tallemant des Réaux*, 2nd. rev. ed. (Paris: Garnier Frères, 1861), Vol. II, pp. 164–65.

**EXAMPLE 9-3a**   E. Gautier, *La Poste*, for lute, transcribed by André Souris

**EXAMPLE 9-3b**   Anonymous, *Gigue*, for harpsichord

pincé

coulé

port de voix

183

doubled at the unison or octave.) It was not necessary to read the usual staff notation to play the lute, since its music was circulated in the form of tablatures, which showed the placement of fingers on frets that marked off semitones on the fingerboard. This made the instrument and its repertory accessible to the musically unschooled. Still, it was not an easy instrument to master, and the tuning of sixteen or more strings was an awesome hurdle. There is probably more than a grain of truth in the complaint of a layman of the time that he had often heard lutanists tuning up but rarely had the privilege of hearing one play. Players of the lute and admirers of its music were an in-group, frequenters of elegant salons, with a mystical reverence for its muffled, intimate, pensive music. Lute fanciers communicated in an almost secret language, assigning to pieces names that had meaning only for initiates, even resorting to initials, as in the title of a piece by Denis Gaultier "A. d. M. L. b." (L'Adieu de Mademoiselle Le Brun). Other pieces had titles such as *l'Immortelle, La Caressante, l'Homicide*, which undoubtedly helped insiders to identify familiar favorites. When a lutanist died, a colleague would compose for him a *tombeau*, a musical epitaph.

Denis Gaultier (c. 1600–1672) was the leading exponent of this tradition in mid-century. His music is conceived expressly in terms of the instrument; there is no pretense at part writing or full harmony. His pieces, rarely more than twenty-four measures long, are, aside from a few unmeasured preludes, almost all in the dance form of two repeated sections, and, whether or not so labeled, they are mainly allemandes, courantes, sarabandes, pavanes, or gigues. The tombeaux are highly abstracted allemandes or pavanes, two dances that are closely related. The tombeau he wrote for his wife (he also wrote one for himself), *Tombeau de Mademoiselle Gaultier* (*TEM* 39), an allemande, exemplifies several features of this category as well as of Gaultier's style generally (Example 9-4). It is written in f♯ minor, the key known to lutanists as *le ton de la chèvre* (key of the she-goat), a tonality reserved for serious, melancholic expressions. It begins with a mysterious succession of chords that one does not suspect until the end of measure 3 is leading to the subdominant. The f♯ pedal, in spite of the frequent repetition of the bass note, must be partly imagined, because the instrument cannot sustain it between its reiterations. Amidst the ornaments, both written-out and implied, the scattering of chord tones, and the delayed and anticipated beats, lurks a simple, recitative-like melody. The first eight measures preserve the neat phrasing of earlier dance pieces, just as this tombeau's total form is the normal one of two repeated sections with a modulation to the dominant in the middle. But out of this conventional wrapping are unfurled explosive little gestures that mark Gaultier's personal manner. Dissonances are strewn about almost recklessly. In measure 1 the G♯ may be an upbeat port de voix; or is it the resolution of an imagined sustained A suspended against the B? In measure 2, the E is less problematic: a passing tone,

EXAMPLE 9-4  D. Gaultier, *Tombeau de Mademoiselle Gaultier*

because the lower F♯ is doubled by the octave string next to it (by convention not shown in transcriptions). There is no simple explanation for the B in measure 3. In this measure as well as in the first the melodic movement traces a b minor chord, while the harmonic movement traces a tonic f♯ minor, a conflict that is resolved in measure 4. This is normal in a passage over a pedal point, but here the surrounding harmony is hinted at rather than sounded, so that the B has the effect of a long appoggiatura. The repercussions of suspended notes, made necessary by the arpeggiated triple stops, add bite to suspended dissonances, as the D and A over the E's in measure 7, or the F♯ and C♯ in measure 10. It is by such ambiguities and sly insinuations that Gaultier plucked poetry from his lute.

## Lute Style in the Harpsichord

The lutanists cast such a spell that harpsichordists enthusiastically copied their mannerisms, willingly cramping their style with the kinds of compromises and deceptions exacted by the recalcitrant lute but unnecessary on their instrument. Along with the manner they adopted the repertory: dances, preludes, tombeaux, and other characteristic pieces. Favorite pieces for the lute were transcribed for keyboard, as in the collection of works of

Ennemond and Denis Gaultier edited by Perrine, *Pièces de luth en musique* (Lute Pieces in Score), Paris, 1680. Thus one art fed on another, propagating an inbred preciosity. French harpsichordists for a time ignored the capabilities of their own instrument to rival the lutanists in their arena. Accompanying instrument that it was, the harpsichord had to prove itself a vehicle for the virtuoso player. The composer who accomplished this transformation was Jacques Champion de Chambonnières (c. 1602–1672), chamber musician to Louis XIV. He founded what is known as the "French clavecin school" (*clavecin* = harpsichord) carried on by his pupils, Louis Couperin (c. 1626–1661), Jean-Henri d'Anglebert (1628–1691), and Nicolas-Antoine Lebègue (1631–1702).

An exact contemporary of Gaultier, Chambonnières strikes some of the same moods, as in his pavane, *L'entretien des dieux*, he parallels the grave lyricism of Gaultier's tombeaux. The beginning of the second part evokes the sound and technique of plucked strings in the arpeggiated chords, the ubiquitous trills, the dropping in and out of parts, and the staggering of chord tones, resulting in frequent suspensions.

**EXAMPLE 9-5**    J. C. de Chambonnières, *Pavane L'entretien des dieux*

But Chambonnières also discovered some of the native resources of his instrument. In Example 9-5 the resonant low strings sustain a strong bass line that descends diatonically more than an octave to produce the climax in measure 19 with an expansive tenth in the left hand. He also tested the instrument's aptness for drawing out contrapuntal lines, as in the imitative opening of *Les Baricades* (Example 9-6). The courante's fickle swaying between alternate divisions of a six-beat measure into either two or three (hemiola) is here exploited to enhance the independence of the voices through metrical conflict. The combination of dotted notes and leaps in this example brings out the harpsichord's lively percussive qualities. On the other hand,

**EXAMPLE 9-6**  J. C. de Chambonnières, *Les Baricades*

the casual changes of register from measure 7 to 8 and from measure 8 to 9 show that Chambonnières was still not writing consistently in distinct parts.

Both these pieces were published toward the end of Chambonnières's life in his *Les Pieces de clavessin, Livre premier*, 1670. The presence, in this book, of old-fashioned dances such as the pavane, galliard, and canary is evidence of loss of contact with the world of the theater and ballroom and reliance upon older models. Some of the compositions both published and surviving in manuscripts, however, do reflect more recent trends. The chaconne in F in the *Manuscrit Bauyn* (*HAM* 212) follows the form of those found in the Lully operas, alternating a refrain in the deep register with couplets varying somewhat freely a different eight-measure pattern. The refrain pattern, heard four times in the refrain, has both a consistent bass and chord succession (I–IV–V–I). The last piece of Chambonnières's second book, of uncertain date, is also modern: a minuet in rondeau form, on an uncomplicated tune (Example 9-7).

EXAMPLE 9-7  J. C. de Chambonnières, *Menuet*

## GROUPING DANCES BY MAJOR-MINOR KEYS

Although Chambonnières did not publish his pieces in suites, their grouping in the two printed books is significant. Each allemande or pavane is followed by a series of dances in the same key, with an occasional shift from minor to major. Each such set contains one or more courantes and usually one sarabande, and closes most often with a gigue but in single cases with either a galliard, canary, or minuet. Five of the sets consist of only an allemande, several courantes, and a sarabande. The only keys used are a, C, d, D, F, g, and G. These are truly major and minor keys, not modes, even though the pieces in d minor have no flat in the signature. On the other hand, in the sumptuous manuscript of fifty-six lute pieces by Gaultier composed in 1652 for the gentleman-amateur Anne de Chambré under the title *La Rhétorique des Dieux* (Eloquence of the Gods), the pieces are arranged by mode, beginning on C (usually called Ionian), here called Dorian. (Some French writers had adopted the numbering of the modes proposed by Zarlino in 1571 in which the C mode was I, D mode II, and so forth.)[4] On inspection, however, it is evident that the pieces of the *Rhétorique*, which the compiler of the manuscript naively arranged to illustrate the power of the ancient Greek *tonoi*, are not in the twelve modes at all but in a small number of major and minor keys.

Indeed, it was French music teachers, unburdened by the Italian academic tradition, who were the first to discard the fiction of the church modes. Jean Rousseau in his *Méthode claire, certaine et facile, pour apprendre à chanter* (Clear, Sure, and Easy Method for Learning to Sing)[5] recognized only two modes, major and minor, although he did make a distinction between "natural" and "transposed" keys and noted that the affective qualities differed depending on the key to which a mode was transposed.

[4]Zarlino, *Dimostrationi harmoniche* (Venice: Francesco dei Franceschi Senese, 1571), Ragionamento V, Definitione xiv, p. 275). Salomon de Caus in his *Institution harmonique* (Frankfurt: Jan Norton, 1615) adopted Zarlino's numbering, as did numerous others in France, including Marin Mersenne.

[5](Paris: author, 1683), p. 78.

Two-manual harpsichord by Michel Richard, Paris, 1688. This instrument has three choirs: two 8-foot and one 4-foot. (Yale University Collection of Musical Instruments, on loan from the Albert Steinert Collection in the Rhode Island School of Design. Photograph by Thomas Brown.)

There are keys [*Tons*] suited to the serious as are d minor [*D la re mineur*],[6] and a minor [*A mi la mineur*], which are natural keys. There arc keys for gay things, and for those that are marked by grandeur, as are C Major [*C sol ut majeur*], which is natural, and D Major [*D la ré majeur*] which is transposed. There are some for the sad, as g minor [*G re sol mineur*], which is natural, and for the tender, as are e minor [*E si mineur*], and G Major [*G ré sol majeur*], which are transposed. For the laments and other plaintive subjects, there are no keys more appropriate than c minor [*C sol ut mineur*] and f minor [*F ut fa mineur*], which are transposed, and for the devout pieces or sacred songs, F Major [*F ut fa majeur*], which is natural, and A Major [*A mi la majeur*], which is transposed, are most suited. I do not wish, nevertheless, to say that one cannot express the various passions of which I just spoke in other keys than these, but it is certain that those that I have cited are more appropriate than any others.

[6] *D la re* and similar formulations indicate the placement of a note in the Guidonian hand. Thus *D la re* (correctly: *D la sol re*) is d', which is *la* in the soft hexachord starting on f, is *sol* in the hard hexachord starting on g, and *re* in the natural hexachord starting on c' (middle C). See the article "Hexachord" in *Harvard Dictionary of Music*.

Thus C and F Major and a, d, and g minor were natural keys; A, D, and G
Major and c, e, and f minor were transposed keys. Elsewhere Rousseau also
mentioned B♭ Major and B♭ and f♯ minor as transposed keys. By natural
keys Rousseau apparently meant that they could be formed by means of
notes found in the Guidonian hand, which includes B♭ in the c, c′, and c″
octaves, but no other sharps or flats. The inclusion of g minor, in spite of the
frequent use of E♭, is explainable by the custom of assigning a key signature
of one flat to it. Charles Masson (*Nouveau traité des règles pour la composition de la musique*, 1st ed., 1694, not extant; 2nd ed., 1699) still assigned only
one flat to g minor and none to d minor, which he considered the primary
minor key. He did away with the distinction between natural and transposed
and gave the "final" (our tonic), "mediant," and "dominant" (which he called
the "essential notes") for nine major keys and nine minor keys. He omitted
G♭, A♭, D♭, E♭ Major, and g♭, a♭, b♭, d♭ minor. He recognized the relative
major of a minor key by implication, when he gave as the main cadences in
major the final and dominant and in minor the final, mediant, and dominant.
He instructed the composer to end the first part of an "air" or "ouverture"
and to begin the second part in the dominant in major but in the mediant in
minor.

   All of these precepts were already clearly at work in the dances of
Gaultier and Chambonnières, and for the latter the modern keys served as
the means to arrange several dances in a group. Such grouping of dances
ending on the same final, which was practiced as far back as the earliest
ballets de cour, suggests that Chambonnières meant to give the harpsichordist
the option of playing the succession of dances within a key in the order given.

   The *Pièces de clavecin*, 1705, of Gaspard Le Roux, also published as
an unbroken series, are even more suggestive in their arrangement of a
deliberate order. The various series of pieces in a given key all begin either
with a prelude followed by an allemande, or with an allemande followed by a
courante with or without a double. Then ensue a variety of dances, frequently including a sarabande and a minuet.


## FRANÇOIS COUPERIN


   François Couperin also grouped his harpsichord pieces by key,
expanding the range to include such keys as A and E Major and b and f♯
minor. He called his groups of pieces *ordres*, and it has been a moot question
whether or not they should be considered suites to be played as a series
without pause and without omissions, like the Italian *sonate da camera* or
the later German suites. The question is somewhat theoretical in that such

music was published for the entertainment of the player rather than for performance in concerts. Most of the pieces have titles like *L'Audacieuse, Les Tricoteuses, L'Arlequine, Les Gondoles, Les Satyres* (the pieces constituting the twenty-third ordre). The first number of an ordre can often be recognized as an allemande or overture, and among the other pieces sarabandes, courantes, gigues, and minuets can usually be discerned. Other pieces have a more abstract relationship to the dance, preserving mainly the binary form. Altogether Couperin published twenty-seven ordres in four *livres* over a period of seventeen years: 1–6 in 1713, 7–12 in 1716–1717, 13–19 in 1722, and 20–27 in 1730.

The eighth ordre in b minor from the second book is considered one of Couperin's greatest and has the advantage for purposes of study of having a number of the dances identified by the composer himself. The first number is entitled *La Raphaèle*, and it is an allemande of the slow, serious variety. In its intense harmonies and sweeping upbeat figures it approaches in spirit the first movement of the French overtures of Lully. Example 9-8 shows the return to the tonic in the second half. The lutelike breaking of chords and the piling up of dissonance and suspensions are reminiscent of Denis Gaultier (see Example 9-4).

The piece that follows is marked *Allemande L'Ausonième* and is of the light, gay variety of allemande in 4/8. The first part is made up entirely of four-measure phrases and announces a straightforward tune, whereas the second part makes an about-face and develops several motives from the tune

**EXAMPLE 9-8** F. Couperin, Ordre 8, *La Raphaèle*

in a headlong series of pedal points, sequences, and chains of suspensions. There follow two courantes, both of which are notable for their use of short passages of both canonic and free imitation. Next is *Sarabande l'Unique*, which is unique not only for its twice-repeated change of tempo and meter but also for its being constructed, up to the first change, entirely out of a three-note motive announced in the first measure. The next two pieces draw inspiration from stage works of Lully: a Gavotte from Lully's *airs tendres*, with their sentimental chromaticism, and a Rondeau from Lully's refrain treatment of the minuet in danced choruses. Next is a Gigue, in 6/4, in which the melody passes frequently from the right to the left hand and back.

The climax of the eighth ordre is a stirring *Passacaille* in rondeau form, with eight couplets. Like the chaconne, the passacaille originated in Spain (*pasacalle* comes from *pasar*, to walk, and *calle*, street). It appears to have been not a dance but walk-on music for actors, singers, and dancers. Its typical harmonic pattern was I–IV–V–i, which was repeated as often as necessary before the act and functioned also as a ritornello between strophes of a song. Couperin's refrain of eight measures repeats the pattern i–III–IV–V–i twice, with a potential ostinato theme in the bass (Example 9-9, mm. 1-8). The couplets, however, do not vary this or any other theme and are not of uniform length. Only the first, second, and seventh couplets make any significant references to the refrain theme. Each of the other couplets is tightly constructed on some characteristic motive of its own that propels the relentless flow of b minor harmonies. One feels the compulsion and constraint but the ostinato is not there. The first couplet is a study in appoggiaturas and chromatic harmony (Example 9-9).

Characteristically, the ordre does not end with this weighty piece but with a light Italian gigue, *La Morinète* (perhaps a favorite of, or dedicated to, the daughter of the composer Jean-Baptiste Morin). A tradition had already developed of ending a set of dance pieces with a lively, lighthearted number; that Couperin should respect it in his ordres generally lends support to the belief that he conceived of them not merely as a collection of pieces in one key from which a player might select a few for a given occasion but a succession that was thought out in terms of contrast, variety, and continuity. The eighth ordre is outstanding for its reflection of the many facets of Couperin's art—the majesty of *La Raphaèle*, the almost folklike melody of the *Gavotte*, the troubled passion of the *Passacaille*, the elegance of the first *Courante*, the delight in exploring the possibilities of a theme in the *Allemande* and the *Gigue*, the courtly grace of the *Rondeau*. There are echoes of Lullian opera, of the theater of the fairs, of popular music, and, although the lutanist tradition was still strong, there is no longer the hermetic, introspective poetry of the hushed chamber.

**EXAMPLE 9-9** Ordre 8, *Passacaille*

## BIBLIOGRAPHICAL NOTES

There is no better introduction to the music of the age of Louis XIV than Wilfrid Mellers's *François Couperin and the French Classical Tradition* (1950, reprinted by Dover Publications, New York, 1968). Robert M. Isherwood's *Music in the Service of the King: France in the Seventeenth Century* (Ithaca, N. Y., London: Cornell University Press, 1973), places musical events in France in the context of the philosophy, celebrations, politics, and social life of the reign of Louis XIV with an impressive array of documentation.

The introductions to the editions listed below are recommended reading, particularly that to the works of Le Roux. There is a French-German-English edition of Couperin's treatise *L'Art de toucher le clavecin* (1716), edited and translated by Anna Linde and Mevanwy Roberts (Leipzig: Breitkopf & Härtel, 1933). Charles Masson's *Nouveau traité* 2nd ed. (1699) has been reprinted by Da Capo Press (New York, 1967), with an illuminating introduction by Imogene Horsley.

The problems of ornamentation in French music of this period have aroused heated controversies. Some valuable interpretations in English are those of Robert Donington, *A Performer's Guide to Baroque Music* (New York: Scribner's Sons, 1973) and Frederick Neumann, *Ornamentation in Baroque and Post-Baroque Music, with Special Emphasis on J. S. Bach* (Princeton University Press, 1978).

Two volumes of music arranged for lute by Robert Ballard have been published: *Premier livre* (1611), edited and transcribed by André Souris and Sylvie Spycket (Paris: Editions du Centre national de la recherche scientifique, 1963), and *Deuxième livre et pièces diverses* (1614), edited by Souris, Spycket, and Jacques Veyrier (same publisher, 1964). Also from the same publisher is *Oeuvres du Vieux Gautier*, edited and transcribed by Souris. Denis Gaultier's *La Rhétorique des Dieux* and other pieces for lute are edited in facsimile by André Tessier and Jean Cordey in *Publications de la Société française de musicologie* (Paris: Librairie E. Droz, 1932), Vol. VI and, transcribed, Vol. VII. The *Oeuvres complètes de Chambonnières* are edited by Paul Brunold and André Tessier (Paris: Éditions Maurice Senart, 1925). There is an excellent new edition of the *Pièces de clavecin* of François Couperin by Kenneth Gilbert as part of the collection of early music *Le Pupitre*, edited by François Lesure (Paris: Heugel). Albert Fuller's edition of Gaspard Le Roux's *Pieces for Harpsichord* (New York: Alpeg Editions, 1956) contains a valuable introduction on the performance practice of clavecin music.

# TEN

# ORGAN AND CLAVIER MUSIC
# IN GERMANY

If the main fact of a French keyboard player's life was the dance, for the typical German one it was the Lutheran chorale. But this does not mean the two could not mix, as they sometimes did in the chorale elaboration.

A striking example of this is the variations set by Dietrich Buxtehude (c. 1637–1707) on the chorale *Auf meinen lieben Gott*, which forms a suite consisting of allemande (untitled) with double, sarabande, courante, and gigue. The notes of the chorale (Example 10-1) are decorated in the uppermost part of the texture, each time according to the borrowed style of a different keyboard dance genre. Example 10-2 shows the beginning of each movement, with the chorale notes marked by x.

To apply this idiom to a chorale may seem to profane the sacred hymn, but by now the standard dances were so thoroughly abstracted from the court ballet that the style was no more out of place in the church than the style brisé of the lute was in the harpsichord, or here the organ (if that, indeed, was the intended instrument). The utter artificiality of the mix, yet

EXAMPLE 10-1   Chorale, *Auf meinen lieben Gott*

the perfect absorption of the chorale into the French style prove Buxtehude's mastery of the art of composition, which, at his moment in history, was judged to a significant degree on the composer's ability to capture the essence of a genre.

If Couperin in France could take pride in achieving in his chamber concerts and sonatas *les goûts réunis*, the blending of the Italian and French styles, in Germany the prize went to those who could keep the two *goûts* clearly distinct, yet somehow transcend the models in rationality and constructiveness.

## JOHANN JAKOB FROBERGER

The process of assimilating Italian and French keyboard styles began in effect with Johann Jakob Froberger (1616–1667). A native of Stuttgart, he studied in Rome with Frescobaldi between 1637 and 1641 on a stipend from Emperor Ferdinand III, whom he served as organist in Vienna through much of his life. He also spent some time playing in London and Paris. In Froberger's work, traces of the two traditions separate neatly according to the keyboard category: the toccatas, fantasias, ricercari, canzoni, and capricci follow the Italian style, while the suites, laments, tombeaux, and similar pieces follow the French manner.

The toccatas are more like Merulo's than Frescobaldi's in that they segregate figural play and fugal development in discrete sections. The toccata in d minor (*HAM* II, 217; No. 8 in Walter's edition) partakes of Frescobaldi's bent for chromaticism but forgoes his spasms of invention for more consistent and thorough development of the imitative subjects, which, as often happens in Froberger's toccatas, evolve from each other.

Froberger's suites mark the crystallization of the standard content of allemande, sarabande, courante, and gigue, though not necessarily placed in that order in the sources. His intended order is in doubt, because none of the

**EXAMPLE 10-2** D. Buxtehude, Chorale variation, *Auf meinen lieben Gott*, BuxWV 179

a) Allemande

b) Double

c) Sarabande

d) Courante

e) Gigue

suites was published in his lifetime. They seem inspired more directly by French lute music, such as that of his friend Gaultier, than by the keyboard music of Chambonnières and his contemporaries. The individual dances follow the binary form with repeats, but often the number of measures of the sections is irregular and unequal, and the dance rhythm is obscured by the *style brisé*, by sudden short runs, by silences on beats that in dancing would receive steps, by ornaments and figuration—sometimes lutelike, at other times springing from keyboard technique. The flavor of the sung dance air is also masked by the stylized instrumental orientation of his writing.

The allemandes, particularly, depart from the usual continuous movement in eighth or sixteenth notes. Example 10-3, from the suite usually numbered 11 in D Major (*DTOe* VI/2, 30–32) from a manuscript dedicated to Emperor Ferdinand III and therefore composed before his death in 1657, shows one extreme of this style. At the other extreme is the straightforward allemande in Suite 22 in e minor (*MM* 35).

**EXAMPLE 10-3**   J. Froberger, *Suite 11 in D Major*, Allemande

The sarabandes do not always emphasize the second beat of three, as was typical, but often the third, which in this event usually bears the cadence. Both Nos. 11 and 22 (see Example 10-4 from No. 11) follow this pattern, though the second half of No. 11 vacillates in this regard. The gigues are almost all in a pseudofugal style and in 6/8 (for example, that of No. 22), but some are written in 4/4 and marked by dotted rhythms, as is that of no. 11.

The most characteristic genre of German organ music, the chorale elaboration, if missing from Froberger's work, was widely cultivated by his predecessors and contemporaries in north Germany—for example, Praetorius, Scheidt, Franz Tunder (1614–1667), Mathias Weckmann (1619–1674), and Buxtehude—and by succeeding generations. The outstanding figures were Scheidt and Buxtehude.

**EXAMPLE 10-4** J. Froberger, *Suite 11 in D Major*, Sarabande

## SAMUEL SCHEIDT

Scheidt was a pupil of Sweelinck (see Chapter Five) and shows his teacher's influence in numerous fantasies and variations on solmization subjects, madrigals, popular songs, and chorales. His *Tabulatura nova* (Hamburg, 1624) contains in three volumes most of his surviving works. Of the variations, the largest number are on Protestant chorales. Those on the chorale *Warum betrübst du dich, mein Herz* (*DdT* I, 33; *Werke*, VI, 48; *GMB* has five selected variations, or *versus*, of the twelve) display a variety of methods that became standard in chorale elaborations. These methods include the following: 1) The chorale is given to the top voice, the lower voices preimitating the first phrase in a fugal exposition (Versus 1); 2) the chorale is in the tenor part with imitative counterpoint woven around it (Versus 3); 3) the chorale is stated in the top voice against free figuration in the lower parts (Versus 5); 4) a *bicinium* is so devised in invertible counterpoint that after each phrase is stated over a florid counterpoint, the upper voice is transposed down an octave and the lower up a fifth (Versus 6); 5) the chorale is highly ornamented in the top voice (Versus 12).

**EXAMPLE 10-5**   D. Buxtehude, Chorale elaboration, *Danket dem Herrn*, BuxWV 181

# DIETRICH BUXTEHUDE

The techniques for elaborating the chorale seen in Scheidt were common to the group of composers who influenced Buxtehude and led the way to Bach, particularly Weckmann, less so Tunder, whom Buxtehude succeeded as organist at the Marienkirche in Lübeck in 1668. Whereas Buxtehude's chorale variation discussed above, *Auf meinen lieben Gott* (Example 10-2), was quite extreme in borrowing French dance styles, he used more traditional methods of cantus firmus and fugue in the chorale *Danket dem Herrn, denn er ist sehr freundlich* (Thank the Lord, for he is very kind; *NAWM* 94). The chorale melody is stated three times in whole and half notes, first in the top "voice," then in the pedal part. Thus the chorale functions as a cantus firmus, and one is not surprised to find a number of conventions and devices borrowed from vocal polyphony.

One is the maintenance of discrete voices throughout, in this case two in addition to the one bearing the chorale. Exceptionally a fourth voice enters momentarily to fill out chords at cadences. Further, material from the chorale melody is developed in the other voices, as was common in motets. For example, in the opening the first three notes of the chorale are decorated to produce a motive passed from the middle to the lowest voice (Example 10-5a). A characteristic device is "foreimitation," in which the first notes of a chorale phrase enter in another part before they are heard in the cantus-firmus voice, usually in diminution. In Example 10-5b, from the second variation of the second line of the chorale, the top part foreimitates the chorale in diminution, while the middle voice uses the same chorale line's first three notes for a counter-motive in sixteenth notes. Although these techniques were borrowed from vocal polyphony, the figuration is thoroughly instrumental, to the point of introducing French-style ornaments, as in measures 23–24.

Another type of chorale elaboration cultivated by Buxtehude has been likened to the motet in that each line of the chorale melody (Example 10-6c) is made successively into a point of imitation. *Ich dank dir schon durch deinen Sohn* (I thank thee, surely, through thy son) may be said to fit this category, provided one realizes that after the first section it departs from the vocal style altogether to assume a variety of instrumental guises more suggestive of the ensemble canzona or sonata than the motet. Each section has a different time signature. But the fractions and signs ¢, C, 3/2, and C cannot imply proportional changes; rather, they should be interpreted as contrasts of tempo governed by the associations they acquired in the course of the seventeenth century. The first section, in ¢, is in the severe *alla breve stile antico*. It does not, however, follow strictly the contrapuntal rules of the "Palestrina style"—for example, in the resolution of the suspension of the minor second in the middle voices of measure 5 (Example 10-6a), which passes chromatically through a major second before reaching the expected consonance in the next measure. The notes of the chorale phrase are stated in full only in the bass part, while the other voices enter with the fugue subject in stretto.

The second section, in C meter, suggests the fugal allegro of the church sonata, with the second line of the chorale migrating as a fourth voice (Example 10-6b). The third section, in 3/2, demands a slow tempo, as it is suggestive of a sarabande, but the chorale is developed in strict fugue throughout (Example 10-6c). The last section, returning to C, a fugue in four parts on the last line of the chorale, has a sprightly countersubject, reaffirming the sonata or canzona character of the piece.

Buxtehude also wrote extended free fantasies on chorales and, most typically, settings in which the chorale is stated only once in the top voice in ornamented form. The latter settings, intended to be played as preludes to congregational singing of the hymns, were consequently called choralepreludes. (See *TEM* 41, *Nun komm, der Heiden Heiland.*) Buxtehude, in short, summed up in his work the whole art of elaborating upon chorales for the organ.

The North German predilection for fugal writing found its purest vehicle in the independent organ piece. The most elaborate fugues were imbedded in toccatas; for example, Buxtehude's Praeludium in D Major (BuxWV 139) contains a thirty-four-measure fugue on a well-shaped subject provided with a tonal answer. There is no time when the subject is not heard in some voice, but there is a modulation to the minor third degree before the fugue closes in the tonic, and the toccata resumes.

## BRUHNS, PACHELBEL, FISCHER

Buxtehude's pupil Nicolaus Bruhns (1665–1697) carried on this tradition, though he tended to inflate his toccatas with virtuoso pedal parts, antiphonal responses among the various divisions of the organ, echoes, rapidly repeated chords, and other somewhat superficial but brilliant effects that exploited the rich organs of the period. The Praeludium in e minor (Stein ed., No. 3; Seiffert ed., No. 3) illustrates all of these traits and is notable for a well-developed fugue (preceded and followed by toccata sections) on a lively subject that is given a tonal answer (Example 10-7a). The one episode (Example 10-7b) utilizes a motive from the subject.

Individual pieces called *fugues* were comparatively rare; two composers who left a large number, however, were Johann Pachelbel (1653–1706) and Johann Kasper Ferdinand Fischer (c. 1670–c. 1746). More than 120 fugues by Pachelbel survive, most of them intended to be performed during

**EXAMPLE 10-6** D. Buxtehude, *Ich dank dir schon*, BuxWV 195; chorale elaboration; a, b, c; the chorale melody: d

a)

b)

c)

EXAMPLE 10-6 (Cont.)

d)

Ich dank dir schon durch dei-nen Sohn, o Gott, für dei - ne Gü - te,

dass du mich heint in die-ser Nacht so gnä-dig hast be - hü - tet.

**EXAMPLE 10-7** N. Bruhns, *Praeludium*

a) Vivace

b)

**EXAMPLE 10-7** (Cont.)

the Magnificat (Pachelbel was associated with several Catholic churches in southern Germany and Vienna). These fugues display a rich variety of moods, subjects, rhythmic and metrical configurations, and keys. The fugues are designated by their Gregorian Magnificat tones and in fact are not in the modern major and minor keys, but the harmonic progressions reflect the current practice, a combination that gives them a hybrid flavor. Inspired perhaps by the liturgical context, the fugues of this cycle show a seriousness of expressive purpose that removes them from the mere playful and ingenious, toward which the instrumental fugue inclined, partly under the influence of the whimsical capriccio. The intensity that Pachelbel built into the counterpoint around the last statement of the pathetic subject of Example 10-8, in the first tone, exemplifies to what a degree the fugue had become a medium for the expression of the affections. Almost every half-note beat bears a dissonance in the form of an accented passing note, a suspension, or an evaded resolution of one.

**EXAMPLE 10-8** J. Pachelbel, *Magnificat primi toni*

Several of the fugues are threefold fugues, such as that for the Magnificat in the eighth tone (G Major), in which the first two fugues each present a different subject, and the third combines the two subjects in the manner of a double fugue. Example 10-9 shows the beginning of the exposition of the third fugue, with the subjects entering in the order in which they first appeared.

**EXAMPLE 10-9**   J. Pachelbel, *Magnificat octavi toni*

Fischer is remembered chiefly for his collection *Ariadne musica* of 1715 containing twenty preludes and fugues ordered according to key. All the major and minor keys are represented except Db and Gb Major, and eb, g#, and bb minor. There are three on E: on the E mode, in e minor, and E Major. (See *GMB* 265 for the Prelude and Fugue on E; all the subjects are given in *MGG*, "Fuge: Thementafel"). Fischer's fugues are compact and made to seem even more so when, as often happens, the answer enters before the subject has been fully stated.

The number of composers in Germany and Austria whose keyboard works would merit discussion is very large. The standard of excellence attained by these composers is one of the wonders of the baroque period; the second half of the seventeenth century deserves to be recognized as a golden age of German organ music.


## *JOHANN SEBASTIAN BACH*[1]


Johann Sebastian Bach left evidence of being a voracious reader of the keyboard music of his predecessors and contemporaries, even of music that was not published. His curiosity about the creative work of others never

[1]See Chapter Thirteen for biographical information.

flagged. It embraced not only German but also French and Italian keyboard writers. Beyond that, Bach drew into the vocabulary of the organ many techniques that originated or flourished in other media, particularly those of the violin, brass instruments, and harpsichord. The process of assimilation had begun before Bach, of course, but the application of nonkeyboard forms to the organ seems to have challenged Bach particularly, as if he were not satisfied with the expressive possibilities of the organ medium as he inherited it.

While court organist at Weimar between 1714 and 1717, Bach consolidated his personal approach to organ composition by synthesizing the many styles that he encountered in the music of others. We saw that he arranged concertos by Vivaldi, originally written for strings, for solo organ, and for one or more harpsichords and orchestra. The style and structure of the Italian concerto appealed to him as a resource that would show off the brilliance of player and instrument and permit an expansion of form. For example, in the Toccata in C Major, BWV 564[2], after a prelude of unison finger-work, there are three sections analogous to the three movements of a concerto: an allegro with contrasts between fuller and sparser textures, an adagio—an ornamented aria over a quasi-ostinato bass—and a concerto-fugue on a violinistic theme.

A subtler infusion of concerto style animates the Praeludium and Fugue in a minor, BWV 543. The prelude begins like the solo of a violin concerto, with figuration that alternates between two strings (Example 10-10). The next section (measures 10–23), on a tonic pedal point, though it fits the two hands marvelously, seems still inspired by violin figuration. The last two measures of the pedal point and the subsequent section, measures 24–35, including virtuoso passages for the pedals, are more characteristically in toccata style. But measures 35–44 hark back to the concerto, this time its tutti.

The theme of the fugue that follows is also violinistic in its rapid leaps and simulated alternating strings (Example 10-10c). The fugue's structure, too, seems modeled on the allegro of the concerto, the expositions functioning as tutti and the episodes as modulatory solos that point the way to the main expositions. Analogous to the tutti, the expositions are in a tight family of keys: relative major (measure 62), subdominant (measure 78), and tonic (measure 95). The last of the episodes, leading to this return of the home key, is especially violinistic in the patterns that submit to sequential development (Example 10-10d). The long cadenza (measures 139–151) is also a concerto device, though the material has the keyboard flourish of the toccata.

Another justly famous creation of the Weimar period, the Passacaglia

---

[2]*Bach Werke Verzeichnis* numbers are used to identify the works of J. S. Bach. They are set forth in the *Thematisch-systematisches Verzeichnis der musikalische Werke von Johann Sebastian Bach*, ed. Wolfgang Schmieder (Leipzig: Breitkopf & Härtel, 1950; 1961; 1977).

EXAMPLE 10-10   J. S. Bach, *Praeludium et Fuga*, BWV 543

a) Praeludium.

b)

c) Fuga.

d)

in c minor, BWV 582, owed a more complex debt to the past. The first half of the theme is from André Raison's *Trio en passacaille*, which is the Christe in his *Messe du deuziesme ton*. Raison's theme (Example 10-11), is an expansion of the passecaille chord patterns found in guitar tablatures, where they provided models for players to strum preludes or ritornellos for singers. (See Chapter Nine.) Raison's implied progression is i–V–I$_6$–iv–V–VI–iv–V.

Bach's first variation may be indebted also to Buxtehude's Passacaglia, one of the few ostinato compositions in the north German organ literature. Buxtehude used rests and suspensions strategically over the ostinato in the opening variation in a manner similar to Bach's. It was by now customary for each variation to be unified by a characteristic figuration. Bach, however, went beyond this to wed several variations together by a single species of figuration or rhythm. For example, counting Example 10-12b as the first variation, variation 2 continues the rests, syncopations, and ornamentally resolved suspensions of 1. Variations 6, 7, and 8 all use sixteenth-note scale figures, as do 10 and 11, while variations 4–5 have mixed sixteenths and eighths. A higher level of organization is also evident. The theme is in the

**EXAMPLE 10-11**   A. Raison, *Messe du deuziesme ton*, Christe, *Trio en passacaille*

**EXAMPLE 10-12a**   D. Buxtehude, *Passacaglia*, BuxWV 161

**EXAMPLE 10-12b**  J. S. Bach, *Passacaglia*

bass in the first ten variations, migrates in the next five, and returns to the bass in the last five. Moreover, the last five variations repeat some of the elements of the first eight in that variation 16, with its rests, resembles 1 and 2; 18, with its rhythm of eighth plus two sixteenths returns to 4 and 5, while 19 and 20 return to the rhythm of sixteenths, though not the precise figures of 6, 7, and 8. The twentieth variation is followed by a fugue on the Raison theme in which the subject is constantly escorted by a countersubject derived from the remaining notes of the passacaglia theme. It is clear that Bach did more than refill an old mold; he created a unique and powerful structure out of partly secondhand material.

Other examples could be given of Bach's testing the relevance of nonorgan genres to the instrument's technique during the Weimar period. The six sonatas for two manuals and pedal (BWV 525–530) adopt the format and content of the trio sonata for two melody instruments and basso continuo. The later clavier works offer other examples—the *Overture nach französischer Art* (Overture in the French Style, 1735; BWV 831) and the *Concerto nach italienischen Gust* (Concerto after the Italian *goût*, 1735, BWV 971).

Like the later "Italian concerto," four of the preludes of the English suites (Nos. 2, 3, 4, and 5) are patterned after the concerto grosso. Chronologically they come after the organ works just discussed. Composed in Cöthen not later than 1722, they were inspired by the French clavecin style but in many ways left it behind. The anomalous appellation "English" that became attached to the suites may be explained by the fact that the prelude of the Suite in A Major is modeled on the gigue in the Suite in f minor by the

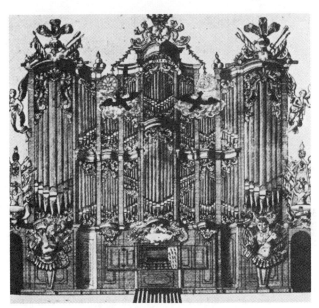

The organ at the Garnisonkirche in Berlin, built by Joachim Wagner, 1724–25, as drawn by that church's organist, Johann Friedrich Walther in his book, *Die Gute Hand Gottes über der Garnisonkirche* (*ca.* 1729). The long pipes at each end constitute the *Pedal* (Pedal Organ), those immediately above the player, the *Hauptwerk* (Great Organ), while those above were known as the *Oberwerk* (Upper Organ). Instead of a *Rückpositiv* placed behind the organist's back (literally "back positive") and found in many Baroque organs, this instrument had a *Seitenwerk* (side-organ) in the lower cases at either side of the console. Each of these divisions had its own manual or pedal keyboard.

composer François Dieupart (c. 1670–1740), who spent most of his life in London. Another connection may be that Dieupart's suites are among the few that consistently followed the sequence prelude, allemande, courante, sarabande, optional dances, and gigue. Bach observed this sequence, and among the optional dances he included were bourrée, gavotte, musette, minuet, and passepied. Certain of the dances are accompanied by one or more doubles, in which the melody is heavily ornamented with agréments (Example 10-13), while other dances are paired—for example two courantes—and each may have doubles.

Bach's "*English*" *Suite No. 1* is the most French of the collection and may well be the earliest. There is an abundance of style brisé in the allemande and the two courantes. The sarabande, on the other hand, is conceived as a trio, and the two bourrées and the gigue are *bicinia*, much in the manner of the two-part inventions. The other suites are overwhelmingly written in this kind of linear counterpoint, relieved only by chordally accompanied arioso in the sarabandes. A characteristic of Bach's treatment of the binary dance form is to delay the first cadence until the end of the first half and to begin the second half in the dominant or relative major in a manner parallel to the

**EXAMPLE 10-13**  J. S. Bach, *English Suite 1*, BWV 806 Courante 2, Double 1

first, but, in the case of the gigue, by an inversion of the subject. There is a further consistency in the first suite, for the allemande and two courantes have parallel beginnings in the manner of the variation suites of Johann Hermann Schein's *Banchetto musicale* (1617). The suites were not specifically destined for the harpsichord and may have been played also on a spinet, virginal, or clavichord; the term *clavier* is used to cover all of these.

The chorale elaboration for organ occupied Bach throughout most of his working life. Toward the end of his stay in Weimar he began the ambitious project of composing a large book of chorales, intended to contain 164 arranged in the order of the liturgical calendar, under the title *Orgel-Büchlein* (Little Organ Book). He had finished only forty-five, however, when he left for Cöthen in 1717. Unlike some of the longer chorale elaborations he had composed up to now in the styles practiced by his predecessors, these are single statements of the melody, intended to show students how to accom-

**EXAMPLE 10-14**   J. S. Bach, Chorale-prelude, *Durch Adams Fall*

pany the chorale with carefully chosen figuration that would bring out the affection and meaning of the text. *Durch Adams Fall ist ganz verderbt* (Through Adam's fall is all undone; *NAWM* 95), BWV 637, from this cycle is outstanding at once for its pictorial effects and for the moving harmonies under the simply stated tune (Example 10-14).

The leaping diminished sevenths in the pedal, falling into notes outside the tonality, may be said to symbolize the fall of man from grace through Adam's sin and the collapse of the harmony between man and his maker. The vacillation between F♯ and F natural may have been intended to denote the fickleness of man. Meanwhile the left hand, perhaps to portray the serpent in paradise that tempted and deceived Adam and Eve, winds tortuously, often by diminished, augmented, or chromatic intervals.

In 1739 Bach published his first organ works in the *Clavier-Übung* (Clavier Practice), Part III, a collection of chorale arrangements that complemented those of the incomplete *Orgel-Büchlein*, with "ordinary" hymns for the first part of the Lutheran Mass. There are two versions of each item, one simple and one elaborate. An example of the elaborate chorale is that composed on the Lord's Prayer, *Vater unser im Himmelreich* (Our Father in heaven), BWV 682. The anonymous melody of 1539 is highly ornamented in the treble part, sometimes with such *galant*-style mannerisms as Scotch snaps and triplets, at other times with French ornaments. The embellished chorale is then duplicated in canon at the interval of four measures in the left hand, or "alto" voice. When the cantus firmus—the simple chorale tune— finally enters in the "second soprano," it becomes evident that what preceded was a compound foreimitation. Two measures later the tenor enters with a canonic duplication of the cantus firmus. The resultant texture, confusing to the ear, may be resolved by the analyst, however, into a trio sonata upon which a chorale-canon has been superimposed, or vice versa. The chorale-canon perseveres throughout, but the other parts, having received their first impetus from the chorale, proceed with their intricate trio without further reference to the tune.

Example 10-15 shows the entrance of the first phrase of the chorale in the "second soprano" (measure 11) and its canonic imitation in the "tenor" (measure 14). It would not be difficult to read into the juxtaposition of canon and sonata an allegory of the sacred and profane, and such a message may have been intended, but it is clear that Bach at this stage was more interested in constructivist strategies than in detailed exegesis.

**EXAMPLE 10-15**   J. S. Bach, *Vater unser im Himmelreich*, BWV 682.

Among Bach's last organ works is the group of arrangements of vocal numbers from his cantatas published by his pupil J. G. Schübler in 1746 as *Sechs Choräle von verschiedener Art* (Six Chorales of Diverse Sorts). That these compositions were addressed to a wide public and perhaps to amateurs is suggested by the presence of instructions for registration and by the melodiousness of the arrangements. A good example is *Wachet auf, ruft uns die Stimme* (Wake up, the voice calls to us), BWV 645, based on the fourth stanza of the chorale-cantata BWV 140 from 1731. The organist's right hand plays the part scored in the cantata for violins and viola in unison, while the left hand has the simple chorale, probably sung by the choir tenors. This work, too, exhibits some modernisms, such as the neat two-measure phrases, the comic-opera upbeat pattern of two sixteenth notes followed by an eighth note at the beginning of a bar, the phrase repetition and balancing, and the smooth lyricism graced by Italian-style trills and turns. One of the modern traits written into the cantata score—the contrasts of *piano* and *forte*—was suppressed in the organ edition, since that would have required frequent changes of registration.

**EXAMPLE 10-16** J. S. Bach, *Wachet auf*, BWV 645

*Das Wohltemperierte Klavier* (The Well-Tempered Clavier) of 1722 and a parallel collection completed twenty years later are tours de force at once of genre-crossing eclecticism and tight fugal design. The first series of twenty-four preludes and fugues, one in each of the major and minor keys, was aimed both to instruct and to entertain, as the composer's title tells us: "for the use and practice of musical youth eager to learn and for the amusement of those already skilled in this study." Despite the didactic and public objective, neither set was printed in Bach's lifetime.

The preludes of the first cycle are studies in manners of composition reduced for the keyboard as well as exericses for the player. There are prelude types—for example, a lute-inspired chordal introduction (No. 1)—toccatas (Nos. 2, 7, 21); trio-sonata movements of the *grave* type (No. 8) and with walking bass (No. 24); and concerto movements, including an allegro (No. 17) and a slow aria (first part of No. 10). There are also among the preludes two- and three-voice fantasies similar to the two-voice counterpoints Bach called *inventiones* and those for three voices that he called *sinfoniae*, descendants of the didactic *bicinia* and *tricinia* of the Renaissance.

The second cycle of preludes explores some newer genres as well as some essayed in the first set. Of the new genres the most important is the Italian bipartite keyboard sonata. This is in the form made famous by Domenico Scarlatti, consisting, like the earlier dance movements, of two repeated sections. Some of the sonata-like preludes contain a recapitulation of the opening material, as in Nos. 5, 12, and 21; others have parallel closing sections, such as Nos. 10 and 15; and still other "sonatas" contain neither of these features, such as Nos. 9, 18, and 20. No. 17 is an Italian concerto-ritornello movement, whereas No. 4 seems to be inspired by the French *concert*. Other movements are dance-derived—No. 5 from the gigue and No. 8 from the allemande—but they lack the binary form.

The fugues of both sets exercise every device of fugue writing, but each, like the Magnificat fugues of Pachelbel, has an individual expressive character, often matched to the traditional moods of certain keys. They are more compact than the big organ fugues, whose leisurely episodes are sacrificed to more learned devices. Their economy of time and material, yet richness of invention and detail, is exemplified in II, 2 in c minor. Within the space of twenty-eight measures this four-voice fugue contains twenty-four statements of the one-measure subject, most of them full. There are a number of strettos, that is, sections in which an answering voice enters before the subject has been stated completely. Example 10-17, which comes after a cadence on the dominant, illustrates the intensity of harmony and modulation that accompanies the concentration of entries, some in augmentation (measure 14), contrary motion (measure 15), and stretto (measure 16) in this climactic buildup of abrasive, tormented counterpoint.

The two sets of preludes and fugues, are Bach's most important legacy to the musicians and composers of later times. During the hundred years between Bach's death and the founding of the Bach Gesellschaft they kept alive his name and also the learned contrapuntal tradition. More than twenty-five different editions of *The Well-Tempered Clavier*, including the second set, were published during this period. When most of Bach's other works were neglected, the keyboard music continued to be studied and played. Even before the Bach Gesellschaft began publishing the complete works, Friedrich K. Griepenkerl and Ferdinand Roitzsch edited a complete collection of the organ works between 1844 and 1847. In his own time Bach was famous mostly for his organ playing and his keyboard compositions. If he had left nothing else, they alone would have assured him an honored place among the great.

EXAMPLE 10-17   *Well-Tempered Clavier* II, 2, Fugue

## BIBLIOGRAPHICAL NOTES

For basic materials on the history of keyboard music, see the Bibliographical Notes for Chapter Five, particularly the books by Willi Apel and Frank E. Kirby.

Thomas Walker tells the fascinating history of the chaconne and passacaglia in "Ciaccona and Passacaglia: Remarks on Their Origin and Early History," *JAMS*, XXI (1968), 300–20, which is supplemented by Richard Hudson, "Further Remarks on the Passacaglia and Ciaccona," *JAMS*, XXIII (1970), 302–14.

Froberger's keyboard works are contained in *DTOe*: IV/1 (1897) and X/2 (1903) contain the toccatas, fantasias, canzoni, capricci, ricercari, and VI/2 (1899) the suites, all edited by Guido Adler. The suites are also available in a new critical edition by David Starke (Darmstadt: Tonos-Musikverlag, 1972) and the organ works in a well-annotated edition by Rudolf Walter, *Toccaten, Fantasien, Ricercari, Canzonen und Capricci*, Suddeutsche Orgelmeister des Barock, VII (Altötting: A. Coppenrath, 1968).

Scheidt's *Tabulatura nova* is edited in *DdT*, I (1892), by M. Seiffert, and in Scheidt's *Werke*, VI, VII (Hamburg: Ugrino Verlag, 1963), by Christhard Mahrenholz.

217

There are two recent critical editions of Buxtehude's organ works: J. Hedar, ed., *Sämtliche Orgelwerke* (Copenhagen: Hansen, 1952); and Klaus Beckmann, ed., *Sämtliche Orgelwerke* (Wiesbaden: Breitkopf & Härtel, 1971–72). To locate individual works the thematic index by Georg Karstädt should be used: *Thematisch-Systematisches Verzeichnis der musikalischen Werke von Deitrich Buxtehude* (Wiesbaden: Breitkopf & Härtel, 1974). For the location of works by Bruhns and Pachelbel, see the "List of Musical Examples and their Sources" at the end of this volume.

Bibliographical notes concerning J. S. Bach may be found at the end of Chapter Thirteen.

# ELEVEN

# OPERA IN FRANCE AND ITALY
# FROM LULLY TO SCARLATTI

French opera was shaped by the magnetic forces of attraction and repulsion exerted by Italian music. As drama, Italian opera could hardly measure up to the vital theater of Corneille and Racine. Its excesses of passion and fantastic flights of imagery and virtuosity offended a French public exhorted to reason, moderation, and decorum by Boileau and the classic critics. Pierre Perrin summed up the inadequacy of Italian opera as a model for French composers in a preface to the text of his musical pastoral, performed in Issy in 1659 and hence known as the *Pastorale d'Issy*, with music by Robert Cambert (1628–c. 1677). Italian operas, Perrin said, were too long and the recitatives monotonous; the poetry was too arty, archaic in its language, and forced in its metaphors; one could not hear the words being sung, so there was no appeal to the mind; the male sopranos and altos—the castrati—horrified women and made men snicker. But perhaps the most important reason the French would not imitate Italian opera Perrin did not mention. The dance was central to the French musical stage, and, though

Stage design and machinery by the architect Giacomo Torelli for the opera, *Le Nozze di Teti e Peleo*, by Carlo Caproli on a text by Francesco Buti, produced in Paris in 1654. Lully participated as a professional dancer. (Phot. Bibl. nat. Paris.)

the ballet was originally imported from Italy, its share in Italian productions was by now minimal.

On the other hand there were aspects of Italian opera that French audiences could not resist. The beautiful spectacles conjured up by architects and machinists like Giacomo Torelli da Fano satisfied the hunger of Parisians for things extravagant and marvelous. And how to express the passions, even if they had to be gently tamed, was a lesson that could be learned from Italian music.

## JEAN-BAPTISTE LULLY

No one was in a better position to steer between the positive and negative poles of the French attitude toward Italian opera than Jean-Baptiste Lully (1632–1687). A native of Florence who went to France as a musician-page at fourteen, he participated in the performance in Paris of two operas of Cavalli, *Serse* (1660) and *Ercole Amante* (1662). He furnished music for the dances added to cater to the French taste. As composer of instrumental music for King Louis XIV from 1653 and a member of the *24 violons du Roy* before he led his own *petits violons*, Lully assimilated the rich French heritage of orchestral music. Moreover, he appeared as a dancer as early as the *Ballet des Bienvenus* in 1655. Between this date and 1661 he composed music for numerous *ballets de cour*, including not only overtures and dances but also airs and récits to the poetry of Benserade. From 1664 to 1671 he collaborated with Molière and Corneille in a series of ballet comedies and one ballet tragedy. For these he wrote in both the French and Italian styles. Thus Lully united in his experience the best of both the French and Italian musical, dance, and literary traditions.

From his very first opera, *Cadmus et Hermione* (1673), Lully proved himself a master of the new synthesis. He was fortunate in having a librettist who also achieved a satisfactory union of French and Italian elements: Philippe Quinault. The action gave abundant scope to the machines and decorations of Carlo Vigarani of Modena. The opera tells of the deliverance of Hermione from her captor, the giant Draco, by Cadmus, King of Tyre. As Francesco Buti in *Orfeo* (Paris, 1647) had made Juno the protectress of Orfeo and Venus that of his rival Aristeo, so Quinault had Mars intercede in favor of the giant, while Pallas Athene and Aphrodite (Amour) sided with Cadmus. Quinault followed the Italian operas, too, in coupling in a subordinate love plot the confidant of Cadmus, Arbas, with Hermione's companion, Charite. To complete this triangle the old nursemaid of Hermione was made to flirt with Arbas. The scenes among these secondary characters are part comic, part sentimental.

High points of the opera are not the scenes between the principals but the interventions of the deities: a dance of gold statues animated by the goddess of love (II, vi); sacrificial dances and choruses to propitiate Mars at the end of Act III; Pallas astride an owl on the wing freezing the giants in their tracks at the end of Act IV, finally the pomp of the wedding of Cadmus and Hermione that fills all of Act V. Such visual and aural diversions were fittingly called *divertissements*.

Less Italian than Quinault's libretto, Lully's music is nevertheless largely based on transalpine models. There is a sharp contrast between recitative and air, but as in Roman and Venetian practice there is the twilight zone of arioso.

The conversation between Arbas and the Tyrian princes (Example 11-1) shows Lully's recitative at its plainest. Like contemporary Italian recitative, it is rapid and full of triadic and repeated-note figures declaimed over sparse chords. The rhythms are at once freer and more constrained than the Italian. Ends of lines are invariably marked by a long value or rest, and accented syllables almost always fall on successive quarters of the measure. Constant shifting of the poetic foot between iambic and anapest in Quinault's

Costume design by Jean Bérain for Hermione in *Cadmus et Hermione* by Lully, Paris 1673. (Copperplate engraving by Le Pautre. Staatliche Kunstsammlungen Dresden, Kupferstich-Kabinett.)

verses requires alternately a duple or quadruple subdivision of the beat, while the changing number of feet per line demands shifting between $\frac{4}{4}$ and $\frac{3}{4}$.

Speeches charged with passion call forth a somewhat more halting delivery and diminished and augmented intervals, such as the diminished fourths of Example 11-2, measures 1 and 4.

Tending toward what some eighteenth-century writers called *récitatif mesuré* are the passages that approach the air in having a uniform meter but lack the musical repetition and closed form of the air. Some of these arioso passages, scarce in *Cadmus* but abundant in later operas, are labeled "Air" in both modern and ancient scores. The movement of the bass is more marked than in the simple recitative, the melodic contour more deliberately molded,

**EXAMPLE 11-1**   J.-B. Lully, *Cadmus et Hermione*, Act III, scene i

1st Prince / 2nd Prince

Tu de -tour- nes bien tes re - gards? As-tu peur du Dra - gon de
*( You turn away your* *gaze.* *Do you fear the Dragon* *of*

Arbas

Mars? La dé - fi - ance est né - ces - sai - re, Il est bon de pré -
*Mars?* *Suspicion is* *necessary.* *It is good to foresee*

voir un fa -cheux ac-ci -dent; On ne doit point i - cy mar-cher en té-mé-rai - re.
*an angry incident; But one must not walk here with timidity.)*

**EXAMPLE 11-2**   J.-B. Lully, *Cadmus et Hermione*, Act II, scene vi

Hermione

Lais - sez moy ma dou - leur, J'y trou - ve des ap -
*( Leave* *me* *pain.* *I find some solace*

pas Dans l'horreur d'un pé -ril ex - trème; Est-ce là le se-cours que l'on me doit of - frir?
*in the horror of a danger extreme. Is this the succor that is being offered me? )*

223

**EXAMPLE 11-3** J.-B. Lully, *Cadmus et Hermione*, Act II, scene i

> En te voy-ant, Bel-le Cha-ri - te, J'a-vais cru que l'a-mourfût un plai-sir char-
> *(When I saw you, lovely Charite, I thought that love was a pleasure sweet,*

> mant Mais lors-qu'il faut que je te,quit - te, J'é - prou-ve qu'il n'est point un
> *But now that I must leave you, I see that it is nothing but*

> plus cru -el tour-ment
> *a cruel torment.)*

and the succession of accented syllables less regular. The caesura, a resting point around the middle of a line, is normally observed as in Example 11-3 at "amour" and "point." Such passages are delivered more slowly and song-fully than the unmeasured recitative and demand a tasteful application of the French graces, such as short trills at the F♯ of "charmant" (measure 4) and at "quitte" (measure 5).

The airs of *Cadmus* reveal Lully as a loyal disciple of the air composer, Michel Lambert (c. 1610–1696), whose daughter he married in 1662. Mersenne once said that airs "are composed particularly and chiefly to charm the mind and ear, and to let us pass life with a bit of sweetness among the bitterness that we encounter . . . not to excite anger and other passions. . . ."[1] Lully's airs are always fitting to the subject and character, but they

[1] Letter of 29 November 1640 quoted in Théodore Gérold, *L'Art du chant en France au XVIIᵉ siècle* (Strassburg, 1921), p. 102.

**EXAMPLE 11-4** J.-B. Lully, *Cadmus et Hermione*, Act I, scene iii

Cet ai - ma - ble sé - jour Si pai - si - ble et si
*(This lovely retreat So pleasant and*

som - bre, Of - fre du si - lence et de l'om - bre, A qui
*sombre, offers some silence and shade, to one*

vent é - vi - ter le bruit et le grand jour.
*who wants to avoid the noise and the sun.*

jour. Ah! que n'est-il aus - si fa -
*Ah! It is not so easy*

ci - le De trou - ver un a - zi - le Pour é - vi - ter l'A -
*to find a refuge to avoid love.)*

**EXAMPLE 11-4** (Cont.)

remain musical interludes rather than dramatic climaxes. They are best for dwelling on some pleasant thought or sensation. Almost invariably they are accompanied only by the thorough-bass instruments, though they may be preceded by a two-violin ritornello. Hermione's air (I, iii) sung to her companions in a delightful garden is typical (Example 11-4). The poet's short lines are knit into a unified rhyme scheme ABBACCA. Lully repeated the music and text of the first twelve measures (the ABBA lines). The next eight measures (set to the CCA lines) go from a minor to the relative major, and the final seven measures, repeating the final three lines of poetry, modulate back to a minor. The exclamation "Ah!" (measures 13, 20, and 21), characteristically on a secondary beat, reminds us that this is a dramatic scene. Two more such airs round out this scene, both of them of a type that has earned them the label "maxim-air." Aglante muses: It is vain to flee love; not to resist saves a lot of trouble. Charite in her air chimes in: Love exempts no one: it is more frightful than evil.

Some of the other French genres represented are the dance songs, such as the famous "Amants, aymez vos chaines," a sung minuet that alternates with an orchestral minuet in the final scene (V, iii), and the comic bass airs accompanied by two violins, such as that of Arbas, "C'est trop railler de mon martire" (II, i). Many of the airs of the divertissements are obvious descendants of the popular genres cultivated in France: *chansons* (popular love songs), *vaudevilles* (city songs), *airs à boire* (drinking songs), and *brunettes* (flirting pastoral songs).

The most distinctive features of the Lully opera are those taken over from the court ballets and comedy-ballets: the overture, the entry music for dancers, the atmosphere and action symphonies, the homophonic choruses, and, of course, the dances. All of this music is scored for a five-part orchestra in contrast to the ritornelli, which are for the traditional Italian ensemble of two treble instruments and bass. The heart of the orchestra is the "twenty-four violins," composed traditionally of six soprano violins (*dessus de violon*), twelve alto and tenor violins of various sizes tuned like the modern viola but playing three separate parts known as *hautecontre, taille*, and *quinte*, and six bass violins, tuned like the modern cello but a tone lower. The Lully operatic orchestra, like Stradella's, thus breaks up into two groups. One is the *petit choeur*, corresponding to the Italian concertino, which plays the ritornelli and accompanies the solo voices. It is made up of two violins or transverse flutes and thorough-bass instruments, including harpsichord, bass viols, and theorbos. The twenty-four violins, with the occasional addition of oboes, bassoons, recorders, and kettledrum, comprise the *grand choeur*, and this corresponds to the Italian concerto grosso.

*Cadmus et Hermione* was a hybrid creation that fell short of realizing a native French opera. As Quinault and Lully subsequently turned away from the Italian tragicomedy toward the French classic tragedy, they developed a new kind of music drama, the *tragédie lyrique*. The political and romantic entanglements and comic episodes of the Italians were cleared away for a simple well-knit plot line. But opera could not simply imitate Racine. As Jean La Bruyère said in its defense, "*Bérénice* and *Pénélope* need neither flights nor chariots nor transformations; opera needs them; and it is proper to this spectacle to hold mind, eye, and ear all equally spellbound."[2] So the simple plot was embellished with a variety of marvelous and magical apparitions and transformations that justified long scenes and entire acts of ballet, characteristic musical pieces, and choral-solo rondeaux. If these added little to the progress of the drama, they at least were woven into it with remarkable ingenuity and pertinence; and by inspiring an aura of wonder they eased the suspension of disbelief.

Beginning with the ballet *Triomphe de l'Amour* (1681) Lully introduced a major innovation, the orchestrally accompanied recitative. His first opera to use this medium was *Persée* (1682), in which it was reserved chiefly for moments of high drama. Merope's invocation of death, for example, is accompanied by the five-part string orchestra (V, i; *GMB* 232). The opening "O Mort! venez finir mon destin déplorable" returns twice as a refrain, giving the monologue the rounded form that Lully was fond of conferring upon important solo scenes (see also *Cadmus et Hermione*, V, i).

The last of the tragedies was *Armide* (1686). Lully was fully himself

---

[2]Quoted from *Les Caractères*, 1688, in Cuthbert Girdlestone, *J.-P. Rameau* (London: Cassel, 1957), p. 110.

and in complete command of the rich resources of his craft. Despite the prodigious number of dances, marvelous scenes, and airs, there is a single-minded continuity and forward movement in this opera. The prologue in praise of heroes leads naturally to the first act's triumphs in honor of Armide, the enchantress who captured the knights of the Crusades. Most of the opera from here is a psychological study of her struggle against a growing attraction to her prisoner Renaud. The enchantment of Renaud during his sleep presents the first opportunity for a divertissement, as demons in the shape of nymphs, shepherds, and shepherdesses cast a spell over him (II, iv).

The first extended continuo-recitative employing fluctuating meters—now less frequent than the measured recitative—is the fine monologue of Armide "Enfin il est en ma puissance" (II, v; *GMB* 234; *NAWM* 73b). The declamation is artfully paced. Based on the quarter note per foot as Armide's fury to slay Renaud builds up, the rhythm breaks into spasmodic exclamations when she realizes that she cannot bring herself to the ugly deed, then slows to a half note per foot at "Est-ce ainisi que je dois me venger aujourd'huy?" as she questions her feelings. Finally the rhythm becomes resolute again when she decides Renaud should be punished with a love he does not seek. Tonally the monologue hovers around e minor and G Major, unlike comparable Italian recitatives, which explore distant tonalities. The recitative leads into a triple-meter air in AAB form, introduced by a ritornello that sums up the melodic material in a direct AB statement.

The entire Act IV is a series of transformation scenes. The desert of Act III, with its monsters and savage beasts, is changed into a fertile countryside by the knight Ubalde through his magic diamond buckler and scepter. The fifth act returns to the personal drama and to the freer recitative. Armide has abandoned herself completely to her passion for Renaud while he, delivered from his spell by Ubalde's magic buckler, finds the strength to forsake the enchantress.

The music of the closing scenes strikes a mood of genuine tragedy. Renaud's farewell (V, iv), in unmeasured continuo-recitative, mounts to a painful climax. Armide's final monologue (V, v) acquires heightened pathos through a string accompaniment. Her bleak unmeasured recitative-with-refrain eloquently voices her wounded soul, but the final measured *récit*, in which she summons the demons to destroy her pleasure dome, falls short of the fury Quinault must have imagined. Its melodizing sequences and refrains, its worn triadic clichés, and its persistent anapests lay bare the limitations of Lully's idiom.

The operas of Lully enjoyed a longevity unparalleled for his age. They continued to be staged and printed for a hundred years. The Lullian opera became such a national institution that a composer who defied its conventions imperiled his reputation. Lully's immediate successors, such as André Campra (1660–1744) and André-Cardinal Destouches (1672–1749),

Armide in her final monologue (Lully, *Armide*, 1686, Act V,
scene 5), furious because her captive lover, the warrior Renaud,
has been released from her power by Ubalde and his magic buckler,
calls upon the demons to destroy her palace. In the foreground,
Renaud, in armor, is taking leave of Armide and joining Ubalde
and the Danish knight. Ink-wash by the designer Jean Bérain.
(Phot. Bibl. nat. Paris.)

departed little from his formula. Campra acceded to the renewed taste for
the ballet spectacle by reviving the type of work, usually called opera-ballet,
represented by Lully's *Le Triomphe de l'Amour* (1681). Campra's first opera-
ballet, *L'Europe galante* (1697), consists of a prologue and four loosely connected ballets, or *entrées*. More significant is his *Les Fêtes vénitiennes* (1710).
Though similarly organized, it gives evidence of fresh receptivity to Italian
music after the death of Lully, whose dictatorial control of the Academy of
Music had excluded it. *Les Fêtes vénitiennes* contains motto arias with da
capo in a modified Italian style, designated *ariettes*, a term that remained

attached to these French adaptations of the Italian aria; each is preceded by secco recitative. The voice in these ariettes is accompanied by two treble instrumental parts for violins, or violins doubled by recorders or flutes, rather than the usual five-part strings.

## JEAN-PHILIPPE RAMEAU

By the 1730s the French style of opera was in danger of being submerged permanently. Unexpectedly, *Hippolyte et Aricie* (1733) of Jean-Philippe Rameau (1683–1764) brought the tradition back to life. So vigorous and enduring was Rameau's re-creation of it that *Hippolyte* was performed 123 times by 1767. Far from being overwhelmed by Italian opera seria or buffa, his French opera stirred up a wave that was eventually to sweep into its fold two principal composers of Italian-style opera, Gluck and Piccinni.

Abbé S. J. de Pellegrin's libretto for *Hippolyte et Aricie*, drawing heavily upon Racine's *Phèdre*, brought the *tragédie lyrique* into closer rapport than ever with the spoken tragedy. Superficially the format closely resembles late Quinault-Lully. The core of the dramatic scenes is sung in recitative, either simple or measured. Short airs frequently break into the recitative. There are scenes of divertissement, with ballets, choruses, and lighter airs, but beyond these superficial parallels Rameau's opera is in a different world. For, if Lully had merged the practices of Cavalli's generation with those of contemporary Frenchmen, Rameau brought into rococo France the advances of the Italian high baroque and glimpses of the new classic style.

In Lully's late works the orchestrally accompanied recitative already crowded that accompanied only by harpsichord. Rameau went a step farther. He adopted the very active orchestra of the Italian *recitativo obbligato*. It volunteers its commentary, for example, when Phèdre's conscience is tortured by the thought that she has caused her stepson Hippolyte's death (IV, iv). (She had falsely accused him of an attempt on her honor, thus bringing down on him the fury of her husband, Hippolyte's father, Thesée.) The restless sallies and tremolos of the strings evoke the internal hell that tears her apart.

Even when the orchestra is less independent, it is intensely active harmonically. Rameau's stirring harmonies alone can convey the despair of a Hippolyte banished by his father (IV, i; *NAWM* 75). Example 11-5 shows the measured refrain of his monologue. It is set off by the meter C from the surrounding unmeasured recitative, which is in ¢ and $\frac{3}{4}$. As in similar passages of Lully, the caesuras and line endings are observed in the refrain and are often marked by decorative ornaments, but the melody is so much more fluid that the anapests are hardly noticed. Forward motion is gained by a harmonic technique Rameau may have learned from Corelli, whose music he analyzed

**EXAMPLE 11-5** J.-P. Rameau, *Hippolyte et Aricie*, Act IV, scene i

Ah! faut-il, en un jour, per - dre tout ce que j'ai -
*(Ah! must I in one day lose all that I*

me? Mon Pè - re pour ja - mais me ban-nit de ces lieux si ché- ris de Di-a - ne
*love? My father forever has banished me from these places so dear to Diane*

mê - - - me;
*herself.)*

while preparing his *Traité de l'harmonie* (Treatise of Harmony, 1722).

It was Rameau's theory that each chord aside from the tonic should carry a dissonance whenever possible. Indeed, every chord of the first four measures of Example 11-5 contains a seventh or ninth from the root except for that on A, the tonic. As conceived by Rameau, a chord progression is determined by its "fundamental bass." This concept assumed that a chord is a collection of pitches with a common "fundamental" pitch. For the major triad this is the acoustical fundamental of which the other notes of the chord are partials, though Rameau learned of this phenomenon only after he had proclaimed his theory.

Rameau invented the names "tonic," "dominant," "subdominant," "supertonic," etc. to describe the place each fundamental chord held in the hierarchy of a key. Each of these chords, he showed, could occur in a number of "inversions." Later Rameau applied the same names to chords according to their tendency or function, without regard to key.

Before Rameau, theorists spoke of harmony in terms of the movement from one interval to the next. Only in cadence patterns did they really recognize chord movement. Rameau showed that the most forceful chord sequences arise from stringing together those movements of the fundamental bass that are made in cadences. He called "perfect" the cadence in which the dominant seventh[3] is followed by the tonic. In a chain of such cadences each temporary "tonic" is turned into a temporary "dominant" by adding a seventh to it. This dissonance destroys the feeling of close, and the cadence is "avoided."

In a more usual progression other types of cadences are mixed with the "perfect." An "irregular" cadence is made by proceeding from a tonic chord to a dominant, or from a subdominant to a tonic. To make a temporary subdominant out of a triad, a sixth is added instead of a seventh. A "broken" cadence consists of a dominant chord followed by a triad on the sixth degree, usually in the first inversion. When a dominant chord proceeds to a dominant a third below, this is called an "interrupted" cadence. These cadences are the source of the most frequent harmonic progressions. Thus the strong though often halting motion of the cadences is offset by the cohesive forward push of the sevenths added to the dominant chords. Example 11-5 shows how Rameau's concepts of the fundamental bass and cadential motion may be applied to the beginning of Hippolyte's monologue.

Although this passage seems to issue straight from his theories, it is misleading to regard Rameau as a founder of a new harmonic practice. His is an interpretation of the rich harmony that was already the common coin of Italian composers and some Frenchmen such as François Couperin and Destouches. If Rameau's harmony seems daring and colorful next to Lully's, this is partly because his predecessor was abstemious; yet Rameau's theories did simplify syntax, and this is reflected in his music. He also found a way to justify theoretically such combinations as ninth and eleventh chords, augmented triads, chords with added sixths, and diminished seventh chords.

---

[3]Rameau called the dominant seventh of a key "tonic dominant" (*dominante tonique*) to distinguish it from other seventh chords, major or minor, that function temporarily as dominants, which he called simply "dominant."

EXAMPLE 11-6   J.-P. Rameau, *Hippolyte et Aricie*, Act II, scene v

Consequently, he could use them without guilt when he needed them in certain dramatic situations. His treatises also pointed up the dynamic resources of modulation. The famous Trio des Parques (Fates) "Quelle soudaine horreur" makes superb use of enharmonic modulation "to inspire dread and horror."[4] Example 11-6 gives the central portion of this trio, scored for flutes, oboes, bassoons, and strings. The trio as a whole is in g minor. Between the opening dominant chord and the end of the excerpt, which closes on a dominant chord, there is a hair-raising series of progressions in which the fundamental bass moves alternately up a third and down a fourth. The one "perfect" cadence is reserved for the end.

It is clear that in Rameau's music chordal harmony ended the hegemony of linear counterpoint. Treble and bass are no longer pulling in opposite directions. Rather, the melody, which in Rameau's view comes out of harmony, is supported by a fundamental bass and its chords. Because the

[4]Rameau, *Code de musique pratique* (Paris, 1760), p. 184.

expressive force of music is seen to lie in harmony, chords must linger long enough to be felt. This results in a slowing of harmonic motion. Rameau thus tended in the direction of the preclassic style.

This tendency is most in evidence in *Platée*, a *comédie lyrique* first performed at Versailles in 1745 and at the Opéra in 1749. This opera had the distinction of eliciting superlative praises from the critics who considered French opera a lost cause, for example Jean-Jacques Rousseau, Jean-le-Rond d'Alembert, and Friedrich Melchior Grimm. Later all of these men sided with Italian opera in the *guerre des bouffons*, the pamphlet war between the detractors and admirers of Pergolesi's intermezzo *La serva padrona*, which opened at the Opéra on August 1, 1752. No longer a novelty elsewhere, Pergolesi's intermezzo had its premiere in Naples in 1733 and had even been done in Paris in 1746 without drawing much attention. The fact that *Platée* showed some of the Italian traits that displeased the pro-French party made it one of the issues in the quarrel. Rameau was accused of deserting the ideals of his ancestors. Thus *Platée* was the Trojan horse that eased the entry of the new Italian style of Pergolesi, Rinaldo di Capua, Nicola Jommelli, and Leonardo Leo into the favor of Parisians during the season of 1752–1753.

The *air de danse* for the "Sad Madmen" (Example 11-7) passes from the sentimental to the comic in a few measures, parodying similar juxtapositions in Pergolesi and his compatriots. The ariette "Aux langueurs d'Apollon" is another masterpiece of parody. Some of the *galant*-style mannerisms imitated are phrase repetition and static harmony, sharp contrasts of mood and tempo, and extended florid passages on certain words. That these words are unlikely ones such as "tombeau" (tomb), "métamorphosa" (transformed), and "outragé" (outraged) betrays Rameau's satirical intent. Even in the scenes not studiously mimicking the new Italian style, it subtly invaded his writing.

Rameau's modernity was not all borrowed from foreign sources, however. A good measure of it was owed to his talent for distilling the essence of what was lasting in French music from the ephemeral. Throughout his music there are fleeting echoes of Lully, Couperin, Lambert, and Boesset. He also owed much to the nameless composers of *brunettes* and other popular forms. But he made all these components very much his own.

Rameau's orchestra grew out of the French tradition. The extra viola part was now expunged, reducing the strings to four real parts, and the winds were assigned their own written parts. Rameau had a particular affinity for winds. Their resplendent music in the operas seems generated almost spontaneously in the instruments, so fitting is it to their characters and capabilities. Winds are the soul of the marine, hunting, and pastoral divertissements of *Hippolyte et Aricie* (III, viii; IV, iii; V, iii). In the dances they often alternate with strings or the tutti. For example, in the March of Act V, scene viii, a group of musettes *a 2*, oboes *a 2*, bassoons, and continuo is contrasted against

EXAMPLE 11-7  J.-P. Rameau, *Platée*, Act II, scene v

the entire orchestra and a chorus *a 5* that repeats the same music. In the chaconne of the same scene the smaller ensembles that alternate with the tutti are delicate mixtures of strings or winds or both, setting in relief the repetitions of the eight- or four-measure ostinato patterns.

This chaconne exemplifies the freedom with which Rameau dealt with the stereotyped French dances. Already in Lully, Destouches, and Campra the chaconne had departed from the conventional repetition of a single four-measure harmonic-bass pattern. (See the chaconne from Campra's *Les Fêtes vénitiennes, TEM* 45.) The chaconne of scene viii has not one but several ostinatos. The first, in minor, is an eight-measure theme varied only three times. A free modulatory passage, which, however, preserves the eight-measure periods, leads to the second main section in the parallel major key. This is the longer part and is based on a succession of four different four-measure ostinatos, culminating in two eight-measure dominant pedal points. Such a dynamic form must have presented the choreographer a better than usual opportunity to construct an open and forward-moving series of dance events.

Inventiveness abounds also in the treatment of the rondeau structure, at the heart of many of the instrumental and choral designs. This is a song form practiced throughout French musical history in which the refrains, repeated unvaried, are separated by varied couplets. The first *air à danser* of *Hippolyte et Aricie* (IV, iii) consists of three refrains separated by two different but allied couplets. The entire rondeau is first played by an ensemble of flutes, oboes *a 3*, and bassoons, alternating with tutti including horns *a 2*, and then sung by a hunting girl accompanied by winds and basso continuo. The same formal scheme underlies the second *air en rondeau*, a gavotte, but this time a huntress and hunter alternate with the chorus in making variations upon the refrain, which is played straightforwardly by the orchestra; the couplets are taken by the huntress. Following this a binary minuet frames a second minuet, a true trio of two oboes and bassoon in rondeau form. This dance music, with its sharp contrasts, its symmetries and neat divisions, looks ahead, like the vocal music, toward the classic period.

## OPERA IN ITALY: ALESSANDRO SCARLATTI

Hardening of the categories, that disease of operatic ripeness, overtook Italian opera in the second half of the seventeenth century. The fluid mixture of recitative, arioso, ritornels, and arias out of which Cesti and Cavalli had built their scenes gradually gave way to formalized schemes. Recitative and aria acquired separate functions and discrete boundaries, while the ariosos grew up to be a kind of aria.

These changes came to a head in the career of Alessandro Scarlatti (Palermo, 1660-Naples, 1725). His early operas, intended for private palaces in Rome, are of small dimensions. Comic episodes relieve the serious action or the reverse. From 1684 to 1702, while Scarlatti was director of the Royal Chapel of the Viceroy of Naples, he wrote about two operas a year for the royal palace or the royal theater of San Bartolomeo. These are large-scale works with complicated intrigue plots, using elaborate scenic designs and effects. The primary characters are usually involved in love relationships, while on a secondary plane are various companions, adventurers, and statesmen. On the fringes are the grotesque antics of two comic characters, who often close an act with a lively duet (e.g., *GMB* 258 from *Gl'Inganni felici*, 1699.)

It is during this period that expansive arias assumed the main burden of the musical and emotional content. This concentration of the lyric content was made possible by a happy meeting of esthetic aims and technical resources. On the esthetic side was the recognition that the chief purpose of music in the artistic complex that was the opera theater was the expression of the affections. Scarlatti confessed to his patron Prince Ferdinand de' Medici that the style of *Il Gran Tamerlano* (1706, music lost) was compounded of three simple elements: "naturalness and beauty, together with the expression of the passion with which the characters speak." And this last, he said, "is the very most principal consideration and circumstance for moving and leading the mind of the listener to the diversity of sentiments that the various incidents of the plot of the drama unfold."[5] Since an affection was understood as a state of mind that could occupy a character's thoughts and sentiments over a period of time until he was moved by dialogue or action to another state, the problem for the composer was to sustain a single mood in a way convincing as music and as affection.

It was to this problem that the technical resources accumulated during the century offered a solution. The sonatas and concertos of the 1670s and 1680s advanced the art of organizing chordal and key relationships around a single center and of developing expansive periods out of the motivic germs of a single subject. Vocal composers, by drawing upon this experience, could exceed the modest limits of the earlier arias without recourse to ostinatos, strophic variations, or rondo forms. The modulatory and thematic contrast afforded by episodes in fugal movements and by solos in concertos could be achieved in the aria through a middle section in a foreign key. Concertolike contrast could be gained also by the alternation of instrumental ritornelli and voice, and during vocal sections through the interplay between the voice and orchestra.

Aria-centered opera at its best may be studied in Scarlatti's *Mitridate Eupatore*.[6] Written for the Teator San Giovanni Crisostomo in Venice in 1707, it has a tightly knit libretto, without comic scenes, by Count Girolamo Frigimelica Roberti. The central action is the revenge of Prince Eupatore and his sister Laodice on their mother, Queen Stratonica. The Queen has murdered Eupatore's father and married her lover Farnace.

A fast-slow-fast sinfonia rather than the Venetian prototype of the French overture favored by Cesti and Cavalli, opens the opera. The movements are analogous to those of the concerto but of reduced proportion. As opposed to the French overture, the sinfonia is harmonically rather than contrapuntally conceived, and it exploits the brilliant tutti-soli contrasts of the Italian concerto. Though not itself a weighty piece, the opera sinfonia is important as a direct ancestor of the concert symphony. (See the sinfonia of Scarlatti's final opera, *La Griselda*, 1721, *HAM* II, 259.)

The principal vocal form is the da capo aria, whose identifying characteristic is the literal repetition of an opening section after a contrasting one, giving an ABA scheme. The name is derived from the practice of marking at the end of the B section the words *da capo* (back to the start). *Fine* (the end)

[5] Mario Fabbri, *Alessandro Scarlatti e il Principe Ferdinando de' Medici* (Florence: Leo S. Olschki, 1961), p. 73.

[6] It is available in a piano-vocal score edited by Giuseppe Piccioli (Milan: Edizioni Curci, 1953). Unfortunately, the five acts are compressed into three and in many other details this edition does not give a true picture of the original.

is often indicated at the end of the A section. Scarlatti's early da capo arias are short, like those of Stradella and his generation. (See the two from Stradella's *Floridoro* in *HMS* V, 14–15.) Those of *Mitridate* are quite fully developed, though not so expansive as some from the period after 1720.

Stratonica's aria "Esci ormai" (Example 11-8) illustrates most of the features of the full-blown species. It opens with a sixteen-measure concerto-like ritornello that makes exceptional demands on the solo violinist. Without anticipating any of the vocal melody, it sets the mood of fiery resolution. The Queen proclaims to her people that she is banishing mother-love from her breast for their sake (though an aside in the preceding recitative tells us that she is actually scheming to sacrifice her son for her lover). From this ritornello are drawn most of the orchestral figures sandwiched between the phrases of the vocal line. These figures provide the main unifying thread. The four lines of text are divided equally between the two sections, as in this diagram:

|   |   |   |   |   |
|---|---|---|---|---|
| A | Ritornello | | 16 mm. | A |
| | A$^1$ | Esci ormai chè più non v'hai loco | 4 mm. | A–E |
| | | Materno amore da questo sen! | | |
| | Ritornello | | 1 m. | |
| | A$^2$ | same text | 8 mm. | E–A |
| | Ritornello | | 5 mm. | A |
| B | B$^1$ | In regio petto un più bel foco | 4 mm. | f♯ |
| | | Amor v'accese del comun ben. | | |
| | B$^2$ | same text | 5 mm. | f♯–E |
| A | | Da capo | 34 mm. | |

The rushing sixteenths on the word "Esci" immediately communicate urgency, whereas the clipped rhythm of the descending eighths sets an imperious tone that dominates the next two phrases (Example 11-8). The beginning of the B section (measure 35) is typical in that it is subtly related to the beginning of A. It inverts the opening rising fifth of the A melody into a descending fifth and preserves some of the rhythmic features. Although the first two lines speak of the suppression of maternal love and the last two of the kindling of regal affection for the Queen's subjects, the common thematic material subordinates the two aspects of her speech to a single mood of heroic sacrifice.

A simpler da capo aria, lacking the elaborate ritornello or the modulation to the dominant in the A section, is Eupatore's "Patri Numi" (*SHO*, 2nd ed., p. 174), which he sings as he prays for strength to punish the traitor. Steady adagio eighth notes in the lowest part and the solemn dotted figure of the two violins throughout both A and B sections sustain a plaintive affection.

EXAMPLE 11-8  A. Scarlatti, *Mitridate Eupatore*, Act III, scene iii

(a)

Stratonica
E - sci    E -sci o-mai che più nonV'hai
*(Get    out    now,    for you have no*

Vls.

B.C.

lo - co    ma - ter - no  A - mo - re    da ques - to
*place,    maternal    love,    in  this bosom! )*

sen!    E - sci

(b)

In Re - gi - o pet - to    un più  bel  fo - co  a-
*(In royal    breast    a  brighter    fire*

EXAMPLE 11-8 (Cont.)

mor v'ac - ce - se del co - mun ben.
*kindles love for the common good.)*

Even the arias without full da capo are influenced by the constructive methods of the da capo aria. Eupatore's aria "Stelle" brings back only the three-measure ritornello after the B section. Throughout this appeal to the stars there is a dialogue between the beautiful coloraturas of the singer and the delicate thirty-second-note figures of the violins (Example 11-9).

**EXAMPLE 11-9** A. Scarlatti, *Mitridate Eupatore*, Act IV, scene i

Eupatore
Stel - - - - le!
*(Stars!*

Vl.I
Vl.II

Vla.
Vlc.
B.C.

EXAMPLE 11-9 (Cont.)

Stel - le, se il vos - tro lu - me ha vir - tù so - vra
*Stars!     if your     ray       has sovereign rule     over*

me, be - ni - gne ar-de -
*me,  benignly        burn.)*

te be- ni - gne ar - de - te.

This enchanting music follows a magnificent procession of Eupatore's soldiers disembarking at dawn to the sounds of two muted trumpets and timpani in the orchestra pit, answered by two trumpets and timpani on the ship. Eupatore has disguised himself as an agent of the Queen and is purportedly delivering his own severed head to her in an urn. The urn is empty, but Laodice, not recognizing her brother, thinks Eupatore's head must be in it. After an impassioned recitative she sings the aria "Cara tomba," which Edward J. Dent rated the greatest in all of Scarlatti's operas.[7]

Again it is not a da capo aria, though it is constructed like a full A section with three ritornelli. The second part modulates from the tonic b minor to d minor instead of to D Major. Example 11-10 shows the return to the tonic. On each first and third quarter of the measure the voice rises to a higher chromatic step. The harmony also gathers intensity, culminating on the diminished seventh chord just before the cadence at "anche con te!" The aria is a perfect embodiment of a sister's tender love and inconsolable grief.

Scarlatti lavished great care on recitative. He once expressed the hope that he might succeed so well in recitative that its "force and efficacy will not make one long for the arias, as usually happens."[8] A short section from the

**EXAMPLE 11-10**   A. Scarlatti, *Mitridate Eupatore*, Act IV, scene ii

---

[7]*Alessandro Scarlatti: His Life and Works* (new ed.; London: Edward Arnold, Ltd., 1960), p. 112. Part of the recitative and the beginning of the aria are printed on pp. 109–12.

[8]Fabbri, *Scarlatti*, p. 78.

speech that precedes the aria (Example 11-11) illustrates the richness of harmony and the swiftness of modulation it is capable of. (See *SHO*, 2nd ed. p. 179, for the subsequent and final portion of this recitative.) Several details deserve notice: the diminished-seventh chords (measures 16 and 18), the augmented and diminished intervals in both voice and bass, and the Neapolitan harmony (measure 17), as the chord formed from the triad on the lowered second degree is called. These harmonies convey the emotion without retarding the speechlike pace of the declamation.

**EXAMPLE 11-11**　A. Scarlatti, *Mitridate Eupatore*, Act IV, scene ii

Two singers performing a cantata or opera duet with the accompaniment of a harpsichord and 'cello playing the continuo. A violin, two recorders, and an oboe play obbligato parts. The complexity of the instrumental parts in eighteenth-century arias and duets, as, for example, in Scarlatti's late operas, reached a point where the conductor—the man with the rolled up music sheet—became necessary. (Engraving by Johann Christoph Steudner after the design by Paul Decker der Ä. Halle, Händel-Haus [GDR])

As is typical of Scarlatti's operas, the chorus is scarce. It sings only in Act III, showering praises on King Farnace, but it is again on stage in Act V to give silent assent to the surprising outcome of Eupatore's conspiracy. Although the plot offered good opportunities for grand choral scenes, Scarlatti was careful not to detract from the solo roles. Instead the chameleonic public is impersonated in Pelopida, King Farnace's loyal minister, who reverses himself to glorify the new King Eupatore. In the manner of the time, there are several such supporting characters who advance the action little but inject welcome variety, particularly of vocal color, adding two alto voices to the three sopranos, Stratonica, Laodice, and Eupatore, and the one tenor, Farnace.

In *Mitridate Eupatore* Scarlatti fought the current of fashion. His fellow composers were on the one hand moving toward a simpler, more popular style of melody, and on the other catering to the exhibitionism of singers. Scarlatti never succumbed to these trends to the degree that his rivals did—for example, Giacomo Antonio Perti (1661–1756), who replaced him as the favorite of the Duke of Tuscany, or Giovanni Maria Bononcini. Nevertheless, Scarlatti's late operas are full of signs of the times. The arias become grander and more detached from the dramatic flow; the B section develops into a two-section form mediated by a ritornello, as for example in

"No, non sospira l'amor d'un Re" in *La Griselda* (1721; I, iii). Coloraturas are less motivated and more than ever long-winded and showy. Harmonic motion slows as the bass becomes less a counterweight, more a supporting girder. The orchestra gives the singer the advantage by staying in the background and complementing rather than competing.

Scarlatti's comic opera *Il Trionfo dell'onore* (The Triumph of Honor, 1718) is his most forward-looking stage work. A semi-serious farce, it is full of witty yet touching songs, duets, and quartets. The foibles of modern society are mirrored in characters and action clearly inspired by the improvised farce, the *commedia dell'arte*. The arias concentrate on unstable sentiments such as the coquettish love of the maid Rosina or the deceptive ardor of a Don Juan named Riccardo. Occasionally Scarlatti satirized the poses of opera seria, as when Leonora, whose honor has been robbed by Riccardo, sings a mock despair aria, complete with plunging string figures, an ominous Neapolitan chord, and a dramatic hold on a diminished seventh chord. But she stops herself before the aria sprouts a full da capo. Realizing it is all in vain, she blushes at her error and faints ("Mio destin," I, i). Another characteristic moment is the short da capo aria "Avete nel volto" (II, i; Example 11-12) sung by Rosina. Pursued by her mistress's fiancé Flaminio, and already the victor of Captain Rodimarte's heart, she is now greedy for Leonora's brother, Erminio. Her tune turns from playful to sentimental with the freedom and impetuosity that mark the comic style. The excerpt in Example 11-12 (the A² section) shows this and other characteristics of the comic manner: frequent syncopations, immediate repetition of short phrases, sudden self-interruptions and changes of mood, static harmony that rocks between tonic and dominant, and additive as opposed to continuously evolving melody. Out of such inherently counter-baroque mannerisms as these, the next generation of opera composers, mostly centered in Naples, forged the new *galant* style.

**EXAMPLE 11-12**  A. Scarlatti, *Il Trionfo dell'onore*, Act II, scene i

# BIBLIOGRAPHICAL NOTES

French operas are well represented in published editions Lully's *Cadmus et. Hermione*, *Alceste*, and *Amadis* as well as numerous ballets and ballet comedies are printed in full score in *Oeuvres complètes*, edited by Henry Prunières (10 vols.; Paris, Editions de *La Revue musicale*, 1930–1939). The Prologue and Acts I and II of *Armide* are in *EP* XIV. Four operas of Rameau, including *Hippolyte et Aricie* (Vol. 6), and several opera ballets are in the incomplete *Oeuvres complètes* (17 vols; Paris: A. Durand & fils, 1895–1913). Many of the same and additional works by Cambert, Campra, Destouches, and others are in piano-vocal editions of uneven reliability in the series *Chefs d'oeuvre de l'opéra français* (Paris: T. Michaelis, c. 1880). A thorough guide to Rameau's works is Cuthbert Girdlestone's *Jean-Philippe Rameau, His Life and Work* (London: Cassel and Co. Ltd., 1957; New York: Dover, 1969). Rameau's pathbreaking *Traité de l'harmonie* of 1722 is faithfully and readably translated by Philip Gossett as *Treatise on Harmony* (New York: Dover, 1971). An exceedingly fine introduction to the social, artistic, and intellectual background of French music during the reign of Louis XIV is Chapters 2 and 3 of Wilfrid Mellers's *François Couperin and the French Classical Tradition* (London: Dennis Dobson Ltd., 1950; New York: Dover, 1968). André Campra's *Les Fêtes vénitiennes* is edited by Max Lütolf in the series *Le pupitre*, No. 19 (Paris: Heugel, 1972) and a selection from his operas is in Campra, *Operatic Airs*, edited by Graham Sadler (London: Oxford University Press, 1973).

For a broad view of France's musical culture in this period, see James R. Anthony, *French Baroque Music from Beaujoyeulx to Rameau* (London: Batsford, 1973; New York: W. W. Norton & Co., Inc., 1974), which contains a good survey of the ballet de cour, pastorale, tragédie lyrique, and opera ballet.

Alessandro Scarlatti's name is far better known than his music. This situation is being remedied by the Harvard University Press series, *The Operas of Alessandro Scarlatti*, under the general editorship of Donald Jay Grout. Issued so far are *Ericlea*, edited by Grout (1975), *Marco Attilio Regolo*, edited by Joscelyn Godwin (1975), and *Griselda*, edited by Grout and Elizabeth B. Hughes (1975).

*Il Trionfo dell'onore* is available in a piano-vocal score (Milan: Carisch, 1941). The Prologue and Acts I and II of *La Rosaura*, edited by Robert Eitner, are in *EP* XIV.

# TWELVE

# DRAMATIC MUSIC IN ENGLAND

Most of the conditions that delayed the rooting of opera in France worked against it also in England. A strong theatrical tradition relegated music to a decorative and occasional function. The court and private masque, which was the English counterpart of the ballet de cour, emphasized spectacle and dance at the expense of dramatic vocal music. There was no Mazarin to promote Italian operas, and the first of them did not begin to trickle in until the eighteenth century. Beside these artistic factors stands the fact that during the Civil War and Commonwealth period (1649–1660) theater practically ceased to exist.

Ben Jonson had made a promising beginning in the Jacobean era with masques magnificently staged by Inigo Jones, set to music partly in recitative style by Nicholas Lanier and later by William and Henry Lawes. The Poet Laureate Sir William Davenant obtained in 1639 a theater patent from Charles I with the intention of establishing a program of extravaganzas using music, drama, and dancing, but civil upheaval prompted the Lords and

Commons to issue an order on September 2, 1642, to close the theaters. Davenant finally succeeded in 1656 in staging ten performances of a "Representation by the Art of Prospective in Scenes, and the Story Sung in Recitative Music" called *The Siege of Rhodes*. The music, by some of the most eminent English composers of the day, is lost. However, a private masque organized three years earlier by Luke Channell in honor of the Portuguese ambassador gives a good sampling of the styles of music then practiced on the stage. This was *Cupid and Death* by the poet James Shirley. An autograph manuscript by Matthew Locke, dating from this masque's second performance at the meeting house of the Military Ground in Leicester Fields in 1659, gives his own music for it and that of Christopher Gibbons.

The music (in *Musica Brittanica* II) consists of entry pieces, dance pieces, pleasant songs that are mainly independent of the action, and recitative passages. Locke's recitative was modeled on an Italian manner long out of fashion in Italy, very unstable tonally and full of arioso outbursts. It was self-contained, not being preparative to arias. The rhythmic freedom, the many cross relations, and free dissonances found here passed into the recitative of John Blow (1648/9–1708) and Henry Purcell.

## HENRY PURCELL

The main deterrent to progress toward a native opera was the absence of a composer of sufficient talent and versatility to cope with its myriad problems. When such a man—Henry Purcell (1659–1695)—arrived upon the scene, the moment of opportunity had passed. A peculiarly English compromise which did not dilute the strength of the masque's dramatic poetry and preserved its visual and musical feast had preempted the stage—the heroic play with music. Although such plays were sometimes advertised as "operas" or "dramatic operas," the musical element was confined to scenes not unlike the divertissements of the French ballet comedies and operas. Among such plays for which Purcell wrote music is John Dryden's *King Arthur* (1691). An inventory of its scenes with music makes plain how accessory to drama were the composer's functions: a sacrifice scene (I, ii), a battle scene (I, ii), spirit scenes (II, III), a pastoral scene (II), a frost scene (III), and forest scenes and triumphs in honor of Britain (V). It must be acknowledged, on the other hand, that the main excuse for such a play was the music.

Two years earlier Purcell had shown in *Dido and Aeneas* (1689) that his powers as a composer were equal to situations of high emotional intensity. Though a miniature opera written for performance by a girls' school, it had a grand sweep, tragic nobility, and swiftness of action that promised a new kind of music drama. It was true to the English stage tradition while drawing freely upon French and Italian musical practices. An unmistakable French flavor pervades the instrumental music, particularly the Triumphing Dance, the Sailors' Dance, the Overture, the Prelude for the Witches, and the Echo Dance of the Furies. Even the arrangement of scenes and the prominence of supernatural happenings seem to be indebted to the French opera. But actually these are masquelike episodes of a sort long cherished by the English, too.

The points of contact with Italian opera are more significant. Prominent among the arias are those on ground basses: "Ah, Ah, Belinda," "Oft she visits," and the final lament "When I am laid in earth." These suggest that the Italian influence came to Purcell through cantatas and operas of the middle of the century, the heyday of the ground bass in Italy. (Cavalli, for example, had used two short laments on chromatically descending basses in only the first act of *Didone* of 1641). Purcell's forms tend to be more extended. For example, by contrast to "Mio ben, teco il tormento" from Luigi Rossi's *Orfeo* (1647), in which a four-measure ground is heard ten times, "Ah, Ah, Belinda" extends a four-measure ground to eleven statements in the tonic, two in the dominant, and eight more in the tonic. Purcell's vocal line avoids the sweet smooth contours of Cesti and Carissimi, whose cantatas he must have known. Instead, the melody preserves the flavor of the earlier Italian monodies. Its angularity, insistent text rhythms, and free dissonance hark back to pre-bel-canto Italian melody. The *accenti*, exclamations, trills, *portamenti*, and similar ornaments taught by Caccini are used for expressive emphasis, as they were in the English airs. Florid lines like that of the following excerpt from "Ah, Ah, Belinda" may be reduced to rather simple terms by removing such ornaments, as in Example 12-1.

**EXAMPLE 12-1** H. Purcell, *Dido and Aeneas*. Act I

Not all of Purcell's arias have this archaic flavor. "Oft she visits" has a walking-type ostinato more frequently found in the second half of the century. (Compare it with "Resta in vita" from *Achille in Siro*, 1672, of Antonio Masini.) Belinda's aria "Pursue thy conquest, Love" is surprisingly modern with its fanfarelike motto, the near canonic relation between the bass and soprano, and its perseverance in a single affection.

The choruses of *Dido* are mainly in a native English style Purcell learned in the syllabic setting of sacred texts. Some of them, though, such as "Fear no danger to ensue," remind one of Lully; and the contemplative choruses "Great minds against themselves conspire" and "With drooping wings ye Cupids come" belong to the Italian madrigal tradition. The models were probably Blow's lamenting choruses in *Venus and Adonis* (1683). Blow's obvious antecedents, in turn, are the lamenting choruses of the Florentine and Roman operas, for example, "Ah! piangete" in Luigi Rossi's *Orfeo*.

Composed only three years later, Purcell's music for the masque *The Fairy Queen* (1692), at least in its dozen or so pieces of obvious Italian derivation, reflects a sure knowledge of the style of the last quarter of the seventeenth century. There are da capo arias, a motto aria, a Siciliano, a trumpet aria, several arias with concerto-style obbligato parts, and such details as Neapolitan harmony. Moreover, the Symphony for Act IV imitates the sequence of movements and manner of the ripieno concerto. The one ground-bass aria, "O, let me weep" (V; *NAWM* 74b), is in the $\frac{3}{2}$ bel canto idiom, the smooth vocality being broken only for affective intervals on words such as "weep" and "sigh." Like most late examples of ostinato, it has a free middle section and a free coda. The tenor song "See, my many colour'd fields" (IV) exemplifies the Italian aria bordering on the arioso. True to type, it uses two violins, expressive intervals like the ascending minor sixth, and imitation in all the parts so contrived as to produce many suspensions. It belongs to the same genre as "Infelice miei lumi" of Scarlatti's cantata *Su le sponde del Tebro*. The continuo aria with much dialogue between voice and bass, "Thus the ever grateful Spring," and the trumpet aria, "Hark! the ech'ing air" (V; both in *NAWM*: 74 a, c), are two more Italian types. The latter, in which the singer imitates the brilliant figures of the trumpet, may be compared to a similar aria, "Con battaglia di fiero tormento," in Scarlatti's serenata "*Il Giardino di Amore*."

Purcell was obviously attracted to the musical qualities and expressive force of the Italian aria styles. Unfortunately, he lacked a proper context to make the most of them. The weak texts Purcell had to set, only too painfully audible because of his careful declamation, dispel most of the illusion of feeling his music achieves. The English stage demanded too little of music. It asked that it paint a little atmosphere, divert the spectator with a few songs, accompany dances, and occasionally set a sad or tender mood or a gay and trifling one. But the task of arousing deep emotions or unfolding a dramatic situation was the prerogative of the poet. Under the circumstances, the English Restoration stage got better music than it deserved in the work of Purcell. A born opera composer in search of an opera house, he might have found one had he not died so young.

## GEORG FRIDERIC HANDEL (1685-1759)

### Operas

When Handel produced his first London opera—*Rinaldo*, in 1711—the English public was already acquainted with Italian-style operatic music not only from Purcell but from various imitations and importations. An Italian libretto translated into English, *Arsinoe, Queen of Cyprus*, was produced in 1705 at the Drury Lane theater with music mainly by Thomas Clayton, who had studied in Italy, and by two others: Nicola Haym (1679–1729), an Italian-born German, and Charles Dieupart (d. c. 1740), a French musician. Clayton later collaborated in *Rosamond* in 1707 with Joseph Addison, who, after this failed, turned to writing acid essays against Italian opera. There were also adaptations of Italian operas, Antonio Maria Bononcini's *Camilla* in English in 1706, and Alessandro Scarlatti's *Pirro e Demetrio* (Naples, 1694), partly in English, partly in Italian, in 1708. The first completely Italian opera was Giovanni Bononcini's *Almahide* in 1710, though it too was garnished with some English intermezzi.

To London, Handel was an Italian composer, but actually he had begun his theatrical career in Hamburg. His first opera produced there, *Almira*, in 1705, was a mixture of German recitatives and airs with Italian arias. (Bilingual opera was normal in this melting pot of musical styles.) Johann Sigismund Kusser (1660–1727), one of the first director-composers of Hamburg's public lyric theater, had spent eight years in Paris and brought in many French practices. French-style overtures and choral and ballet scenes thus found their way into *Almira* and other Handel operas. The main exponent of the Italian style in the Hamburg repertory was Agostino Steffani (1654–1728), the court music director at Hanover, whom Handel replaced in 1710 for a short time. What Handel knew of Italian opera at this time he must have learned from Steffani's example. The Italian style in *Almira* naturally dominates the arias in Italian, but it invades most of the German airs too. One of the best examples of this is the furious aria with da capo, "Der Himmel wird strafen dein falsches Gemüth" (The heavens will punish your false heart, II, xii). The orchestra, however, is a German ensemble, richer and busier than the Italian, and a distinctly German church-cantata uniformity and stiffness characterize the recitatives. Some of the German airs in *Almira* have the form and flavor of the seventeenth-century German lied, simple in melody and hewing closely to the poetic form. These German traits bear the stamp of the theater's director Reinhard Keiser (1674–1739), whose operas Handel regarded highly. Four years in Italy (1706–1710) converted Handel almost completely to the melodious Italian manner, although his predilection for counterpoint, choral writing, and elaborate instrumentation never left him.

Handel wrote about forty operas for London between 1711 and 1741. A close look at two of his best works, one composed at the height of his success—*Giulio Cesare* (1724)—and the other during his struggle for survival as a composer of opera—*Alcina* (1735)—will reveal some of their outstanding characteristics.

The author of the fine libretto of *Giulio Cesare* was Haym, the composer, cellist, and bibliographer who supplied eight or more librettos for Handel. Haym took some liberties with the facts of Caesar's sojourn in Egypt to permit each character to contribute significantly to the denouement. Ptolemy's rule over Egypt is threatened by his sister Cleopatra's plot to unseat him. She strives to win Caesar to her side through womanly wiles. King Ptolemy too hopes to gain Caesar's favor by presenting him with the head of Pompey, whom Caesar has pursued to Egypt. Pompey's wife, Cornelia (in reality he was married to Julia, Caesar's daughter) and her son Sesto seek revenge for Pompey's murder. Caesar, shocked by Ptolemy's brutal deed, joins Cleopatra in the second act to fight the forces of Ptolemy. In Act III Ptolemy's forces are victorious over Cleopatra's and she is made prisoner. Caesar escapes by swimming out to sea. On returning he finds Achilla, who has turned against Ptolemy because the King did not reward him with the beautiful Cornelia as promised. Together with Sesto they gain entry into the palace and liberate Cleopatra. Sesto stabs Ptolemy (in history he accidentally drowned in the Nile) and Caesar crowns Cleopatra.

The disposition of arias, and consequently the action, was controlled by a protocol imposed by the reign of the virtuoso singers. Once brought on the stage, a principal singer had to be given an aria, after which he normally made an exit, he hoped amidst swells of applause. Exceptions were made, as when Cleopatra moves to leave after an aria but is detained by Nireno to observe Cornelia's plaint over Pompey's tomb (I, vii). The plan of Act I may be represented by the diagram on page 253.

The part of Caesar was written for the famous alto castrato Senesino. Castrated male sopranos and altos were Handel's preferred voices for heroic parts such as that of Caesar. (If operated upon before his voice changed, a boy possessing a naturally good voice, could with age and training develop a powerful, smooth, agile projection, while preserving the high pitch. When Handel could not find a good castrato, he sometimes wrote a youthful male role for a woman soprano, but he usually preferred women for female roles.)

As the *primo uomo*, Caesar has the largest number of arias—eight—of which six are followed by exits. In addition he has a duet with Cleopatra before the final chorus, which is actually an ensemble of soloists. Cleopatra, the *prima donna* part, first sung by the great Francesca Cuzzoni, likewise has eight arias besides the duet, five of them exit arias. Both Caesar and Cleopatra have two accompanied recitatives apiece. Cornelia, sung by Mrs. Robinson,

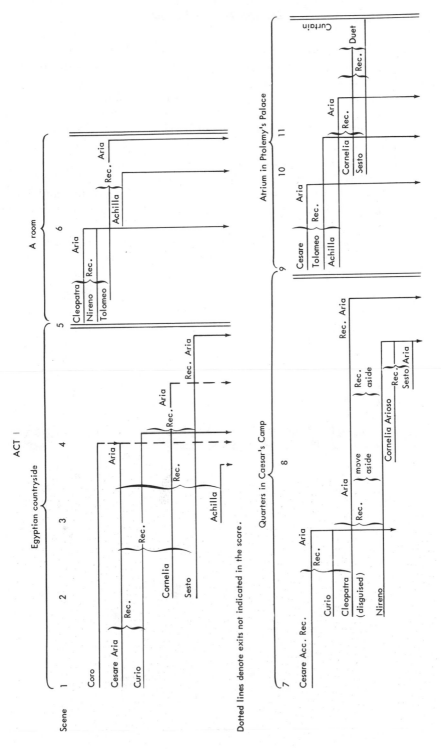

Dotted lines denote exits not indicated in the score.

has three exit arias and two ariosi, and she shares the duet-finale of Act I with Sesto. Sesto, sung by Margherita Durastante, a soprano famed for male roles, gets one exit aria per act.

Because of the exit convention, the arias are mainly static culminations of the preceding recitative, but this does not mean the opera is an undramatic succession of arias separated by recitatives. Characters profess their love or scorn, conjure conspiracies, murder, and win and lose battles in natural, vivid, and swift encounters. The economy of the recitatives gives room for the real drama: the conflicts and interactions among the aspirations, attitudes, and emotions expressed in arias. Deeply felt and finely wrought characterizations succeed each other with dazzling brilliance and variety. A few of these may be singled out.

Sesto's revenge aria, "Svegliatevi nel core," has two contrasting sections. In the first (Example 12-2a) concertato strings play against vigorous, almost instrumental leaps in the voice. The B section (Example 12-2b) is a plaintive largo in bel canto style, with flutes added to the orchestra. Here Sesto prays for his father's ghost to come to his aid.

**EXAMPLE 12-2**   G. F. Handel, *Giulio Cesare*, Act I, scene iv

Cleopatra's reflections on the pleasures of love, "Tu la mia stella sei," is at the opposite pole. Its simply accompanied, short-breathed, and absolutely vocal phrases imitate the lighter style of the younger Italians (Example 12-3). In similar vein is the sarabande aria "V'adoro pupille," daintily accompanied by an orchestra divided in concerto-grosso style. The concertino consists of oboes, muted violins, viola, and a continuo group made up of viola da gamba theorbo, harp, bassoons, and cellos. The concerto grosso calls for muted strings.

There are three fine "simile" arias. In this type the A section usually paints what appears to be an extraneous vignette until the B section relates it to the character's situation. In "Va tacito e nascosto" (Example 12-4), Caesar, suspecting that Ptolemy has some kind of treachery up his sleeve, compares him to an astute hunter stealing up to his prey. The orchestra is dominated by the horn's hunting theme, which is imitated by the voice. The repeated eighths in the theme suggest the measured steps of the hunter.

Another simile aria is Sesto's "L'angue offeso mai riposa" (The hurt snake never rests, II, vi), which includes among its picturesque devices a winding snakelike concertato figure in the violins and a long run on "spande"

**EXAMPLE 12-3**  G. F. Handel, *Giulio Cesare*, Act I, scene viii

**EXAMPLE 12-4**  G. F. Handel, *Giulio Cesare*, Act I, scene ix

Va ta - ci - to e nas - co - sto, Quand' a - vi - do è di pre - da, L'a
*(He moves silently and concealed,    when he's intent upon his prey,    the*

stu - to cac - cia - tor,
*astute hunter. )*

(spills) to describe the emptying of poison into the offender. Caesar in "Quel torrente, che cade dal monte" (III, v) compares himself to the torrent from the mountains that sweeps all before it as he sings long runs on "atterra" (sweeps down) and the violins play cascading figures.

Cleopatra has two great laments. The aria "Se pietà," preceded by an accompanied recitative, expresses her sorrow after Ptolemy's conspirators break in to murder Caesar (excerpts in *SHO* 2nd ed., pp. 165–67). The drooping obbligato figure, the intense harmony, and the angular coloraturas make one think of Bach. She sings the second lament, "Piangerò" (III, iii), when she herself is taken prisoner. A descending-fourth ground bass is treated freely in the A section, whereas the B section is in the furious concertato style.

The Siciliano, a Sicilian dance usually in $\frac{12}{8}$ meter, finds its way into every Handel opera to express feelings of either tender melancholy or bucolic bliss. A representative of the first is the Sesto-Cornelia duet "Son nata a lagrimar" (I am born to weep, I, xi) in largo tempo. The final idyllic duet of Caesar and Cleopatra, an allegro non troppo, illustrates the second type. Another dance is at the basis of the final "chorus" in four parts sung by the octet of principal singers. It is a gavotte with trio, the latter sung as a duet with basso continuo by Cleopatra and Caesar, doubled by two oboes.

One significant departure from the recitative-aria pairing in a number of Handel's operas is the grand scene reserved for principal singers. Caesar has an impressive one on a beach after slipping from Ptolemy's murderers by swimming (III, iv; *NAWM* 77). It begins with a string sinfonia describing a gentle sea breeze. Caesar asks in accompanied recitative where he must go to find his legions. Next he addresses the breeze in a bel canto aria, "Aure, deh per pietà" (Breezes, for pity's sake), as the strings recall the previous breeze music. In the B section Caesar speaks of Cleopatra in interjections punctuated by fragments of the breeze music. Then instead of the da capo we hear an accompanied recitative, and only after this does the A section return.

About one-fourth of Handel's London operas are, like *Giulio Cesare*, based on Roman history. Fewer than one-fourth of them are on mythological, magical, and Persian themes. About a third are derived from medieval romances or the Renaissance epics and pastorals by Ariosto, Tasso, and Guarini. *Alcina* (1735), for example, is drawn from Ariosto's *Orlando furioso*.

Alcina herself is a counterpart of Tasso's Armide, an enchantress who captures Christian knights and turns them into beasts. But she falls in love with her prisoner, Ruggiero, thereby losing her magic powers. Without them she is easily overcome by "Ricciardo" and his followers. "Ricciardo" is actually Ruggiero's fiancée Bradamante, who has come to search for him. Exchanges of sex of this sort were facilitated by the custom of placing men's parts in the soprano or alto voice. For example, Ruggiero's part was written for a male soprano, whereas Bradamante's was for a female alto.

Most of *Alcina* is in the high baroque style, but many of the arias are in a *galant*, or nearly *galant*, style.

There are several fine baroque arias. Ruggiero's "Sta nell'ircana pietrosa" (She waits in her stony lair, III, iii) is a splendid grand da capo simile aria. A concertino of two horns paints a hunting scene as Alcina is compared to a tigress poised staring at a hunter, debating whether to abandon her young and flee or take him on. Alcina's "Tornami a vagheggiar" (Come back to woo me, I, xv) develops a graceful rhetorical figure inspired by the word "vagheggiar" into a maze of coloratura. Bradamante's "Vorrei vendicarmi" (I want my revenge, II, ii) is one of Handel's most powerful concertato furious arias.

Otherwise *Alcina* is impressive mostly for the arias in the new style. The instruments in Alcina's "Dì, cor mio" (I, ii) appear to be busily engaged in baroque fashion, but they are really only punctuating the slow harmonic rhythms of a squarely periodic melody. The sixteenth-note turn beginning on the downbeat, as on "mio," is a cliché of this style (Example 12-5).

**EXAMPLE 12-5**  G. F. Handel, *Alcina*, Act I, scene ii

EXAMPLE 12-5 (Cont.)

mostra il bos - co, il fon - te, il ri - o,
*show him the woods, the brook, the river)*

A sad affection is treated lightly as Morgana pleads with Oronte to take her back after she has neglected him for Ricciardo (III, i). The opening two-measure phrase (Example 12-6a) is expanded to three measures in the A² section (12-6b) by means of an effusion of coloratura dominated by the triplet figure, a characteristic rhythm of the *galant* style.

A mocking tone is achieved in "La bocca vaga" (The lovely mouth, I, xi) when Ruggiero dismisses as mad raving "Ricciardo's" confession that "he" is Bradamante.

These are a few of the many arias in which Handel sets aside the heroic bigger-than-life passions of the baroque to treat with equal care and a good measure of sophistication the everyday sentiments of mortals. He must have found a fresh stimulus to creation in this new idiom, for he indulged in it frequently in his last operas, particularly in *Serse* (1738).

Handel's seeming capitulation to the new fashion from Naples was partly stimulated by competition from younger composers, but there were other circumstances. Handel lost a loyal supporter when King George I died in 1727. The Royal Academy of Music at the King's Theater, for which Handel staged his operas, failed financially in 1728. The same year a ballad opera, *The Beggar's Opera* (excerpt in *NAWM* 78), reminded the English public how entertaining musical theater could be in their own language. This saucy satirical comedy by John Gay had songs set to popular, operatic, and other borrowed melodies. It ran for sixty-two nights and had more than a hundred sequels, though none was as successful as the original. When Handel and the stage manager, Johann Heidegger, opened again with their own company in 1729, they had to face competition not only from the new English comedies but also from a rival Italian company. Patronized by the Prince of Wales and the Duke of Marlborough, it had a master of the *galant* style, Nicola Porpora (1686–1768), as the principal composer. In spite of occasional artistic successes, both companies failed in 1737. Handel continued to struggle against dwindling audiences until 1741.

The new *galant* style did not bring the public back. The music may have suited the rising middle class in Italy, but it was not the answer to a

EXAMPLE 12-6  G. F. Handel, *Alcina*, Act III, scene i

(a)

Cre - de - te al mio do - lo - re, Lu - ci ti - ran - ne e ca -re!
*(Believe in    my aching heart,    yes,    both cruel    and dear.)*

(b)

Cre - de - te al mio do - lo - - - - - - re.

similar social phenomenon in London. The newly wealthy had little taste for foreign opera, and the nobility preferred the old Handel. By 1741 Handel finally faced the fact that his English oratorios were much more in demand than his operas, and he returned to the high-baroque style of that form.

## Oratorios

Handel's English oratorios have rather slight connection with the Latin or Italian oratorios of the seventeenth century or even with Handel's own *La Resurrezione* (The Resurrection, 1708). It is futile to generalize about them as a class or to group them in various categories. At one end of the spectrum are those, such as *Messiah* (1742) and *Israel in Egypt* (1739), that are lacking in dramatic thread; at the other end, those that are virtual operas. For example, the so-called secular oratorio *Semele* (1743), if staged with action, costumes, and scenery, would be a true English opera. That the oratorio was not so staged is an essential point of distinction. Staging was avoided largely because after a revival of *Esther* with staging in 1732, in which the children of the Chapel Royal performed, the Bishop of London, Dr. Edmund Gibson, was said to have forbade further theatrical performances of this biblical story.

The English oratorios had the same ingredients as the opera, mixed in somewhat different proportions. The overture, recitatives, ariosos, and arias functioned as in the opera, but the chorus took on a more important role, and it is the choral writing particularly that linked the oratorio with the English musical tradition, for it came out of Handel's experience with the anthem. During the period between 1717 and about 1719, when Handel served as composer to James Brydges, Duke of Chandos, at his residence in Cannons, he wrote twelve anthems known as the "Chandos Anthems." In these he showed that he had studied the anthems of Purcell, who, in turn, had absorbed the heritage of the Protestant anthem literature that can be traced back to the Renaissance motet.

Though perhaps not the best of Handel's oratorios from any point of view, *Solomon* (1749) presents three important facets of the Handelian oratorio. It has, with *Messiah*, some of Handel's greatest choruses. Like the ever-popular *Judas Maccabeus*, it is largely ceremonious. Not as exciting a biblical drama as *Saul*, it tells in one important scene one of the most captivating Old Testament stories, that of Solomon's judgment between two mothers.

The whole is a paean to King Solomon and by implication to King George II of England. Act I celebrates the inauguration of the newly built Temple and dwells upon the idyllic relationship between Solomon and his young queen. Act II praises the wisdom of Solomon through a dramatization of his legendary judgment in the case of a child contested by two women. Act III is a display of the magnanimity, prosperity, and pomp of the monarchy by way of an entertainment—a kind of masque—for the visiting Queen of Sheba.

The choruses show a rich variety of approaches. The magnificent opening double chorus, "Your harps and cymbals sound," combines several techniques in a most original way. It begins with all the choral basses proclaiming a theme. Only after this statement, as in some motto arias, does a concerto-style ritornello begin. It is Vivaldi-like in its grouping of figures in $4 + 2 + 4$-measure segments. But the chorus is organized more like a concerto-fugue without exposition than a concerto-allegro. A subject set to the words "To great Jehovah's praise" roves among the parts in the fugal sections, while in the episodes short homophonic exclamations bounce between the two choruses against reiterations of ritornello material.

The double chorus "With pious heart and holy tongue resound your Maker's name" begins like a solemn accompanied recitative against a constant beating of orchestral chords that modulate with daring intensity and rapidity. This is followed by a polychoral motet in German style on a simple tune set to the words "Till distant nations catch the song." The inevitable but evocative melismas on words such as "flame" and "glow" remind one of Schütz.

Act I ends with a haunting lullaby for Solomon retiring with his queen. It is the famous five-voice "Nightingale Chorus," "May no rash intruder disturb their soft hours." This is the greatest nature picture of the many Handel wrote. It is compounded of simple elements that are stocks in trade of many French ariettes (e.g., *Hippolyte et Aricie*, V, iii)—birdlike figures in the flutes and slow trills in the strings over pedal points to suggest hot breezes and droning insects. Yet Handel's alchemy transforms these clichés into a beautifully integrated structure that is a perfect rendering of the words.

The chorus that opens Act II, "From the censer curling rise, grateful incense to the skies," is one of those shining glorifications that Handel created with ease. A four-part fugue with partly polychoral episodes is framed between a double chorus in concerto style and its expanded recapitulation.

Of the pieces in the masque of Act III, which develops the theme of the powers of music, the outstanding chorus is "Draw the tear from hopeless love." It is a choral adaptation of the slow arioso style with imitations and suspensions.

The arias of *Solomon*, as of Handel's late oratorios generally, pale next to the choruses. Many of them are written in a pleasant, melodious style strongly penetrated by the English air and popular song. Gone are the potent affections of the Italian operas. The anonymous libretto is partly accountable, for the poetry is pretty and picturesque but timid and blurred in its emotional focus. A sameness of mood winds its way through numerous airs. For example, several of the arias are dominated by an expression of pleasure, wonder, and delight at nature that is genuine enough but more soothing than stirring: the queen's "Bless'd the day when I was brought to behold this favour'd spot," "With thee th'unshelter'd moor I'd tread," the duet between Solomon and his queen "Welcome as the dawn," and the Queen of Sheba's "Ev'ry sight these eyes behold." Even the scene of the two women of Act II backs away from any deep feeling, though the trio "Words are weak" is cleverly contrived and pointed in characterization and even caricature.

It seems as if Handel had become overly considerate of his audience's sensibilities and his singers' limitations. While reaching back for successful formulas of the past, he also turned his back on certain aspects of the baroque—its violent contrasts and bold gestures, its concertato accompaniments, grand da capo forms, and vocal virtuosity. Handel's melody reached at the end of his life a classic serenity, a purity of line and near abstractness of expression that in spirit had much in common with the rising classicism. But musically it cleared a private path that no one was to seek again until after the nineteenth-century revival of his music.

## BIBLIOGRAPHICAL NOTES

The most authentic edition of Henry Purcell's *Dido and Aeneas* is that by Margaret Laurie and Thurston Dart (London: Novello, 1961). An older edition of this as well as other dramatic works is in *The Works of H. Purcell*, 26 vols. (London: Novello, Ewer, 1878–1928), which is being continued by the Purcell Society in a new series that includes several volumes of anthems (London: Novello, 1957–). Among the several books on Purcell, especially recommended are Robert E. Moore, *H. Purcell and the Restoration Theater* (London: Heinemann, 1961); J. A. Westrup, *Purcell* (London: J. M. Dent & Sons, 1937); and *H. Purcell: His Life and Times* (London: Macmillan & Co., 1967) and *H. Purcell, An Analytical Catalogue of His Music*, both by Franklin B. Zimmerman (New York: St. Martin's Press, 1963).

Other aspects of the English scene are covered in Edward J. Dent, *Foundations of English Opera* (Cambridge: The University Press, 1928), and Andrew J. Sabol, *Four Hundred Songs and Dances from the Stuart Masque* (Providence, R. I.: Brown University Press, 1978). Three masques, *The Triumph of Peace*, *The Triumphs of the Prince d'Amour*, and *Britannia triumphans*, with texts by John Shirley and William Davenant, designs by Inigo Jones, and music by William Lawes, introduced and edited by Murray Lefokowitz, are in *Trois masques à la cour de Charles 1er d'Angleterre* (Paris: Éditions du CNRS, 1970).

Handel's works in the edition of the Deutsche Handelgesellschaft, edited by Friedrich Chrysander (Leipzig, 1858–1903), have been reprinted by the Gregg Press of Ridgewood, New Jersey. A new scholarly edition is in progress: the *Hallische Händel-Ausgabe* (Kassel: Bärenreiter-Verlag, 1955–). The monumental study by Paul Henry Lang, *George Frideric Handel* (New York: W. W. Norton & Co., Inc., 1966), contains a great wealth of fresh insights into his music and surroundings. An excellent collection of shorter guides is Gerald Abraham, ed., *Handel: A Symposium* (London: Oxford University Press, 1954). Winton Dean's *Handel's Dramatic Oratorios and Masques* (London: Oxford University Press, 1959) is a gold mine of information and commentary, and his *Handel and the Opera Seria* presents a rather personal view (Berkeley: University of California Press, 1969). All essential source material is in *Handel, A Documentary Biography* by Otto Erich Deutsch (London: Adam and Charles Black, 1955).

# THIRTEEN

# JOHANN SEBASTIAN BACH

## (1685–1750)

### BACH'S CAREER

An eighteenth-century composer's output was largely conditioned by the demands made upon him by patrons, employers, and public. Bach's output, aside from the works of his youth and old age, was channeled into the media required by three positions: court organist at Weimar (1708–1717); Director of Music for Prince Leopold of Anhalt at Cöthen (1717–1723); and Cantor of St. Thomas Church and Director of Music for the City of Leipzig (1723–1750).

At Weimar, Bach was principally an organist, and it was natural that he should write a large number of organ and keyboard compositions, including arrangements of Italian concertos. He also served as a violinist and eventually concertmaster or director of chamber music to the duke, Wilhelm Ernst, a very pious but art-loving man. During the latter part of his stay in

The Collegium Musicum that Bach led in Leipzig made up of university students gave evening outdoor concerts like this one in 1744 in honor of a professor by the Collegium Musicum of the University of Jena portrayed in this painting. (Hamburg, Museum für Kunst und Gewerbe.)

Weimar, Bach also took over some of the duties of the aging choirmaster, Samuel Drese. In this role he was charged in 1714 to compose and direct a new cantata each month for the ducal chapel. Thus he was stimulated to produce about thirty such works.

Prince Leopold in Cöthen required of Bach mainly chamber and orchestral music. It was during his residence there that he composed his Brandenburg concertos, the *Well-Tempered Clavier*, Book I, the first four French Suites, and much other harpsichord, clavichord, and chamber music. He also wrote approximately twelve cantatas for the duke's birthdays and New Year's Day, of which only three survive (BWV 173a, 134a, 202).

During his first years in Leipzig Bach dedicated himself to fulfilling the need for a repertory of cantatas for each Sunday and feast day of the church year. He wrote a new one weekly or, when hard pressed, reworked an older cantata if he had a suitable one. After 1727 he reduced his output in this medium drastically and embarked on a variety of other projects, such as the composition or compilation from earlier compositions of large-scale works such as the St. Matthew Passion and the Mass in b minor. Beginning in 1729, when he took over the direction of the Collegium musicum, an association of Leipzig University amateurs, he composed a large quantity of secular music for its weekly concerts. During the final decade of his life, Bach felt free to indulge in the compilation of Book II of the *Well-Tempered*

*Clavier* and the composition of studious and nonfunctional music, such as *The Musical Offering*, the *Goldberg Variations*, and *The Art of the Fugue*.

Two media that occupied Bach throughout his life were the keyboard and the concerted solo-choral medium known as the cantata. Though chronology of the keyboard works (see Chapter Ten) remains uncertain, a well-documented chronology of the cantatas has been worked out in the past fifteen years. The cantatas will therefore serve as the principal repertory for a discussion of Bach's stylistic development.

## MUSIC IN THE LUTHERAN CHURCH

The duties of a Lutheran church musician during Bach's lifetime were particularly demanding. The liturgy was simple compared with that of the Catholic church (see Seay, *Music in the Medieval World*, pp. 26–31). But congregational participation by way of hymn singing complicated the organist's task, and preparing the long piece of concerted music customary in the Sunday morning service was a major weekly project during most of the year.

In his *German Mass and Order of Divine Service* of 1526, Luther reduced the number of services to three: the *Frühgottesdienst*, or morning service, which combined Matins, Lauds, and Prime; the *Hauptgottesdienst*, or principal service, which united Terce, Sext, and None; and the *Nachmittagsgottesdienst*, or afternoon service, which took the place of Vespers and Compline. Local practices varied. Most churches preserved only a skeleton of Luther's order of service, but Leipzig's churches were extreme in hewing to it quite strictly. When Bach visited Leipzig in 1714, its order of service so impressed or confused him that he jotted down the service for the First Sunday of Advent on the reverse of the title page of the cantata he performed there, *Nun komm, der Heiden Heiland*, BWV 61.

According to this outline (see the facsimile) the organist began with a prelude. Then motets were sung by the choir. The organist played a prelude on the Kyrie, which was sung with instruments. After an intonation at the altar (Collects), the Epistle was read and the Litany was sung. The organist then played a prelude on the chorale, which was sung (by the congregation). The Gospel was then read. After another prelude, the principal music (usually a cantata) was performed. The Creed was sung, after which came the sermon. After the sermon (about an hour long), several verses of a hymn were sung and the words of institution pronounced. Once again the organist made a prelude to the music that was to follow (what this music was is unclear, since only a few cantatas had a second part). Finally the organist alternated preludes with congregational chorales until the end of the Communion. This service—and the list given here is not complete—lasted from about 7:00 to 11:00.

# BACH'S CANTATAS

Erdmann Neumeister (1671–1756), whose devotional poetry established a new trend in sacred music, described a cantata as resembling "a portion of an opera, made up of recitative style and arias."[1] He called *oratorio* a composition that mixed excerpts from the Bible and occasional chorales with madrigal-like poetic texts for arias and duets. Neumeister's earliest texts for the Sunday service were of the oratorio type, but the first published annual cycle of 1700 consisted of what he called cantatas. Later cycles compromised between the two types, and these suited composers better, for they were more in line with the Lutheran musical tradition of chorale concerto and concerted motet. It is this combination of biblical texts, chorales, recitatives, and arias that constitutes the cantata as practiced by Bach from his Weimar period on and by many of his contemporaries.

Only five cantatas by Bach on Neumeister's texts have been authenticated: BWV 18, 24, 28, 59, and 61,[2] but a large number were on texts inspired by Neumeister's models. The term *cantata* was applied by the editors of the collected works of Bach to all the composite works of concerted music intended for the principal service, whether they were of the kind Neumeister designated *oratorio* or *cantata* or were closer to the older chorale concerto and motet. This loose employment of the term *cantata* tends to obscure the fact that the Italian chamber cantata, which was written for one or two solo voices, usually as a succession of recitatives, arias and duets, without chorus, was only one of the models for the Bach cantatas. The Bach works were not, however, modeled on the Italian sacred cantata, such as Rossi's *Giuseppe*, for this was a continuous narrative-dramatic work, although its components were also recitatives, arias, and choruses or ensembles.

Bach's earliest concerted sacred works were of the type Neumeister called oratorio, made up of scriptural extracts and chorales. Such a one is *Gottes Zeit ist die allerbeste Zeit* (God's time is the very best time, BWV 106), an *actus tragicus*, or mourning music, probably dating from 1707. The texts are selections, elaborated possibly by Bach himself, from the Psalms, Acts, Isaiah, St. Luke, and other Biblical sources. To these were added the first strophe of the chorale "Mit Fried und Freud ich fahr dahin" by Luther (1524) and the seventh strophe of "In dich hab ich gehoffet, Herr" by Adam Reusner (1533). The style of the musical setting is a composite of concerted motet, chamber dialogue, and chorale elaboration. In common with other early "cantatas," it has no fully developed closed forms; rather, it is a suc-

---

[1] Erdmann Neumeister, *Geistliche Cantaten*, 1704, cited in *DdT* 53/54, lxxvi.
[2] The numbering of the cantatas in *BWV* and elsewhere follows the arbitrary order of publication in the volumes of the Bachgesellschaft's edition (Leipzig: 1851–1899).

cession of short sections. The entire cantata follows a nearly symmetrical key plan: E♭–c–f–b♭–A♭–c–E♭.

An opening "sonatina" for the ensemble of two recorders, two violas da gamba, and continuo sets the somber mood and the key of E♭ Major. Though seemingly independent, the sonatina is subtly related motivically to several of the subsequent numbers. There follows a choral motet with solo episodes in an archaic North German style that is most fitting, since the text expresses the old covenant of death as the irrevocable destiny of man. The closing section of this motet is an ingenious three-voice fugue over a walking bass on the words "It is the old covenant: Man must die." The first episode by a solo soprano on the words "Yes, come Lord Jesus, come" is accompanied, on a recorder, by the melody of the chorale "Ich hab' mein Sach' Gott heimgestellt" (I have left all my cares with God), an allusion of a kind Bach enjoyed in his early works.

The new covenant of salvation in Christ is represented by what appears to be a dialogue between the departed soul (alto) and the Savior (bass) in modern Italian style. The alto begins. She sings a continuo aria, with quasi-ostinato accompaniment and imitations between voice and continuo, that is of a type found frequently in seventeenth-century Italian chamber cantatas. After the bass's reply, "Today, you will be with me," the chorus's alto section sings the chorale "With peace and joy I pass away," while the bass simultaneously continues with a varied strophe of his aria, now joined by the two violas da gamba playing counterfigures derived from the aria. The final chorus is an orchestral and choral elaboration of Seth Calvisius's melody (1581) for the Reusner chorale. Its last phrase is expanded into a double fugue climaxed by a statement of this phrase in augmentation. The young Bach seems to have been eager to display every trick of his craft in this work. Nevertheless, it glows throughout with a natural, energetic, and overflowing expressiveness.

Belonging probably to the same period is the ever-favored Easter cantata *Christ lag in Todesbanden* (Christ lay in death's bondage, BWV 4). It is the strictest chorale cantata Bach ever wrote. Every one of the seven stanzas of Luther's Easter hymn is set, and each setting is a variation upon its tune of 1524 (Example 13-1a), which, in turn, was based on the Easter Sequence, *Victimae paschali laudes*. Although the cantata was revised during the Leipzig period, from which the copies date, on stylistic grounds it has been assigned to Bach's tenure as organist at St. Blasius's Church at Mühlhausen between 1707 and 1708.

Numerous traits mark BWV 4 as an early work. There is an independent sinfonia citing fragments of the chorale melody. There are no da capo arias but only the shorter quasi-ostinato and walking-bass types that Bach knew before becoming acquainted with eighteenth-century Italian music. The special treatment given the last lines of the chorale in versus 1 and

4 remind one of *Gottes Zeit*, BWV 106, as does the extreme emotional intensity and display of contrapuntal virtuosity. Like BWV 4, its overall structure is symmetrical but not with respect to key—for BWV106 is all in e
minor—but with respect to voice groupings: sinfonia-chorus-duet-solo-
chorus-solo-duet-chorus.

If *Christ lag in Todesbanden* is conservative with respect to Bach's
canon, the imaginative variety of treatment, the strong infusion of secular
methods, and the masterful craftsmanship are striking when it is compared
with the similarly strict chorale concerto *Vom Himmel kam der Engel Schar*
(From heaven came the angel host) of Johann Schelle (1648–1701), one of
Bach's predecessors in the cantorship of St. Thomas in Leipzig[3] Unlike
Schelle, who made verse 1 and 6 almost identical and 2 and 5 very similar,
Bach strongly characterizes each stanza through instrumental figures appropriate to its central affection, idea, or conflict of ideas. In verse 1, the descending-step motive drawn from the opening notes of the chorale dominates
the first four lines of the stanza to convey the thought of Christ's bondage in
death. Running figures in thirds and imitations on a bright syncopated
"Hallelujah" theme mark the last four lines of rejoicing over the resurrection.
In verse 2 (that is, the second strophe) the continuo never lets go of the
descending-step motive from the chorale's first notes (Example 13-1b), now
sung to the words "Den Tod." The obsession with death even pervades the
closing "Hallelujah" that ends this and every other stanza. For verse 3, which
speaks of the victory over sin and death, Bach drew again from the opening
notes of the chorale to form a cascading figuration in the manner of a furious
or triumphal opera aria (Example 13-1c). A hopping dotted-rhythm ostinato
(Example 13-1d) captures the gist of verse 6, "So we celebrate the high feast/
With hearty joy and rapture." Thus in each of these movements Bach ingeniously coerced the sixteenth-century text and the heterogeneous melodic
fragments of the hymn into serving the baroque ideal of unity of affection.
Verse 4 is in a retrospective style of the chorale-motet, but the fiercely independent lines vividly evoke the "marvelous war between death and life."
Verse 5, unified only by a walking bass, is freest of baroque constraints
though most bound by the melody and words of the hymn, which Bach
illustrated with graphic rhetorical figures.

In Weimar, Bach turned to the type of cantata espoused by Neumeister, although he preferred the somewhat more subjective librettos of
Salomo Franck, Secretary of the Protestant Consistory in Weimar, which
were modeled on those of Neumeister. It is instructive, nevertheless, to study
one of the two Neumeister cantatas Bach set there: BWV 61, *Nun komm, der
Heiden Heiland* (Come, Gentiles' Savior, 1714; the entire work is in *NAWM*
88), intended for the First Sunday of Advent. The libretto is a combination

---

3 *DdT*, *58/59*, p. 167.

**EXAMPLE 13-1**   J. S. Bach, BWV 4, *Christ lag in Todesbanden*

of 1) a chorale strophe as the opening chorus; 2) an iambic stanza of irregular line lengths intended for recitative; 3) an iambic tetrameter stanza of five lines for a da capo aria; 4) a prose quotation from Revelation 3:20 for recitative; 5) a trochaic tetrameter stanza for a da capo aria; and 6) the last four lines of a different chorale from the first, for a final chorus. The poetic texts are based on the Epistle of the day (Romans 13:11–14), in which St. Paul exhorts the Romans to shake themselves out of their wantonness, for the day of salvation is nigh.

Bach hit upon a brilliant solution for the problem of opening the cantata without an instrumental prelude. The functions of the traditional sinfonia or sonata and of the concertato chorus that usually followed are united in a single movement. This takes the form of a choral French overture. In many subsequent cantatas the opening chorus takes the form of an Italian concerto allegro imposed upon a chorale elaboration, as in BWV 62 (1724) on the same chorale as the present cantata. The chorale tune of *Nun komm, der Heiden Heiland* is the ancient melody of the Ambrosian hymn *Veni redemptor gentium*, which Luther translated in 1524 to produce this chorale. The four melodic phrases are accommodated to the slow-fast-slow pattern of the French overture. The first two lines accompany the slow section. The third line is treated fugally in an extensive triple-time section marked *Gai*, and the fourth line, which brings back the opening melodic phrase, accompanies the return of the slow section. To begin this cantata with an overture was all the more appropriate because the First Sunday of Advent opened the new liturgical year, the chorale hailing the coming of Christ as the overture saluted the arrival of the King of France, Louis XIV, at the performances of Lully's stage works.

The first recitative for tenor is of a type popular in seventeenth-century Italian chamber cantatas, a *recitativo con cavata*. A little aria is drawn (*cavata*) from the last two lines of recitative text. It is usual to call this kind of writing arioso. The tenor aria with unison strings "Come, Jesus, to your church," spins out a Siciliano theme (Example 13-2) that is the quintessence of warm invitation. The form is an aria da capo without the repeat of the opening ritornello before the return of $A^1$: Rit. $A^1$ Rit. $B^1$ Rit. $B^2$ $A^1$ Rit.

**EXAMPLE 13-2**   J. S. Bach, BWV 61, *Nun komm der Heiden Heiland*

Komm, Je - su,   komm      zu  dei - ner  Kir - che
*(Come, Jesus,    come      to  thy       church)*

The bass recitative "Lo! I come now. I stand before the door and knock thereat" surrounds the words of Christ with a halo of five-part strings (Bach still used two viola parts in Weimar). Four pizzicato chords in each measure are meant undoubtedly to suggest the knocking at the door. The effect of a closed door is achieved throughout a recurrent dominant-seventh chord over a tonic e minor pedal. A sudden shift to the dominant of the closing tonality G dramatizes the word "*hören*" (hear) (Example 13-3).

The following soprano aria translates the incident told in the recitative into the experience of the individual worshiper, who opens her heart to the knocking Christ. Despite the motto beginning and quasi-ostinato of the A section, it has the flavor of a simple seventeenth-century German continuo-lied. This simplicity is deceptive, because both continuo and voice grow out of the same stepwise rising three-note figure. The means by which the motive is expanded is shown in Example 13-4 by the added stems and beams. The B section, by contrast, is an impassioned arioso.

The final chorus elaborates the last four lines of the last strophe and the melody of the hymn *Wie schön leuchtet der Morgenstern* in a mere

**EXAMPLE 13-3** J. S. Bach, Cantata BWV 61, *Nun komm der Heiden Heiland,*
No. 4, Recitative

Sie-he, sie-he, ich ste-he vor der Tür und klop-fe an, und klop-fe
*(Lo! I come now I stand before the door and knock thereat.*

Strings pizz.

an. So je-mand mei-ne Stim-me hö-ren wird
*If any man hear my voice.)*

**EXAMPLE 13-4** J. S. Bach, BWV 61, *Nun komm der Heiden Heiland,* No. 5, Aria

5. Aria

tr

Off-ne dich, mein gan-zes Her - ze,
*(Open I my whole heart)*

fourteen measures. Bach did not refrain from using more than one chorale
melody in a cantata at this time. The present one is rendered appropriate by
the thought "Come, you beautiful Crown of Joy" that sums up this stanza.
Bach seems to have been intent on describing the beautiful crown in the
soaring violin part, the only instrumental part that does not play along with
the singers.

Neumeister, who held numerous positions as a Lutheran pastor, confessed that he was accustomed to relax after preaching a sermon by writing poetry in which he tried to compress the sermon's most important ideas. Thus the cantata, coming as it did after the reading of epistle and gospel but before the sermon that took its theme from these, prepared the worshipers emotionally and spiritually for the more discursive commentary of the preacher. Cantata 61 fulfills this function magnificently.

Bach was responsible in Leipzig for the performance of a cantata each Sunday and lesser feast day at either St. Thomas or St. Nicholas and on certain greater feasts at both churches. When he arrived in Leipzig he had only a small reserve of cantatas that he considered to be in a suitable style. So he embarked on a schedule of composing one for each Sunday or feast day for which he did not have one from Weimar or elsewhere. When he used an older cantata he often rewrote parts of it or added to it. He kept up this rigorous schedule for two annual cycles, each commencing with the first Sunday after Trinity (late May or early June) and ending on Trinity Sunday. After June 1725 he was less regular, and during 1726 he performed in place of his own music seventeen cantatas by his cousin Johann Ludwig Bach (1677–1741). His production picked up again from June 1726 until the end of that calendar year. From January 1727 either his cantatas do not survive in as great a number or, more likely, he turned to other genres of composition. Moreover, some of the cantatas of this period are parodies, that is, earlier secular cantatas, such as those written in Cöthen, in which religious words have been substituted.

During the latter part of the first Leipzig cycle and during most of the second cycle Bach relied heavily on chorale texts. In the first cycle several different chorales often serve as the basis of music and text in a single cantata. The second cycle has been called the chorale cycle, because almost every one of the texts is based on a single chorale. In the commonest type Bach set verbatim the original hymn stanzas in the first chorus and final chorale, and the music was likewise based on the chorale melody. For the recitatives and arias an anonymous poet paraphrased the remaining strophes of the chorale. Usually the chorale melody is not found in these. However, some of the cantatas of this cycle contain more than two numbers that take over hymn strophes verbatim, and sometimes with them the chorale melody.

Such a work is BWV 92, *Ich hab' in Gottes Herz und Sinn* (I have in God's heart and mind [/delivered my heart and mind]), first performed on Septuagesima Sunday, January 28, 1725. Strophes 1, 5, and 12 of the hymn by Paul Gerhardt are set verbatim in Nos. 1, 4, and 9 of the cantata. The tune with which this hymn was published in 1647 appears in all of these. (It is the tune that accompanied "Was mein Gott will, das g'scheh allzeit" in a collection of 1572, but goes back to the French chanson "Il me suffit de tous mes maulx" published by Pierre Attaignant between 1529 and 1534.) Moreover, the lines of strophes 2 and 10, in Nos. 2 and 7, are interspersed with poetry intended for recitative. The chorale melody is used in these also. The thoughts of strophes 4, 8, 9, and 11 are freely used in the poetry for Nos. 3, 5, 6, and 8, respectively. These numbers are free of the chorale melody.

The opening chorus is a prize example of the high-baroque composer's submission of every detail, no matter how diverse the raw material, to a reigning idea and affection. Neither the chorale text nor the melody presents a unified theme. Yet Bach's chorus does. It has a character of humble resignation, summed up in a six-note motive announced in the first measure ("a" in Example 13-5). The entire tissue that surrounds the chorale melody grows from this motive and preserves this attitude. Motive b is derived by inverting motive a. Motive c projects the rhythm of a. Motive d inverts the descending diminished fourth of a. Example 13-5 shows the first oboe d'amore and the bass, omitting the other instruments of the sixteen-measure ritornello. Like

**EXAMPLE 13-5**   J. S. Bach, BWV 92, *Ich hab' in Gottes Herz und Sinn*, No. 1, Chorus

many of Vivaldi's, this ritornello is divided into two- and four-measure segments, the last of which brings the head-motive back in the bass.

Returns of the ritornello material alternate with the choral sections accompanying the eight phrases of the chorale melody. Thus the chorale segments fulfill the function assumed by the solos in the concerto. Only the soprano states the chorale melody, and in the manner of a cantus firmus. The other voices do not, as in many of Bach's opening choruses, fore-imitate the chorale segments or counterpose distinct motives to fit the words. Rather, the lower voices develop always the same motive, the head-motive a. Against the voices the orchestra of two oboes d'amore and strings develops all of the four motives. This dependence upon the material of the ritornello makes of the chorale melody almost a foreign body, but it also sets it in high relief.

The chorus as a whole has the form AAB. This it inherits from the chorale, which, as is often the case, is in the *Bar*-form of two *stollen* and an *abgesang*. Within this scheme the alternation of ritornello and chorale produces the following design (R stands for Ritornello, Ch for Chorale phrase and the small letters for the motives): R (abcda) Ch 1 R(b) Ch 2 R(abcda) Ch 3 R(b) Ch 4 R(abcd) Ch 5 R(bcd) Ch 6 R(abc) Ch 7 R(bc) Ch 8 R(abcda).

This concentration of material is carried over into the second number, a two-faceted chorale elaboration. Poetic elucidations of the chorale text's meaning set in recitative style are interpolated between musical elaborations of the chorale melody. All the segments of the chorale tune are accompanied by the same quasi-ostinato bass derived from the first phrase of the chorale. This example illustrates one of the perennial features of Bach's recitative, the leaping along the notes of a seventh or diminished seventh chord (Example 13-6). This habit gives Bach's recitative a strongly hypertensive and suspenseful dynamism.

The florid basso continuo part under the recitative makes of this almost a recitativo obbligato, as when, for example, at measure 5 the keyboard reflects the "angry bursts." Another descriptive detail in this recitative is the sixteenth-note keyboard figure in measures 17–23 (Example 13–6b): Bach originally wrote repeated sixteenth notes here, but in revising realized that a turn better described the word "Wellen" (waves).[4]

Number 7 is another double commentary on a chorale, but this time the chorale is sung by a four-voice ensemble, while each of the voices takes a turn at the recitative. The whole is loosely tied together by a walking-bass accompaniment that undergirds the chorale segments.

The remaining chorale movement aside from the closing one is No. 4 for alto and two oboes d'amore. Bach took as his cue the idea expressed in

---

[4]Concerning this autograph revision, see Robert L. Marshall, *The Compositional Process of J. S. Bach* (Princeton, N. J.: Princeton University Press, 1972), I, 113.

**EXAMPLE 13-6** J. S. Bach, BWV 92, *Ich hab' in Gottes herz und Sinn*, No. 2, Recitative and Chorale

the first two lines: "In Him is wisdom and understanding beyond all measure." This omniscience is symbolized in highly intricate counterpoint. A quasi-canonic relationship is maintained between the two oboes d'amore. Against these sounds a concertante bass part, making of the instrumental ensemble's music a virtual trio-sonata movement. Almost an interloper, the alto breaks into this elegant music-making intermittently with its simple rendering of the chorale phrases.

Two of the arias of this work are among the most modern in Bach's sacred cantatas: the tenor aria, No. 3, "Seht, seht, wie bricht," and the soprano aria, No. 8, "Meinem Hirten bleib' ich treu." Both depart significantly from the da capo form, as Bach's arias tended to do at this time. The bold and dramatic sweep of No. 3 is worthy of a late Handel opera. The headlong runs that bridge the leaps in the violins and the athletic leaps of the voice present two sides of the last two lines of the text "Let Satan storm, rage, and crash./The mighty God will make us invincible." As the instruments describe a Satanic upheaval raging unchecked, the voice registers the unshaken confidence of the faithful in God's protection. Example 13-7 shows the parallel vocal and instrumental themes.

**EXAMPLE 13-7**   J. S. Bach, BWV 92, *Ich hab' in Gottes Herz und Sinn*, No. 3, Aria

seht,        seht! wie reisst, wie bricht, wie fällt . . .
(See,        see   how it tears, how it breaks, have it falls)

The broad strokes of the first violin are matched by what for Bach was a slow rate of harmonic change, mostly every half note. The drive is rhythmic rather than harmonic, because the same chords keep returning. Forward motion is conserved by avoiding a return to the tonic except at the end. Bach remained in the relative major through to the B section, after which he made the return to the tonic b minor through f♯ minor. Thus the loss of momentum inherent in the da capo form's return of A² to the tonic is avoided. Redundancy is further offset by recapitulating only the ritornello.

The soprano aria No. 8 is modern in another sense. The melodic construction is based not on the baroque method of continuous expansion of a germ motive but on a process common among *galant* composers of compounding short-breathed phrases into a longer line. At the root of the rhythmic and melodic impulse is the dance phraseology of the minuet. The soprano line (Example 13-8) comprises a series of antecedent-consequent groups in which each member is four measures long. Further, each of the first two members (measures 13–20) can be split into a two-measure antecedent followed by a two-measure consequent. Unlike the *galant* composers, however, Bach avoided a cadence until the end of the eighteen-measure period. The process of modulation then begins at once and is unremitting until the cadence on A in measure 32.

Anti-baroque also is the loose coupling of melody and words. This is not one of those arias so typical of Bach in which the music is custom-tailored to the affection, images, and even individual words of the poetry. At most the aria gets across the simple-minded peasant's faith expressed in the words "To my shepherd I remain true./ Will he fill my chalice full?" As often happens in the last aria of the chorale cantatas, it is now the individual

**EXAMPLE 13-8**   J. S. Bach, BWV 92, *Ich hab' in Gottes Herz und Sinn*, No. 8, Aria

worshiper's turn to speak, feel, and meditate. Thus the individual singer, speaking for the worshiper in the pew, prepares the congregation's return to an active role in the service to sing the final chorale.

As observed, the opening chorus is indebted to the concerto-ritornello technique, the alto chorale aria to the trio sonata, and the soprano aria to the minuet. This subjection of vocal music to the constructive methods of instrumental music was seen already in Bach's Weimar period in the opening chorus of Cantata 61. It became increasingly evident in the birthday and other occasional cantatas of the Cöthen period, insofar as these are available or can be reconstructed from later "parodies." It reached its height in the chorale cantatas of the Leipzig period. Here, with the religious component of the work solidly entrenched in the chorale text and melody, Bach must have felt particularly free to explore the secular resources of instrumental music. The enlargement of the vocabularly of sacred music that he achieved by this search must be reckoned as one of Bach's great contributions.

Cantata BWV 92 promises for Bach's music a shift of style like that undergone by Vivaldi and Handel in the late 1720s and early 1730s, but in fact no such shift is observable. Bach rejected the new approach to musical composition while at times embracing certain of its techniques that appealed to him. This rejection is epitomized in the work that most abounds in *galant* mannerisms, the Peasant Cantata BWV 212, *Mer Hahn en neue Oberkeet* (We have a new Squire). It was written in honor of Karl Heinrich von Dieskau, newly appointed lord of a manor on the outskirts of Leipzig in 1742. Subtitled by Bach *Cantate burlesque*, it is a spoof on modern composers. Bach satirized the Germans who wrote arias on dance and folk models by coupling this style with the most trivial and vulgar texts. He also parodied the new style of Italian da capo aria very charmingly in "Klein-Zschocher müsse" but showed that he also appreciated the ludicrousness of misplaced erudition and rhetoric in the *Coffee Cantata*, BWV 211 (1732–1735), when he set the words "Maidens of hard disposition are not easily won" to a tangled succession of augmented and diminished intervals against a quasi-ostinato bass that uses all twelve tones of the chromatic scale within two and a half measures. This occurs in the aria "Mädchen, die von harten Sinnen" about a girl addicted to coffee, whose father would like to cure her of the habit by finding her a husband.

Despite Bach's apparent indifference to musical fashion, some of the modern tendencies seen in BWV 92 occasionally reappeared in his later works. In the Mass in b minor, much of which consists of reworkings of numbers composed in the 1720s, some of the freshly composed sections illustrate these trends. In the solo arias and duets the human voice is favored both by giving it more flowing and less breathless music than Bach was used to writing and by subduing the loquaciousness of obbligato instruments. In several arias Bach carefully marked the dynamics of the instruments to keep them under the voices, most characteristically in the duet "Domine Deus" of the Gloria, where he could not resist writing an almost continuous florid counterpoint for the flute against the voices. A tendency toward periodic phraseology and slower harmonic rhythm is also present in some of the late works. Some good examples are the aria "Schweight ihr Flöten" in the wedding cantata BWV 210, *O holder' Tag, erwünschte Zeit* (O lovely day, o welcome time, 1742–1744), which also illustrates a mixing of triplet rhythms with duple time; in the aria "Seid beglückt" in the same cantata; and in "Heute noch" in the *Coffee Cantata*.

The concerto-ritornello form continued to be the mainstay of Bach's grand choruses, whether based on chorales, like the opening chorus of BWV 140, *Wachet auf ruft uns die Stimme* (Wake up, calls the voice, 1731), or without chorale, like BWV 34, *O ewiges Feuer* (O eternal fire), a wedding cantata of around 1726 turned in the 1740s into one for Whitsuntide. Two brilliant choruses of the Mass in b minor, the "Gloria in excelsis" and "Et resurrexit," may be reworkings of purely instrumental concertos of the Cöthen period. Several of the other choruses in the Mass followed concerto procedures.

Despite these witnesses to Bach's awareness of contemporary practices and taste, the late works impress one with their conservatism, their insistence upon the old values and venerated procedures. In terms of the categories "strict style" and "free" or "*galant* style" posited by the noted Bach pupil, Johann Philipp Kirnberger, Bach was a loyal partisan of the "strict style." Of the movements of the Mass for which no earlier models have been found, the Kyrie and the "Laudamus," "Quoniam," and "Cum sancto Spiritu" of the Gloria are in strict style. They were probably composed shortly before or around 1733. Of the *Symbolum Nicenum*, or Credo, which was compiled or written around 1747, almost all of the music is retrospective in technique, particularly the opening "Credo," a cantus-firmus composition, and the "Confiteor," which harks back to the walking bass adagio of the Corelli trio sonata, a texture here expanded to five voices and basso continuo. Bach must have instinctively realized that for one who had so fully mastered the resources of the strict contrapuntal method and could draw from it every last measure of beauty and expression it would have been sacrilege to lay it aside for an ill-formed, undisciplined technique that had its origins mainly in comic opera.

## BACH AND HIS CONTEMPORARIES

Among the few reviews that give an inkling of how Bach's music was regarded by his contemporaries are those of Johann Adolph Scheibe (1708–1776), editor and author of one of the earliest journals of music criticism.

Scheibe placed Bach with Handel at the top of composers of keyboard music, a field in which he found Germans preeminent because of their superior working out of structure and ornamentation. As an organist, harpsichordist, and clavichordist, Bach was esteemed by Scheibe as unsurpassable, and rivaled only one other, Handel. After Bach's Italian Concerto was published in 1735 in *Clavier Übung* (Keyboard Exercise), Part II, Scheibe proclaimed it a perfect model of a well-constructed concerto for keyboard alone, one deserving the imitation of all great composers. Foreigners, though, Scheibe warned in his chauvinistic way, would try in vain to match it. When other commentators, such as Johann Mattheson (1681–1764), wrote of Bach, they too singled out his organ music and organ playing.

This one-sided picture given by contemporary critics of Bach's output is understandable. Keyboard music traveled more easily than cantatas, passions, and similar works. Many musicians on trips to Leipzig did hear performances of Bach's church works and admired them. Still, many probably sympathized with a remark made by Scheibe: "Bach's church compositions are always more artificial and laborious, but by no means of such effect, conviction, and reasonable reflection as the works of Telemann and Graun."[5]

Georg Philipp Telemann (1681–1767) was the first choice of the town council of Leipzig when the position of Cantor of St. Thomas became vacant by the death of Johann Kuhnau in 1722. Beside Telemann, most Germans would have placed Johann Adolph Hasse (1699–1783) and Karl Heinrich Graun (1704–1759) at the head of any list of the most celebrated and admired composers. Today the music of these last two is all but forgotten, however undeservedly. (Their music will not be discussed in this book, because they belong more properly to a history of the early classic period.) The reluctance of Bach's contemporaries to grant him the credit that the perspective of two centuries shows to be his due is an important historical fact that must not be lost in the enthusiasm for his music.

It is Scheibe again who presented the clearest statement of what people found least pleasing in Bach's music. It is, he says, unnatural, overly artful, and confused in its style. Both vocal and instrumental music are written as if meant for his own remarkable technique on the organ. He writes out all the ornaments instead of leaving them to the player and in so doing covers up the beauty of the melody and obscures the harmony. Instead of assigning the melody to one principal voice, he makes all voices equally busy and difficult. These tendencies make his music turgid, artificial, and somber, whereas, Scheibe proclaimed, it should be natural, simple, and noble.[6]

The criteria by which Scheibe judged Bach were obviously not those of a baroque musician but of one converted to the new Italian style. He saw

[5]Hans T. David and Arthur Mendel, *The Bach Reader*, rev. ed. (New York: W. W. Norton & Co., Inc., 1966), p. 238.
[6]David and Mendel, *The Bach Reader*, p. 238.

Germany's mission in music as the improvement of this recently imported Italian fashion.

> Indeed, we [Germans] have finally found in music too the true good taste, which Italy never showed us in its full beauty. Hasse and Graun, who are admired also by the Italians, demonstrate by their richly inventive, natural, and moving works how fine it is to possess and practice good taste.[7]

In defending Bach against Scheibe's criticism, another editor of a musical periodical, Christoph Lorenz Mizler, made in 1738 a penetrating comment on Bach's historical position. "If Mr. Bach at times writes the inner parts more fully than other composers, he has taken as his model the music of twenty or twenty-five years ago."[8] Italian, French, and German music of the first decades of the eighteenth century, as Mizler perceived, was indeed the source of Bach's compositional practice, but he realized its possibilities in ways no one else had conceived.

Is Bach's music, then, a culmination of the baroque period? To say so would be misleading. The baroque did not rise to a triumphant climax in Bach's work, for it was already in decline when Bach began his major compositions. The mainstream of the baroque style after around 1715 branched and trickled in countless directions and finally dried up. Bach's music, shooting off before the dispersion began, grew in strength and consistency, remaining baroque to the last. What he did with the resources of the style was a personal triumph. However, to the period in general Bach's mature works were, like Handel's oratorios, a postscript. The course of mid-eighteenth-century music would have been much the same without either. It is the late eighteenth, nineteenth, and twentieth centuries that would not have been the same.

## BIBLIOGRAPHICAL NOTES

The first collected edition of Bach's work was published by the Bach-Gesellschaft (Bach Society) between 1851 and 1900 (46 vols.; Leipzig: Breitkopf & Härtel). This was reprinted by the J. W. Edwards Company of Ann Arbor, Michigan in 1947. A new edition has been in progress since 1954, the *Neue Ausgabe sämtlicher Werke* (New Bach Edition) under the sponsorship of the Johann-Sebastian-Bach-Institut of Göttingen and the Bach-Archiv of Leipzig (Kassel and Basel: Bärenreiter-Verlag. 1954–). The cantatas in this edition are grouped according to the liturgical calendar or other performance destination. Some of the contents of this new collected

---

[7] *Critischer musicus*, 15. Stück, 17 September 1737.
[8] David and Mendel, *The Bach Reader*, p. 249.

edition are available in separate miniature scores and in a format suitable for performance.

The best bibliographic guide to the works of Bach is Wolfgang Schmieder's *Thematisch-systematisches Verzeichnis der musikalische Werke von Johann Sebastian Bach, Bach-Werke-Verzeichnis* (Leipzig: Breitkopf & Härtel, 1950), which locates each work in the Bach-Gesellschaft edition. A piece for which the melody is known but not the number or name may be located through May DeForest McAll's *Melodic Index to the Works of J. S. Bach* (New York: C. F. Peters Corp., 1962). Translations of the cantata texts are in Charles Sanford Terry, *J. S. Bach, Cantata Texts* (London: Constable & Co., 1926).

Because the research that has accompanied the new edition has uncovered so many new facts and has led to a complete revision of the chronology of Bach's works, all of the older biographies and studies of Bach's music are of limited usefulness to the student. Fortunately Karl Geiringer's *Johann Sebastian Bach* (New York: Oxford University Press, 1966) incorporates the new research in a book that is exemplary in every way.

Documents concerning Bach's life and works, annotated and translated into English, are presented together with a short portrait of the man and an essay on the rediscovery of his music in the *The Bach Reader, A Life of Johann Sebastian Bach in Letters and Documents*, rev. ed: edited by Hans T. David and Arthur Mendel (New York: W. W. Norton & Co., Inc., 1966).

The most significant recent addition to the Bach literature in English is Robert L. Marshall's two-volume work, *The Compositional Process of J. S. Bach, A Study of the Autograph Scores of the Vocal Works* (Princeton, N. J.: Princeton University Press, 1972), in which the revisions Bach made in his hand are transcribed, analyzed, and interpreted to reveal his working methods.

For the cantatas discussed in this chapter the following miniature scores are available in both Eulenburg and Broude Brothers editions: BWV 4, 34, 106, 140, 211, 212; BWV 61 is available in both Eulenburg and Bärenreiter editions, the latter reprinted in *NAWM* 88; 34 in all three editions; and 92 only in the Eulenburg. A particularly valuable compilation is the Norton Critical Score of Cantata No. 4, edited by Gerhard Herz, which unites with the score critical, analytical and historical essays (New York: W. W. Norton & Co., Inc., 1967).

# LIST OF MUSICAL EXAMPLES
# AND THEIR SOURCES

All of the realizations of the basso continuo, usually placed in these examples on the same staff as the bass, are by the author. They are not intended as models of good keyboard accompaniment but to ease the student's perception of the chordal content of the example whether in playing at the keyboard or in silent reading.

Examples covered by copyright are printed with the permission of the publishers cited below.

1-1. Bach, BWV 21. *Werke*, Vol. V/1. Leipzig: B&H, 1860.

2-1. Willaert, *O magnum mysterium. Sämtliche Werke*, ed. Hermann Zenck, I, pp. 54–55. Wiesbaden: B&H, 1950. Note values halved.

2-2 to 4. Monteverdi, *Ohimè se tanto amate. Opere*, ed. G. F. Malipiero, IV, pp. 55–56. Vienna: Universal Edition, No. 9606.

2-5. De Rore, *O sonno. Tutti i madrigali a 4 voci*, pp. 20–21. Venice: A. Gardano, 1577. Note values quartered, barring revised, time signatures added.

2-6. Dalla Casa, *Il vero modo di diminuir*, p. 32. Venice: A. Gardano, 1584.

2-7. Cavalieri, *Godi turba mortal*. Cristofano Malvezzi, *Intermedi et concerti*, Canto, p. 34, Nono, p. 16. Venice: G. Vincenti, 1591. Note values halved.

2-8. *Aria de sonetti*. Florence, Biblioteca Riccardiana, Ms F. III. 10431 (written by Vincenzo Galilei). Note values halved. Text from Francesco Petrarca, *Le Rime*, p. 312, No. CCXIX. Florence: Sansoni, 1946.

2-9. Caccini, *Chi mi confort'ahime*. *Le nuove musiche*, fols. 38v–39r. Florence: Marescotti, 1602. Note values halved.

3-1 to 2. Peri, *Euridice*. *Le musiche sopra l'Euridice*, pp. 17, 19–20. Florence: G. Marescotti, 1601. Values halved, barring revised.

3-3 to 6a; 7b. Monteverdi, *Orfeo*. *L'Orfeo*, pp. 39, 40, 28, 33, 52–53, 65. Venice: R. Amadino, 1609. Barring revised.

3-6b. Peri, *Euridice*. *Le musiche . . .* , p. 26. Values halved.

3-6c. Marco Cara, *Se de fede hor vengo*. Herbert Rosenberg, "Frottola und deutsches Lied um 1500" in *Acta musicologica* XVIII (1946), p. 61. Values quartered.

3-7a. Laurana, *Aer de capituli*. *Strambotti, ode, frottole, sonetti, et modo de cantar versi latini, Libro 4*, fol. 5v. Venice: Petrucci, 1505. Barring added.

3-8. D'India, *Là tra le selve*. *Le musiche di Sigismondo d'India da cantar solo*, No. 13. Milan: Simone Tini & Filippo Lomazzo, 1609.

3-9. De Rore, *Calami sonum ferentes*. Charles Burney, *A General History of Music*, ed. Frank Mercer, II, p. 256. New York: Dover. Values halved.

3-10. Gesualdo, *Moro, lasso al mio duolo*. *TEM* 33. New York: W. W. Norton & Co., Inc., 1959, and London: Faber and Faber, Ltd.

3-11, 12. D'India, *O dolcezz'amarissime*. Same as 3–8, No. 42. Values halved.

3-13. Monteverdi, *Ohimè dov'è il mio ben* (*Romanesca*). *Opere* VII, 1928, pp. 152–53.

4-1. Gabrieli, *O Domine Jesu Christe*. *Opera omnia*, ed. Denis Arnold, I, p. 93, where original values are halved. Rome: American Institute of Musicology, 1956.

4-2 to 3. Gabrieli, *Hodie completi sunt*. *Opera*, III, 1962, pp. 46, 45, and 56, where values are halved.

4-4. Gabrieli, *In ecclesiis*. C. von Winterfeld, *J. Gabrieli und sein Zeitalter*, Part III, pp. 75–77. Berlin, 1834. Editor's barring halved, instruments omitted.

4-5. Viadana, *Exaudi me, Domine*. *Cento concerti ecclesiastici*, Op. 12, p. 1. Venice: Vincenti, 1602. Values halved, barring added.

4-6. Cavalieri, *Lamentationes Hieremiae Prophetae*. Rome, Biblioteca Vallicellana, Ms 031, fol. 6r. Values halved, barring original.

4-7. Monteverdi, *Pulchra es. Opere*, XIV, pp. 171–72. Editor's barring regularized. Values halved in C, quartered in $\frac{3}{2}$ ($= \frac{6}{8}$).

4-8, 9. Monteverdi, *Nisi Dominus. Messa a quattro voci et salmi.* Venice: Alessandro Vincenti, 1650.

4-10. Monteverdi, *Laetatus sum.* Ibid.

4-11. Monteverdi, *Laudate Dominum omnes gentes. Opere*, XV, 492.

5-1, 2. Bull, Pavana. *Parthenia or the Maydenhead of the first musicke that ever was printed for the Virginalls*, No. 12. London: G. Lowe, c. 1611.

5-3. Dalza, *Pavana alla venetiana.* Ed. Imogene Horsley in *JAMS* XII, p. 119. Values halved.

5-5. Galilei, *Pass'e mezzo.* Florence, Biblioteca nazionale, Landau-Finaly Ms Mus. 2, fol. 7v. Values quartered.

5-6. Frescobaldi, *Partite sopra l'aria della Romanesca. Toccate d'intavolatura di cimbalo et organo*, p. 41. Rome, 1637. *HAM* II, 192.

5-7a. *John come kiss me now.* Text from William Chappel, *The Ballad Literature and Popular Music of the Olden Times*, p. 148. London, n.d. [1855–1859].

5-7b. *The Fitzwilliam Virginal Book*, ed. J. A. Fuller Maitland and W. Barclay Squire. New York: Dover, 1963.

5-8a. Walsingham. Text from Chappel, see 5–7a, p. 123.

5-8b. Bull, *Walsingham. The Fitzwilliam Virginal Book*, I, i.

5-9. Spinaccino, Ricercar. *HAM* 1, 99b.

5-10. Sweelinck, Fantasia chromatica. *GMB* 158. Used by permission of B&H, Wiesbaden.

5-11. Merulo, Toccata. *Toccate per organo*, ed. Sandro Dalla Libera, II, p. 2. Milan: Ricordi, No. E.R. 2638 (1959). 2 measures = 1 of ed.

6-1 to 2. Schein, *Erschienen ist der herrliche Tag. Sämtliche Werke*, VI, p. 115. Leipzig: B&H, 1919. Editor's values quartered. Barring revised accordingly. Used by permission of B&H, Wiesbaden. Herman chorale after Johannes Zahn, *Die Melodien der deutschen evangelischen Kirchenlieder*, I, No. 1743. Gütersloh: C. Bertelsmann, 1889. Barring added.

6-3. Schütz, *Der 121. Psalm. Sämtliche Werke*, ed. Philipp Spitta, II, p. 130. Leipzig: B&H, 1886. Editor's values halved.

6-4 to 6. Schütz, *O quam tu pulchra es. Neue Ausgabe sämtlicher Werke*, XIII, pp. 80–87. Kassel: Bärenreiter, 1957.

6-7. Schütz, *Was hast du verwirket?* Same ed., X, 1963. p. 16.

6-8. Schütz, *Saul, Saul. Sämtliche Werke*, ed. P. Spitta, XI, 99, pp. 103–4. Leipzig: B&H, 1891.

7-1 to 3. Rossi, *Del silentio*. Oxford, Bodleian, Christ Church Ms 952, fol. 1 ff. $\frac{3}{2}$ sections reduced to $\frac{3}{4}$.

7-4, 5. Carissimi, *Lamento di Maria Stuarda*. London, British Museum, Ms Harley 1265, fols. 1–12v.

7-6. Cesti, *Alpi nevose e dure*. Ed. David Burrows. Wellesley College, 1963. $\frac{3}{2}$ sections reduced to $\frac{3}{4}$.

7-7. Carissimi, *Jephte*. Ed. Balilla Pratella, pp. 21–24. *CDMI*, Quaderni 17–18. Milan: Istituto editoriale italiano, 1919.

7-8, 9. Monteverdi, *L'incoronazione di Poppea*. Venice, Biblioteca nazionale di S. Marco, Ms It. Cl. 4. N. 439, fols. 17r, 37v. Sections in $\phi$3 reduced to $\frac{6}{8}$, with values reduced eightfold.

7-10 to 15. Cesti, *Orontea*. Romes, Santa Cecilia, fols. 188r, 188v, 119r, 120; 98r, 153r–154r, 154v–155r. In 7–15 and 7–16, values halved.

8–1. Marini, *Sonata per il violino per sonar con due corde. Sonate, Symphonie, Canzoni*, op. 8. Venice: Magni, 1628.

8-2. Merula. Canzone "La Strada." *Canzoni overo Sonate concertate per chiesa e camera, Libro 3*, Op. 12, p. 25. Venice: A. Vincenti, 1637.

8-3a, 3b. Legrenzi, Sonata "La Cornara." *Sonate a 2, e 3*. Venice: F. Magni, 1655.

8-3c. Legrenzi, Sonata "La Raspona." Ibid.

8-3d. Legrenzi, Sonata. *Sonate a 2, 3, 5, e 6 stromenti, Libro 3*, Op. 8. Bologna: G. Monti, 1671.

8-4, 5. Legrenzi, Sonata, Op. 10, No. 4, Allegro. *La Cetra. Libro 4 di sonate a 2, 3, e 4 stromenti*, Op. 10. Venice: F. M. Gardano, 1673.

8-6. Cazzati, Sonata "La Pellicana," Presto. *Sonate a 2 instrumenti*, Op. 55, fol. 9. Bologna: 1670.

8-7. Corelli, Sonata da chiesa, Op. 3, No. 11, Grave. *Les oeuvres de A. Corelli*, ed. J. Joachim and F. Chrysander, II, p. 178. London: Augener, nos. 8441–8445.

8-8. Corelli, Sonata Op. 5, No. 3, Allegro. Ibid., III, p. 29.

8-9. Purcell, Sonata II (Z. 791), [Allegro]. Sonnata's of III. Parts. London, 1683. *The Works of Henry Purcell* (London and New York: Novello, Ewer and Co., 1893), V, p. 9. Interpretive marks removed.

8-10. Purcell, Sonata II (Z. 791), Adagio-Vivace. Ibid., V, p. 14.

8-11a. Purcell, Sonata III (Z. 804), [Grave]. *Ten Sonata's in Four Parts*. London, 1697. Ibid., VII, p. 23.

8-11b. Corelli, Sonata, Op. 3, No. 7, Grave. *Sonate da chiesa a tre*. Modena, 1689. *Les oeuvres*, II, p. 160.

8-12. Biber, "Mystery" Sonata 11, Aria con Variazioni. *DTOe*, XII/2, pp. 45–46, 48. Concert-pitch transcription added.

8-9. Stradella, Serenata a 3 con strumenti *Qual prodigio è ch'io miri. Händels Werke*, ed. F. Chrysander, *Supplemente*, p. 21. Leipzig, 1888.

8-10. Vivaldi, Concerto, Op. 3, No. 8, Allegro. Amsterdam: Estienne Roger, n.d.

8-11. Vivaldi, Concerto for violin, Op. 9, No. 2, F. I, 51, p. 214, Largo. *Opere*, Vol. 126, p. 18. Milan: Ricordi, 1952.

8-12, 13. Vivaldi, Concerto for violin, Op. 12, No. 5, F. I, 86, p. 344, Allegro. *Opere*, Vol. 183, pp. 2–3, 7–9. Milan: Ricordi, 1954.

8-14. Vivaldi, Concerto for strings and harpsichord, F. XI, 4, p. 235, *Opere*, Vol. 8, p. 17. Milan: Ricordi, 1957.

8-15, 16. Bach, Brandenburg Concerto No. 5, Allegro. *NBA*, Ser. VII, Vol. 2. Kassel: Bärenreiter, 1956.

9-1. F. Couperin, Ordre 13, *La Persévérance, sous le Domino Gris de lin. Pièces de clavecin*, ed. Kenneth Gilbert, III, p. 11.

9-2. R. Ballard, *Ballet de la Reyne*, second *chant*. Robert Ballard, *Premier livre*, 1611, transcribed and ed. André Souris and Sylvie Spycket. Paris: Éditions du CNRS, 1963, p. 14.

9-3a, b. E. Gautier, *La Poste. Oeuvres du vieux Gautier*, ed. and transcribed by André Souris. Paris: Éditions du CNRS, 1966, Nos. 63, 85, pp. 83, 111.

9-4. D. Gaultier, *Tombeau de Mademoiselle Gaultier*. Denis Gaultier, *La Rhétorique des Dieux*, facsimile, ed. André Tessier and Jean Cordey. Publications de la Société française de musicologie, VI (Paris: Librairie E. Droz, 1932), p. 27.

9-5. J. C. de Chambonnières, *Pavane L'entretien des dieux. Oeuvres complètes de Chambonnières*, ed. Paul Brunold and André Tessier. Paris: Éditions Maurice Senart, 1925, pp. 20–21.

9-6. J. C. de Chambonnières, *Les Baricades*. Ibid., p. 14.

9-7. J. C. de Chambonnières, *Menuet*. Ibid., p. 53.

9-8. F. Couperin, Orde 8, *La Raphaèle. Pièces de clavecin*, ed. K. Gilbert, II, p. 39.

9-9. F. Couperin, Ordre 8, Passacaille. Ibid., p. 52.

10-1. Chorale, *Auf meinen lieben Gott*. Johannes Zahn, *Die Melodien der deutschen evangelischen Kirchenlieder* (Gütersloh: C. Berteslman, 1889–1893), I, 30, no. 2164. Transposed up a whole tone; bar lines, fermatas added.

10-2. Buxtehude, Chorale variation, *Auf meinen lieben Gott*, BuxWV 179. *Sämtliche Orgelwerke*, ed. Klaus Beckmann, II, 150–51. Wiesbaden: B & H, 1972.

10-3. Froberger, Suite 11 in D major, Allemande. *Suiten und andere Stücke für Klavier*, ed. David Starke, pp. 26–27. Darmstad: Tonos-Musikverlag, 1972.

10-4. Froberger, Suite 11 in D major, Sarabande. Ibid., p. 29.

10-5. Buxtehude, Chorale elaboration, *Danket dem Herrn. Orgelwerke*, BuxWV 181, ed. Klaus Beckmann, II, 8–9. Wiesbaden: B & H, 1972.

10-6a, b, c. Buxtehude, Chorale elaboration, *Ich dank dir schon durch deinen Sohn*, BuxWV 195. Ibid., p. 14.

10-6d. Zahn, I, 67, no. 247b, incorporating some variants therein.

10-7. Bruhns, *Praeludium. Gesammelte Werke*, ed. Fritz Stein, II, 78. Das Erbe deutscher Musik, 2. Reihe, Bd. 2. Copyright 1939 by Henry Litolff. Reprint permission granted by C. F. Peters Corporation, New York.

10-8. Pachelbel, *Magnificat primi toni. Orgelwerke*, ed. Traugott Fedtke, III, 10. Copyright 1974 by Henry Litolff. Reprint permission granted by C.F. Peters Corporation, New York.

10-9. Pachelbel, *Magnificat octavi toni*. Ibid., p. 49.

10-10. Bach, Praeludium et Fuga, BWV 543. *BG*, XV, 189, 192.

10-11. Raison, *Messe du deuziesme ton*, Christe, Trio en passacaille, *Livre d'orgue*, Paris, 1687. F. A. Guilmant and A. Pirro, *Archives de maîtres de l'orgue*, II, 37. Mainz: B. Schott's Söhne.

10-12a. Buxtehude, Passacaglia, BuxWV 161. *Sämtliche Orgelwerke*, ed. Klaus Beckmann, I, 134. Wiesbaden; B & H, 1971.

10-12b. Bach, Passacaglia, BWV 582. *BG*, XV, 289.

10-13. Bach, English Suite 1, BWV 806. *BG* XLV, 9.

10-14. Bach, chorale-prelude, *Durch Adams Fall*, BWV 637, *BG*, XXV/2, 53.

10-15. Bach, chorale elaboration, *Vater unser im Himmelreich*, BWV 682. *BG*, III, 217.

10-16. Bach, chorale-elaboration, *Wachet auf*, BWV 645. *BG*, XXV/2, 63.

10-17. Bach, *Well-Tempered Clavier*, II, 2, Fugue, BWV 871. *BG*, XIV, 99.

11-1 to 4. Lully, *Cadmus et Hermione*. Paris: chez le Sieur Foucault, 168–. Collated with *Oeuvres complètes, Les Operas*, ed. Henri Prunières, Vol. I, pp. 122, 121, 91, 62. Paris: Éditions de *La Revue musicale*, 1930.

11-5, 6. Rameau, *Hippolyte et Aricie*. Paris: the author, n.d.

11-7. Rameau, *Platée*. Paris: the author, n.d.

11-8 to 11. Scarlatti, *Mitridate Eupatore*. Library of Congress M 1500.S28M5 case, fols. 91r–92v; 121v–123r; 131v–132r; 127r–127v.

11-12. Scarlatti, *Il Trionfo dell'onore*. Milan: Carisch, 1941.

12-1. Purcell, *Dido and Aeneas*, ed. Margaret Laurie and Thurston Dart. London: Novello, 1961.

12-2 to 4. Handel, *Giulio Cesare*. *Werke*, ed. Friedrich Chrysander, Vol. 68. Leipzig: Deutsche Handelgesellschaft, 1875.

12-5 and 6. Handel, *Alcina*. Same series, Vol. 86, 1868.

13-1a Chorale, *Christ lag in Todesbanden*. Johannes Zahn, *Die Melodien der deutschen evangelischen Kirchenlieder*, Vol. IV, no. 7012. Gütersloh: G. Bertelsmann, 1891.

13-1b to d. Bach, BWV 4. *Werke*, Vol. I. Leipzig: B&H, 1851.

13-2 to 4. Bach, BWV 61. *Neue Ausgabe sämtlicher Werke*, Ser. 1, Vol. 1. Kassel: Bärenreiter, 1954.

13-5 to 8. Bach, BWV 92. Same ed., Ser. 1, Vol. 7, 1956.

# ABBREVIATIONS

*ARC* *Archive Production*, History of Music Division of the Deutsche Grammophon Gesellschaft.

*BG*  Johann Sebastian Bach, *Werke*. Leipzig: Breitkopf & Härtel, 1851–1900.

B&H  Breitkopf und Härtel, Leipzig.

BuxWV  *Thematisch-Systematisches Verzeichnis der musikalischen Werke von Dietrich Buxtehude*. Wiesbaden: Breitkopf & Härtel, 1974.

BWV  Bach-Werke-Verzeichnis. Wolfgang Schmieder, *Thematisch-systematisches Verzeichnis der musikalische Werke von Johann Sebastian Bach*. Leipzig: Breitkopf & Härtel, 1950.

*CDMI*  *I Classici della musica italiana*. Milan: Società Anonima Notari 1918–1921.

*CMI*  *I Classici musicali italiani*. Milan: Fondazione Eugenio Brevi, 1941–1956.

CNRS  Centre nationale de la recherche scientifique.

*CW    Das Chorwerk.* Wolfenbüttel: Möseler Verlag, 1929–.

*DdT   Denkmäler deutscher Tonkunst.* Leipzig: Breitkopf & Härtel, 1892–1931.

*DM    Das Musikwerk* (Anthology of Music). Cologne: Arno Volk-Verlag, 1951–.

*DTOe   Denkmäler der Tonkunst in Oesterreich.* Vienna: Artaria, 1894.

*EP*   Robert Eitner, ed. *Publikationen älterer praktischer und theoretischer Musikwerke, vorzugsweise des XV und XVI Jahrhunderts.* Berlin: Bahn; Leipzig: Breitkopf & Härtel 1873–1905.

*GMB   Geschichte der Musik in Beispielen.* Leipzig: Breitkopf & Härtel, 1931; New York: Broude Bros., 1950.

*HAM*   Archibald T. Davison and Willi Apel, eds., *Historical Anthology of Music.* Cambridge, Mass.: Harvard University Press, 1950.

*HIM    History of Italian Music.* RCA italiana.

*HM    Hortus musicus.* Kassel and Basel: Bärenreiter-Verlag, 1948–.

*HMS    History of Music in Sound,* record albums and booklets. London: Oxford University Press, 1957.

*JAMS    Journal of the American Musicological Society,* 1948–.

*IMAMI   Istituzioni e monumenti dell'arte musicale italiana.* Millan: G. Ricordi, 1931–1941.

*MGG    Die Musik in Geschichte und Gegenwart.* Kassel and Basel: Bärenreiter-Verlag, 1949–1979.

*MM*   Carl Parrish and John F. Ohl, eds., *Masterpieces of Music before 1750.* New York: W.W. Norton & Co., Inc., 1951.

*MR*   Gustave Reese, *Music in the Renaissance.* New York: W.W. Norton & Co., Inc., 1954.

*MQ    The Musical Quarterly,* 1915–.

*NAWM*   Claude V. Palisca, ed., *Norton Anthology of Western Music.* New York: W. W. Norton & Co., Inc., 1980.

*NBA*   Neue-Bach-Ausgabe. J. S. Bach, *Neue Ausgabe sämtlicher Werke.* Kassel and Basel: Bärenreiter-Verlag, 1954–.

*TEM*   Carl Parrish, ed., *A Treasury of Early Music.* New York: W. W. Norton & Co., Inc., 1958.

*SHO*   Donald Jay Grout, *A Short History of Opera,* 2d ed, New York: Columbia University Press, 1965.

*SR*   Oliver Strunk, *Source Readings in Music History.* New York: W. W. Norton & Co., Inc., 1950.

# INDEX